HONOR
BOUND

HONOR BOUND

MY JOURNEY TO HELL AND BACK WITH
AMANDA KNOX

RAFFAELE SOLLECITO
WITH ANDREW GUMBEL

G

GALLERY BOOKS

NEW YORK   LONDON   TORONTO   SYDNEY   NEW DELHI

G

Gallery Books
A Division of Simon & Schuster, Inc.
1230 Avenue of the Americas
New York, NY 10020

First Gallery Books hardcover edition September 2012

GALLERY BOOKS and colophon are registered trademarks
of Simon & Schuster, Inc.

For information about special discounts for bulk purchases,
please contact Simon & Schuster Special Sales at
1-866-506-1949 or business@simonandschuster.com.

The Simon & Schuster Speakers Bureau can bring authors
to your live event. For more information or to book an event
contact the Simon & Schuster Speakers Bureau at 1-866-248-3049
or visit our website at www.simonspeakers.com.

Designed by Julie Schroeder

Manufactured in the United States of America

1   3   5   7   9   10   8   6   4   2

Library of Congress Cataloging-in-Publication Data

Sollecito, Raffaele.
Honor bound : my journey to hell and back with Amanda Knox /
Raffaele Sollecito with Andrew Gumbel.
p.   cm.
1. Sollecito, Raffaele.   2 Knox, Amanda.   3. Kercher,
Meredith.   4. Murder—Italy—Perugia.   5. Homicide investigation—
Italy.   6. Trials (Murder)—Italy.   I. Gumbel, Andrew.   II. Title.
HV6535.I83P485   2012
364.152'3092—dc23   2012025856

ISBN 978-1-4516-9598-4
ISBN 978-1-4516-9640-0 (ebook)

This book is dedicated to the Italian state bureaucracy, and to those public servants who unwittingly put their own interests ahead of the lives of others.

It is dedicated to anyone ensnared in epic, backbreaking legal battles, and to those who desire true justice but lack the money and the support to bring the truth to light.

And it is dedicated to you, Papà, because you fought for me from the depths of your soul, with a determination and a single-mindedness few possess. I love you.

CONTENTS

PREFACE

We don't have the evidence, the hard facts; but by God the truth must be out there somewhere!

—Luigi Pirandello

This is the story of two ordinary people who stumbled upon an extraordinary circumstance, the brutal murder of a British student in Italy. Neither Amanda Knox nor I had anything to do with the crime, but we came perilously close to spending the rest of our lives in prison because the authorities found it easier, and more convenient, to take advantage of our youth and inexperience than to mount a proper investigation.

It's that simple. And that absurd.

On November 1, 2007, Amanda and I were carefree students at the beginning of a cross-cultural love affair in a beautiful Umbrian hill town. Within days, we were thrown into solitary confinement in a filthy prison, without access to lawyers or loved ones, accused of acts so heinous and disturbing we may never be able to banish them from our thoughts, or our nightmares.

In the newspapers and on the nightly news, we were turned into monsters, grotesque distortions of our true selves. It did not matter how thin the evidence was, or how quickly it became apparent that the culprit was someone else entirely. Our guilt was presumed, and everything the prosecution did and fed to the media stemmed from that false premise. By the time we had dismantled the case and demonstrated its breathtaking absurdity, we had spent four of what should have been the best years of our lives behind bars.

Amanda and I certainly made our share of mistakes. At the beginning we were too trusting, spoke too frivolously and too soon, and remained oblivious to the danger we were courting even after the judicial noose began to tighten. Amanda behaved in ways that were culturally baffling to many Italians and attracted a torrent of gossip and criticism. We were young and naive, unthinking and a little reckless. Of that much we were guilty.

But what we did not do—and could not have done, as the evidence clearly showed—was murder Meredith Kercher.

Meredith was Amanda's friend, a fellow English speaker in the house they shared with two Italian women just outside Perugia's ancient city walls. She was twenty-one years old, intelligent, and beautiful. She and Amanda knew each other for a little over three weeks, long enough to feel their way into their new surroundings and appreciate each other's interests and temperaments. I never heard about a single tense moment between them. On the contrary, they toured the sights and went out for meals and music and dancing.

Meredith, of course, suffered infinitely worse luck than we did: she came home, alone, on an ordinary Thursday night and had her throat slit by an intruder hoping to steal the household rent money. But the roles could easily have been reversed. If Meredith's Italian boyfriend had not gone away for the weekend and if Amanda had not started sleeping over at my house, she—not Meredith—might have been the one found in a pool of blood on her bedroom floor. That reality was quickly lost amid the hysteria of the media coverage. But it continued to hover over both of us—Amanda especially—as we sank into the legal quagmire and struggled in vain to overcome the public image of us as heartless killers.

This should not have been a complicated case. The intruder was quickly identified as Rudy Guede, an African immigrant living in Perugia with a history of break-ins and petty crimes. His DNA was found all over Meredith's room, and footprints made in her blood were found to match his shoes. Everything at the crime scene pointed to a lone assailant, and a single weapon. Guede repeatedly broke into houses by throwing a rock through a window, as happened here, and he had been caught by the authorities in the past with a knife similar to the one that inflicted Meredith's fatal wounds.

Guede did not call the police, as Amanda and I did, or volunteer information, or agree to hours of questioning whenever asked. Rather, he fled to Germany as soon as the investigation began and stayed there until his arrest two and a half weeks later.

Guede's apprehension and eventual conviction on murder charges should have been the end of the story. But by the time Guede was identified, the police and the public prosecutor's office had convinced themselves that the murder was, incredibly, the result of a sexual orgy gone wrong, in which Amanda and I had played leading roles. Their speculations ignited a media firestorm, inspiring sensationalist headlines across the world about the evil lurking behind our seemingly innocent faces.

The authorities had no shred of evidence to substantiate this story line, only erroneous suppositions and wild imaginings. We had an alibi for the most likely time of death, and none of the initial forensic evidence tied us to the scene of the crime. Nothing in our backgrounds gave any hint of a propensity for violence or criminality. We were both accomplished, hardworking students known to our friends and families for our gentleness and even tempers. Yet the authorities stuck to their guns. They fed the media a steady diet of sensationalist stories of how Amanda, the promiscuous American she-devil, and I, her sex-and-drug-addled Italian helpmeet, had tried without success to drag Meredith into our depravity and punished her by plunging an outsize kitchen knife into her neck.

It might have been funny if the consequences had not been so devastating. Listening to the tortured language of the prosecution—"one can hypothesize that . . . ," "it is possible that . . . ," "one can imagine that . . . ," "this scenario is not incompatible with . . ."—it became clear that the authorities, like the media, were treating our case with the bizarre levity of an after-dinner game of Clue, or an Agatha Christie mystery. Everyone, even the judges in their black robes, had theories they were itching to air. It could have been Colonel Mustard in the drawing room with the revolver; instead it was Amanda and Raffaele in the bedroom with the kitchen knife. How was it conceivable that a democratic country known for its style and beauty and effortless charm—the Italy of the Renaissance and *la dolce vita*—could allow two young people to be catapulted to international notoriety and convicted of a horrific crime *on the basis of nothing at all*?

The answer has something to do with the grim embrace that developed between the prosecutor's office and the sensationalist media. Like addicts constantly looking for the next fix, each fed the other's insatiable appetite for titillation and attention. The casual cruelty of "Foxy Knoxy" and her Italian lover became too good a story line to abandon, even when it became apparent it was overheated and unsustainable. Our suffering was the price to be paid for the world's continuing entertainment.

The meandering complexities of the Italian legal system, where speculation and hearsay are allowed to run rampant and time invariably slows to a maddening trickle, did little to help our cause. For reasons deeply embedded in the country's history, the concept of proof beyond a reasonable doubt scarcely exists in Italy, and the very notion of undisputed fact is viewed with suspicion, if not outright aversion. Few in Italian society wield as much unfettered power as the robed members of the judiciary, whose independence makes them answerable to nobody but themselves. Many Italians retain a healthy skepticism about the reliability of their procedures and rulings. The courts—tainted by politics, clubbishness, pomposity, and excruciating delays—are the most reviled institution in the country.

Because the Italian legal system is almost completely blind to precedent and relies on a tangle of impenetrable codes and procedures, prosecutors and judges have almost boundless freedom to spin their cases into any shape they please and create legal justifications on the fly. Often, they are more interested in constructing compelling narratives than in building up the evidence piece by piece, a task considered too prosaic and painstaking to be really interesting. Prosecutors and judges are not independent of each other, as they are in Britain or the United States, but belong to the same professional body of magistrates. So a certain coziness between them is inevitable, especially in smaller jurisdictions like Perugia. Defendants unlucky enough to be held in pretrial detention are effectively condemned before any charges are brought and serve long terms regardless of the outcome because cases invariably grind on for years.

* * *

Even though Amanda and I shared the same unjust fate, the case was always about her. Amanda, Amanda, Amanda: to this day, nobody in Italy can utter that name without thinking reflexively about *that American.* In the popular imagination she was Amanda the temptress, the sinner, the whore of Perugia. She was Amanda the heartless when she didn't cry over Meredith's death and Amanda the hysterical manipulator when she did. Whatever she did—practice yoga, play Beatles songs, buy underwear—it was held against her.

For the prosecutor's office, Amanda was a bonanza they did everything to cash in on. It wasn't just the thrill of the hunt, the kudos of nailing a fresh-faced, young American and seeing the story endlessly relayed across the world. She also represented a way out, a grand distraction for Giuliano Mignini, our lead prosecutor, who was facing a separate trial of his own on misconduct charges and was fighting for his career and his reputation.

What about me? By the end, I vanished so far from public view I thought of myself—or rather my *other* self, the one unaccountably on trial for killing a student I barely knew—as Mr. Nobody. In court, Mignini didn't bother to ascribe a motive to me, dismissing me merely as Amanda's *fidanzatino*, her "little boyfriend," who would follow her anywhere and do whatever she wanted.

I don't think the prosecution or police ever seriously thought of me as a murderer. They had one overriding reason to arrest me, throw me into solitary confinement, and threaten me with life imprisonment, and that was to pressure me into rolling over and testifying against Amanda. The police made that pretty clear on the night of my arrest. Stop protecting that *cow,* that *whore,* they said, or we will make your life a living hell. On this they proved true to their word.

I heard much of the same for the next four years. Why, people asked, would I defend Amanda when I had known her only a few days and could not be sure what she might have done? Did I not realize that by losing my head over her I was throwing my whole life away?

The police were not even the ones exerting the most pressure.

I was bombarded by my lawyers, my family, the people I spent the most time with and felt closest to in the world. I don't know what would have happened if I had caved and concocted some half-truth I knew to be dishonest. Perhaps it would have been my ticket out of prison. Perhaps, to save face, the authorities would have continued to prosecute me anyway.

But I do know this: if I had changed my testimony, Amanda would have remained behind bars for the rest of her life, not just the twenty-six years to which she was originally sentenced. There would have been no saving her. And that was something my conscience could never permit. The only hope was for me to stick to the truth and pray that my family and my lawyers could demolish the prosecution's case piece by piece until the courts had no option but to set both of us free.

It was a high-wire act, every step of the way. And this is how we did it.

I

LOVE AND DEATH

*Nessun maggior dolore che ricordarsi
del tempo felice nella miseria.*
No greater pain than to remember happy times in a state of misery.

—Francesca da Rimini in Dante's *Inferno,* canto 5

I can still pinpoint the moment I fell in love with Amanda Knox.

In Italian, we have an expression for moments like these, moments when you connect with a kindred spirit with whom you may not, on the face of it, have much common ground—language or otherwise. Yet you find yourselves locking eyes and exchanging smiles and feeling an instant connection. We call this moment *un colpo di fulmine*, a lightning bolt.

That's what I felt the night I met Amanda.

It didn't hit me right away. Rather, it crept up on me, almost unawares, like a beautiful dream. I'm a romantic by nature, I'll admit it, but when I met Amanda, I was also a shy, awkward twenty-three-year-old with limited experience of approaching girls, let alone having them sweep me off my feet so suddenly, so unexpectedly. So it all seemed vaguely unreal, even when we were standing and holding each other close under a star-filled Perugian sky in Piazza Italia, overlooking the rooftops of the city and the Tiber River valley below. When I leaned in and kissed her for the first time, it was intense and beautiful and seemed to last forever.

I don't know what it is about a first kiss that makes it so much more powerful than the thousands that may follow. It's as if one kiss can bind you to someone forever—it may be in friendship, it may be in love, it may be by some kind of cosmic connection that has no name in English or Italian, and it may be nothing at all. All that matters is living in the moment and experiencing life when you are young and alive and bright, with nothing but promising futures ahead of you.

* * *

It was October 25, 2007. I'd just finished the last undergraduate exam for my bachelor's degree in computer science at the university in Perugia, and while I still had a thesis to complete, I felt relaxed for the first time in weeks. That night, a musician friend invited me to a classical-music concert at the Università per Stranieri, the University for Foreigners, which attracted tens of thousands of young people from all over the world. Even though I was dog-tired and looked a mess, with shaggy hair, several days' growth of beard, and the same jeans and sneakers I'd been wearing all day, I didn't care—I was ready for a break, and zoning out to some live classical music sounded like the antidote to all those long hours of studying.

The concert was held in the university's Great Hall, a marble-floored room adorned with early-twentieth-century art, and refreshments were served in a magnificent side room with a gilded rococo ceiling. Most of the audience were Rotary Club members my father's age. My friend and I sat at the back of the room and settled into the music, starting with Astor Piazzolla's spectacular "Grand Tango," arranged for viola and piano.

At intermission, as the audience dispersed in search of refreshments, I glanced across the room and spotted, looking in my direction, the only other person under fifty years old. She was pretty; beautiful actually, with long, blondish-brown hair and striking eyes.

Normally, I would have been too anxious and reticent to consider approaching her, but I was in a great mood and figured I had nothing to lose, particularly in this crowd.

"*Ciao, sono Raffaele. E tu?*"

"Amanda."

"Amanda," I repeated. She wasn't dressed like an Italian and she didn't sound like one either. So I switched to English, dusting off the little I'd learned in school. "Where are you from?"

"*Sono americana.* Sorry . . . my Italian isn't very good. I just got here."

"It is not a problem. Where in America?"

"Seattle," she replied. "Do you know it?"

"Seattle! Of course. That's fantastic. I'm a computer scientist, and Seattle, for us, *è come Mecca per i musulmani* . . . it's like Mecca for the Muslims."

Amanda laughed, and we chatted until the lights started flickering to signal the end of intermission. I asked if my friend Mauro and I could sit next to her for the second half, and she agreed. Mauro, or Tozzetto, as I knew him, gave me the hairy eyeball when I called him over. "Come on," I urged. He sat next to us with all the enthusiasm of a sullen teenager.

The second half of the program was Schubert's *Trout Quintet*. With each movement, Amanda noted the change of tempo by whispering the few Italian words she knew—*allegro, andante, lento, presto*. I laughed and whispered encouragements back. Every now and again she would bob her head in time to the music, almost as if she were alone in her room with no one around to see her. Something about her was undeniably eccentric, but I didn't dislike it at all. I'd never met someone with so few inhibitions, yet she had this goofy charm that drew me to her and made me feel immediately comfortable.

When the concert ended, Amanda said she had to go to work. She had a part-time job handing out flyers and serving drinks in a cellar bar called Le Chic. Apparently, Thursdays were one of their busiest nights.

"Will you give me your number?" I asked.

"Come by the bar later on and we'll see." With that, she headed home to change her clothes.

Tozzetto was already feeling like a third wheel, and he wasn't enthusiastic about tagging along to Le Chic. But I didn't want to go alone—I'd never set foot inside before and it wasn't the kind of place that I frequented. So I offered to buy him a drink. Tozzetto said he wanted to call two other friends and go out with them instead. I wouldn't take no for answer. In the end, I paid for everyone.

The bar was dark and poky, and the customers were not my kind of people. It belonged to a Congolese immigrant named Diya Lumumba, whom everyone knew as Patrick. His crowd was transient—foreigners, musicians, people passing through for reasons both good and maybe not so good. Amanda had been introduced to Patrick through an Algerian named Juve, who also worked at Le Chic. From what Amanda told me, Juve was the kind of guy who latched onto every girl in sight. She gave me no reason to feel any better about being there.

The place was crowded, but we found a couch to squeeze onto. As the last of Tozzetto's friends sat down, a lever on the side of the couch suddenly fell with a clunk—just as Amanda walked up to greet us. Her face fell and her mood changed immediately. She looked around furtively, clearly worried that her boss would blame her in some way for breaking the furniture. So I sprang up and offered to fix it. For several minutes I struggled with the lever on my hands and knees and eventually screwed it back into place. To my surprise, the entire bar broke out in spontaneous applause. For a moment I felt embarrassed, but then I saw Amanda beaming and it dawned on me I might actually have a chance with her.

"Do you want to go for a walk or something after you finish your shift?" I asked.

She smiled and said she would.

My friends took that as their cue to leave, and I was left staring at the ceiling and wondering how to pass the time until she was free. Eventually I wandered over to the bar and chatted with Patrick, who was perfectly amiable. I'm not a big drinker and didn't want another beer, so I ordered a tonic water and waited until well after midnight.

Perugia was full of foreign students, and a lot of my fellow Italians saw the women as easy targets—good for a quick roll in the hay, or a discreet affair on the side, with a built-in guarantee that sooner or later they would head back where they came from. But that wasn't at all how I felt. I'm too dreamily romantic to think of using women that way. For me, it's always been true love or nothing. Given my overprotected childhood and my introverted personality, "nothing" had been the prevailing story line to that point—for which my friends teased me incessantly. When I came back from a year abroad in Munich, in 2006, they laughed that I was the first person in the history of the Erasmus student-exchange program to leave home a virgin and come back still a virgin.

I'd only had one girlfriend before Amanda, another transplant from my home region of Apulia, on the Adriatic coast. We met at a birthday party a few months after I returned to Perugia from Germany. Neither of us knew entirely what we were doing—she was as inexperienced as I—but we muddled our way through our first time, both rather pleased to have got it out of the way. The relationship was short-lived; when my grandmother died, a month after we started seeing each other, I headed home for the funeral and broke up with her before I returned. Getting into a serious relationship was the last thing on my mind—I didn't have the headspace for it. I was happier focusing on my studies and kickboxing and thinking about my future.

Now that graduation was upon me, I was planning to leave Perugia for good in a few weeks. Foremost in my mind was the pressure I was feeling from my father to apply for a nine-month internship at a prestigious university in Milan. He was planning to take me there as soon as we'd celebrated my graduation. We talked about it incessantly, usually several times a day. As he knew, I was more interested in enrolling in a master's degree program in Ireland, and working toward my dream of becoming a video-game designer. But my father, a doctor specializing in urology and my only living parent, was both highly protective and a difficult man to say no to. So I agreed to apply to Milan. The last thing I wanted was to start one of my family's notoriously melodramatic fights, which some of my relatives seemed to thrive on but which always left me feeling debilitated. I did want to make my father proud; that much was important to me. But figuring out how to please him while also establishing my independence was a skill I had yet to master.

I can now say, looking back, that meeting Amanda was a glorious escape from these concerns. She was an accomplished student, like me, but also quite unlike anyone I had ever met. As she told me on the walk we took after she finished her shift at Le Chic, she was a third-year student at Seattle's University of Washington and was studying German as well as Italian. So we had another language in common. She, like me, was the child of divorced parents, and she too was close to her family—stepparents, stepsiblings, and all. She had arrived in Perugia a month earlier and found a room in a house just outside the city walls, which she shared with two Italian women at the beginning of their legal careers and a young English student named Meredith Kercher.

Meredith had, in fact, accompanied Amanda to the concert but left at the interval, just before Amanda and I set eyes on each other. If Meredith had stayed, chances are we would never have started talking and things would have worked out very differently.

* * *

Our walk seemed to last for hours. We strolled down Corso Baglioni toward the piazza where we shared our first kiss. We admired the views and talked about our families and exchanged many more kisses until we were too cold to continue. I asked Amanda if she wanted me to walk her home, or if she'd like to come back to my place to watch a movie.

I wasn't expecting her to accept my invitation; it's just one of those questions that Italian men feel compelled to ask.

"Okay," she answered, "I can come to your house."

Her answer took me completely by surprise. Where I was brought up, in the traditional-minded Italian South, women who say yes on the first date are regarded as suspect, and men are warned against getting involved with them. But Amanda didn't seem to be one of those girls. She was gentle and genuine, and even my bafflement couldn't mask how thrilled I was that the night was turning out so well.

"Aren't you afraid to be out with me?" I asked. "How is it that you trust me?"

"I don't know," she said, "but I trust you." Then she took me by the hand and smiled, and my heart melted. The lightning bolt had hit its target.

* * *

I took Amanda back to my one-room apartment on Corso Garibaldi, just a few steps away from the University for Foreigners. At night, the area attracted drug dealers and street bums, but they mostly kept to themselves and were easy to avoid; for all the subsequent talk about this being a *brutta zona,* a bad neighborhood, it never struck me as particularly dangerous. I showed Amanda around and invited her to plop down on the bed while I loaded a film on my computer. Of course, by the time I settled in next to her, all thoughts of the movie were quickly forgotten and we pulled each other's clothes off before the opening credits finished rolling.

When I woke up the next morning, Amanda still had her arms wrapped tightly around me. I remember feeling safe and warm in a way I hadn't since I was a little kid. We related in a sweet, almost childlike way, maybe because we didn't share a native language. I helped her with her Italian, she corrected my English, we found common ground in German, and everything felt fresh and new. Amanda brought me back to my childhood, a time of purity and carefree abandon long since overshadowed by family disputes and reversals of fortune, none worse than the death of my mother in 2005. It was as if Amanda had found an old dresser, dusted it off, and opened a drawer full of toys and beautiful objects that had been locked away for a long time.

Did I fall hard for her? Absolutely. Did she feel as strongly about me? No, but as we first got to know each other, I preferred not to let that trouble me. I was floating high in a pristine, azure sky, and I just wanted to keep floating.

* * *

I didn't know what I should tell my family about Amanda, so for a day or two I said nothing at all. I knew I wouldn't be able to hold back for long because my father called several times a day and he would have sniffed out any real reticence in about two minutes flat. Besides, we were in the habit of discussing everything, even the most intimate parts of our lives. That's a Southern Italian thing; families in my part of the world are all over each other's business and treat everyone's ups and downs as their own. But we Sollecitos had also developed a special bond because of my mother's sudden death. She and my father had been divorced for years, but once she was gone, he went into protective overdrive with me and my older sister, Vanessa. We didn't always welcome his intrusions and fought bitterly with him from time to time. Vanessa would sometimes cut off communication for weeks or months and insist on going her own way, but not me. I kept right on talking, no matter what.

By the time I did talk about Amanda, she and I were more or less inseparable. We shopped together, cooked together, strolled around the town's center, and unfailingly slept at my apartment every night. We were apart only when she had to go to class or I had an appointment with my thesis director. Such instant closeness felt right to me. We didn't have a plan; we just took care of each other and lived in the moment. I would climb in the shower and help her get clean, and afterward I would comb out the knots in her long, straight hair.

When I told my father about this, he said I treated her more like a doll than a girlfriend, and he had a point. I did not have much experience being in a relationship, but playing with dolls was something that came naturally. When I was a kid, Vanessa was not remotely interested in her Barbie collection—she was too much of a tomboy—so I played with them instead. I was an unusual child that way. Barbie and I went on adventures together, faced down monsters, and had our romantic moments. A little odd, I will admit. But as a child I had a limitless imagination and didn't see much difference between Barbies and superheroes and the fantasy characters I encountered in video games.

Papà was not hugely enthusiastic about Amanda, but neither was he entirely negative. He was touched that I had found someone who made me happy, but he also wanted to make sure I was getting on with my work. "You need to finish your thesis," he admonished, "and, remember, you're going to Milan." I had not forgotten. Vanessa, being Vanessa, was much blunter. "What do you think you are doing?" she railed. "You're going crazy for someone who is going to go back to America, and you'll never see her again."

She would keep up a similar barrage against Amanda for the next four years.

* * *

I visited Amanda's house at number 7, Via della Pergola the day after I met her and went back twice more over the next week. It was just a few minutes' walk from me, down Corso Garibaldi to Piazza Grimana and the University for Foreigners, then around a corner to the left where the city walls gave way to a large ravine and a dramatic vista. The house felt a little isolated, perched on the edge of the wilderness across the street from a large city parking lot. Inside, though, it was a typical student dwelling, filled with books and computers and cheap furniture. Everyone went about their business and talked mostly when they ran into each other. The four women occupied the upper floor of the house; downstairs were four male students, who were quite a bit rowdier and kept pot plants in one of their bathrooms.

Laura and Filomena, Amanda's Italian roommates, welcomed me warmly, and we often chatted together in our native language. Once or twice, I brought food and cooked them lunch. Laura was the more cynical of the two, all skin and bones and nervous energy and ear piercings; I remember her wondering aloud whether love and sex could really coexist. Could a man be relied upon to commit to a relationship, she asked, or was it better to look for a friend with benefits? I didn't have a whole lot to say on the subject and suspected she was poking fun, however gently, at the way Amanda and I were joined at the hip. *Piccioncini* was how she later characterized us in court. Little lovebirds.

Amanda and Meredith, meanwhile, talked in English—at a speed I couldn't have kept up with even if I tried. Still, I didn't get much of an impression of Meredith the few times I saw her at the apartment. She was well-mannered but a little distant, as English people can often be. The one time I offered her food, she had already eaten and politely turned it down. I noticed one day that she was wearing men's jeans, and she told me they belonged to a boyfriend she had left behind at home. I found that oddly endearing.

Mostly, I craved time alone with Amanda, and for that reason we were much more often at my house. My father reminded me that when I first moved to Perugia, he and my stepmother, Mara, and I had toured some of the hill towns in the area. "Why don't you take Amanda to some of the same places?" he suggested.

Right, a date, I thought. I was more than happy to take him up on the suggestion. A month earlier, I had bought a brand-new, black Audi A3, half of it an early graduation present from my father and the other half paid out of the rental income I received from my mother's estate. I was proud of my new car and loved the idea of touring Amanda around in it. Our first stop was to be Assisi, the spiritual home of St. Francis.

This was maybe three or four days into our relationship. The night before we left, I noticed she was chatting on Facebook with an American friend. I asked who he was. Right away, she explained that she, like Meredith, had left behind a boyfriend when she came to Italy. His name was David Johnsrud, known as D.J., and they were still in regular contact. In fact, they chatted or e-mailed almost every day. D.J. was spending his junior year in China, and given the distance, it hadn't made sense for them to stay together as a couple.

I could tell just by looking at Amanda that she was still attached to him. Even though we'd known each other only a few days, I had fallen for her—and it hurt.

"But we're no longer together, Raffaele," she said.

I had no reason to doubt her, but I also knew she wasn't over him and wasn't able to give her heart fully to me. As the conversation went on, I learned she had just bought a ticket to China to visit D.J. later in the year, and my suspicions were confirmed.

If I felt crushed, I was not about to admit it. *So I met a nice girl,* I told myself, *and we had fun for a few days. Whatever. It's not as though she was the love of my life. So what if I was just some guy to keep her company and nothing more? We had some nice moments together, but this wasn't exactly the romance of the century. If it's finished, I'll get over it.*

At least, that's what I told myself.

* * *

I took her to Assisi anyway. The decision wasn't destined to win the respect of my friends or family, but I followed through just the same.

If an Italian man feels there's more than one other person in a relationship, then his pride should—in theory—lead him to turn his back and say good-bye. Right away. I was brought up to believe that a strong sense of belonging is at the heart of all relationships. It's absolute commitment, or nothing. If the woman is looking over her shoulder or thinking about someone else, it's tantamount to cheating. For the man to stay with her is to be branded a cuckold or a fool—which is exactly how my friends saw me.

But I knew that my days with Amanda were numbered, one way or another, and I was having far too much fun to give her up so soon. I decided I'd take it day by day and felt comfortable with that approach. *If you don't live while you can,* I thought, *what's the point?*

In Assisi, I took particular pleasure in visiting St. Francis's tomb, which had been closed when I was there with my parents. Amanda and I strolled around, ate pizza, and bought incense. A perfect day out.

Back in Perugia, we settled into long, carefree evenings watching movies and listening to music. Sometimes I'd work on my thesis, while Amanda strummed her guitar and sang Beatles songs or did her yoga stretches on the floor. We made elaborate dinners. When I didn't know how to cook something, I would call my father's house to get the recipe. Amanda called herself my sous-chef. We were both *Harry Potter* fans and read to each other from the German edition of the first book, which Amanda brought round to my house. Bizarrely, it became a significant piece of evidence at trial. *Harry Potter und der Stein der Weisen.*

The days began to blend into each other. We went to bed a lot, but neither of us slept well. I wasn't used to having a woman in my bed and woke up several times a night. Amanda tended to be up at 5:00 a.m. every morning, which she chalked up to the aftereffects of jet lag. So our time together felt a little restless and blurry. That did no harm to our romance, but it was lousy preparation for witnesses in a murder case.

* * *

October 31 was the first day since our meeting that Amanda and I spent almost completely apart. In the morning I was invited to a friend's graduation ceremony, and I went to another friend's house for much of the afternoon. Amanda had class, then focused on her plans for Halloween, a big deal for Perugia's foreign students, though it meant nothing to us Italians. She and I did not meet up until late afternoon, at which point she drew cat whiskers on her face in makeup and, knowing my passion for Japanese comics, scrawled an abstract design on me. I didn't feel like going out, so I worked on my thesis while Amanda walked over to Le Chic to meet up with some of her friends there. She had hoped to spend the evening with Meredith, but Meredith's British girlfriends didn't like her—they found her too unrestrained in the way she acted and talked and burst into song whenever she felt like it—and Meredith never responded to her text suggesting they meet.

Late that night, around 1:00 a.m., Amanda called me from the fountain in Perugia's main piazza and asked me to accompany her back to my house. She'd been out drinking with a Greek friend, Spiros, whom I greeted cautiously as I took her by the arm. He ran an Internet café near the University for Foreigners and was a little too familiar with her for my liking.

We slept in the next morning, which was All Saints' Day, November 1, a national holiday. Many people were taking advantage of its being a Thursday to create a "bridge" to the weekend and take four days off. Because of the coincidence of All Saints' and All Souls' Day, they called it *il ponte dei morti,* the bridge of the dead. When Amanda headed back home midmorning to take a shower and change—she did not like the shower at my apartment, saying it was too cramped—she learned that Laura had already left for her hometown north of Rome, and Filomena was making plans to spend the weekend with her boyfriend at his place on the other side of Perugia. The boys in the downstairs apartment were all gone as well.

Amanda had to work that night, but otherwise we were looking forward to a long, lazy weekend with no plans in particular, except to drive to Gubbio, three-quarters of an hour northeast of Perugia, for a little sightseeing. By the time I showed up at her apartment for a late lunch around two, only Meredith was still in the house. Her chin still showed signs of the fake blood she had used for her Dracula costume the night before. We asked her to join us for lunch, but she had a shower instead, did some laundry, and left around 4:00 p.m. without saying where she was going.

It was the last time I ever saw her.

Amanda and I smoked a joint before leaving the house on Via della Pergola, wandered into town for some shopping before remembering we had enough for dinner already, and headed back to my place. Shortly before six, a Serbian friend of mine named Jovana Popovic rang the doorbell and asked if I'd mind driving her to the bus station at midnight to pick up a suitcase her mother was sending. I said that would be fine. When she left, Amanda and I sat down at the computer to watch a favorite movie, *Amélie.*

We had to stop the film a few times as the evening wore on. First, Amanda got a text from Patrick telling her it was a slow night because of the holiday and he didn't need her to come in after all. It was like getting an unexpected snow day—we were thrilled. Amanda texted back: *Certo ci vediamo più tardi buona serata!* Sure. See you later. Have a good evening.

Then my father called. He and Mara had just seen the Will Smith movie *The Pursuit of Happyness,* and he told me how beautifully it portrayed the relationship between a father and his son. My father was always making phone calls like this. It was sweet that he wanted to share his experiences, but he also made everything he said sound vaguely like an order, as if laying out the parameters of how I should react to things before I'd had a chance to form my own opinion. But he never stayed on the line for long—he is too nervy and impatient—so I listened calmly and the call was over in less than four minutes.

In the meantime, Jovana dropped by again and told Amanda that I didn't need to drive her to the bus station after all. Now we didn't have to leave the apartment. The evening was ours, and we couldn't have been happier. We switched off our cell phones, finished watching *Amélie,* and discussed what to make for dinner.

* * *

Shortly before eight o'clock, a video surveillance camera in the parking structure across from Amanda's house captured a man walking briskly past the security barrier and onto Via della Pergola. Of course I had no idea of this at the time; this was material my family gathered during the investigation and the trials. I'm mentioning it here because it was one of many facts that the prosecution and the media chose to overlook, and because it helps make sense of what did and did not occur on that fateful evening.

The man in the video footage was wearing a black coat with high wing-tip lapels and sneakers with white trim. He had his back to the camera and his head was covered with a woolen cap, making him difficult to identify. But his height, gait, coat, and shoes were all a plausible match for Rudy Guede, a twenty-year-old drifter of Ivorian origin who often shot hoops at the basketball court next to the University for Foreigners and was acquainted with the boys who lived downstairs from Meredith and Amanda.

Guede had an extraordinary past: an abusive childhood; a mother who abandoned him as a baby and a father who abandoned him as a teenager; an improbably idyllic period under the protection of one of Perugia's richest families, who sent him to private school in a chauffeur-driven limousine; and, more recently, a budding career as a cat burglar. According to eyewitnesses and police reports, Guede liked to break into houses by smashing a window with a rock and using his considerable athletic skills to scale the wall and climb inside. Often, his victims said, he would help himself to food and drink from the kitchen before looting the electronics and hard cash.

The previous Saturday, the director of an English kindergarten in Milan had caught Rudy red-handed sitting at her office computer and making the place his own. When the police searched his backpack, they found a knife he had lifted from the kitchen, a woman's gold watch, and a laptop and cell phone later traced to a lawyer's office in Perugia that had been burgled two weeks earlier. Guede was taken to police headquarters and questioned for four hours.

All indications were that he was about to be arrested. That is, until a call was placed to the Perugia police and the interrogation stopped. Instead of facing charges, Guede was put on a train back to Perugia, no more questions asked. To many independent observers in law enforcement, the only explanation for this was that Guede was working as a police informant; the Perugia authorities were apparently more interested in continuing his services than in prosecuting him for just a few hundred euros' worth of stolen items. It's a supposition officials in Perugia have never confirmed but it goes a long way to explain their behavior in the weeks and months to come.

On the time-stamped surveillance tape, Guede—or his doppelgänger—vanished into the night just moments after he appeared. But the camera picked up a pair of similar shoes crossing the street toward Meredith and Amanda's house about half an hour later. My defense team would later conclude he must have spent the intervening time formulating a plan to break into the house and making sure he was unseen.

It was a propitious moment to strike. First, Guede could reasonably assume that the occupants of the house were either out for the night or away for the long weekend. Second, he had previously stayed over in the boys' apartment downstairs—he fell asleep on the toilet one night in early October and ended up sprawled on the couch—so he knew the lay of the land. He had even met Meredith and Amanda briefly. And, third, since it was the first of the month, chances were good that the accumulated rent money for November was sitting in a pile somewhere in the house.

In the upstairs apartment, Filomena took responsibility for gathering everyone's cash and handing it over to the landlady. And it was Filomena's bedroom window that would soon be smashed with a large rock—most likely a few minutes after those white-rimmed sneakers were captured loping across the street around eight thirty.

Meredith, meanwhile, was finishing up an evening with her British friends, Amy Frost, Robyn Butterworth, and Sophie Purton. They had met early, tucked into a pizza at Amy and Robyn's house, watched a movie, and snacked on ice cream and apple crumble. Meredith announced that she was tired from the previous night's partying. She asked to borrow a history book and headed home.

Just moments before nine o'clock, the video surveillance camera at the parking lot captured a trace of someone walking across the street toward the house on Via della Pergola—exactly the hour that, the prosecution and defense would later agree, Meredith crossed her threshold for the last time.

* * *

When *Amélie* ended, I went into the kitchen to take care of some dishes left over from breakfast before we started making dinner. I soon realized that water was leaking out of the pipe under the sink, and I cursed under my breath. I'd had a plumber come and fix the sink just a week earlier, and he had made me buy all sorts of replacement parts that clearly were not put together properly. I suspected he had left them loose on purpose to force me to pay for another visit. As Amanda and I threw kitchen towels onto the puddle on the tile floor, I decided I was going to let my landlady deal with it from now on.

"Don't you have a mop?" Amanda asked. I did not. She offered to pick one up from Via della Pergola the next morning and bring it round.

We cooked a fish dinner, did our best to wash the dishes again, and tumbled gratefully into bed in each other's arms. Only later, when I lay in the dark, unable to sleep, did it dawn on me that Papà had broken his usual habit of calling to wish me good night.

It turned out he did so out of consideration. He had been about to pick up the phone when my stepmother talked him out of it. "Stop bothering him," Mara said, as they got ready for bed around eleven o'clock. "He's with Amanda, and they want to be alone. Why don't you send a text instead?"

My father took her advice, but because my cell phone was turned off, I didn't receive the message until six the next morning.

It was a desperately unlucky combination of circumstances. If my father had tried my cell and then called me on the home line—which he would have done, because he's persistent that way—I would have had incontrovertible proof from the phone records that I was home that night. And the nightmare that was about to engulf me might never have begun.

* * *

My father called my landline a little before nine thirty the next morning to make sure we would be ready for our day trip to Gubbio. I was too groggy to talk. I'd been up several times in the night—listening to music, answering e-mail, making love—and wanted only to go back to sleep. Amanda got out of bed and said she was going home to shower and change her clothes, so I walked her to the front door, gave her a kiss, and crawled back under the covers.

By the time she returned, I was up and in the kitchen making coffee. I could tell something was bothering her, but she didn't say what it was. She'd brought the mop, so I spent some time wiping up while she poured our coffee. Then we sat down to breakfast.

Only when we were close to finishing our cereal did she finally tell me what was on her mind. "I saw some strange things over at the house."

"Strange how?" I asked.

"Well, the front door was open when I arrived, but nobody seemed to be home. At first, I just assumed someone had taken out the garbage or gone to the corner store."

Amanda looked increasingly worried as she began detailing the things she'd found out of place. The open front door was concerning, but not alarming—the latch was broken and the only way to keep it shut was to lock it. But Amanda also found Meredith's door closed, which was unusual. She knocked, but nobody answered. Was she asleep? Or away? Amanda didn't quite know what to think.

Amanda went ahead with her shower, only to notice a small bloodstain on one of the washbasin taps. It looked like menstrual blood. Was Meredith, who shared the bathroom with her, having some sort of problem? It was unlike her to leave things less than immaculate. Maybe she'd run out to a pharmacy. Then again, it was just one small stain; perhaps she missed it.

After she came out of the shower, Amanda went to the other bathroom, the one shared by Filomena and Laura, to use the hair dryer and noticed that somebody had defecated in the toilet and neglected to flush. The bowl was stuffed with toilet paper. Amanda knew Filomena and Laura were scrupulously clean; neither of them would have left that kind of mess. What was going on? Nobody could accuse Amanda of being overanxious, but even she was starting to freak out. Why had the person who left the front door open not come back? Where was Meredith? Amanda decided she didn't want to stay in the house a moment longer. So she grabbed the mop from the closet and left, taking care to lock the door properly on her way out.

* * *

Of all the things Amanda did that day, none attracted more criticism than her failure to raise the alarm as soon as she saw so many things out of place. It wasn't just the police who attacked her. Many Italians, including most of my family, could not fathom how she could go ahead with her shower after finding blood on the tap, much less put her wet feet on the bath mat, which was also stained, and drag it across the floor. When Filomena found out, she called Amanda *cretina,* an idiot.

All I can say is, I was as distracted as she was that morning and might have done the same in her position. I'm not a worrier by nature and just did not think through what Amanda was telling me. After she had finished her story, I shrugged it off, saying there had to be a simple explanation. I was so unconcerned I even asked if she was ready to leave for Gubbio. A stupid question, of course, which Amanda found a little jarring as well.

"Perhaps we should drop the mop off at the house and take another look," she suggested. "It won't take more than a few minutes."

I agreed and suggested she call her housemates to see if they had any idea what was going on.

On the walk over, Amanda reached Filomena at a holiday fair on the outskirts of Perugia. They muddled through the conversation in a combination of Amanda's bad Italian and Filomena's sketchy English. The upshot, though, was clear. Filomena was alarmed and urged Amanda to go back to the house as quickly as possible. "Do a check!" she said more than once. She promised to get there as soon as she could, probably within the hour.

Amanda also tried the two cell phones that Meredith was careful to keep close at all times: the British one she used to call her family, and an Italian one Filomena had given her for local calls.

There was no answer on either.

*　*　*

A few minutes' walk from Amanda's house, Elisabetta Lana and her family were increasingly bewildered by what they feared was an attempt to break into their three-story villa overlooking the Fosso del Bulagaio, the same ravine that extended behind the house on Via della Pergola. The previous night, Elisabetta had received a jarring phone call announcing a bomb in one of her toilets. She had called the Polizia Postale, the postal police, who scoured every inch of the house and grounds and turned up nothing. Still, she asked her son Alessandro to come over and spend the night in the house. They had been burgled a number of times before.

Shortly after breakfast on November 2, Alessandro stepped outside to talk to his girlfriend on the phone and noticed a Motorola flip phone lying facedown on the lawn about sixty feet from the wall separating the property from the street. The phone was switched off. He and his mother assumed, at first, that it must belong to one of the police officers who had visited the night before, and they decided to bring it in. They needed to make an official statement about the threatening call anyway. After Elisabetta completed the paperwork, the police asked her to wait while they extracted the phone's SIM card and traced the owner. Twenty minutes later, they had a name: Filomena Romanelli.

Elisabetta had never heard of her. She called home and nobody, not even the maid, knew who she was either. A few minutes later, while Elisabetta was still out shopping, she received a call from her son announcing that a *second* cell phone had just been found in the garden. Elisabetta's daughter, Fiammetta, and the maid heard it ringing in the underbrush about twenty feet from the property line. By the time they retrieved it, the ringing had stopped.

It was a Sony Ericsson, Meredith's British phone. They brought it into the house, and a couple of minutes later, it rang again. Alessandro looked at the display, which flashed up the name *Amanda*.

* * *

Amanda and I decided to go through her house room by room. Filomena called and said she had spoken to Laura at her family's house near Rome, so only Meredith remained unaccounted for. Her bedroom door was still locked.

I agreed with Amanda, the kitchen and living room looked normal. So did Laura's room; a couple of drawers were pulled open, but that didn't strike me as out of the ordinary. Amanda's room was apparently untouched; she had left the previous night's clothes strewn over her bed, and her other things were less than tidy, but nothing seemed to be missing. Then I pushed open Filomena's door, which had been left slightly ajar, and saw that the place was trashed. Clothes and belongings were strewn everywhere. The window had a large, roundish hole, and broken glass was spread all over the floor.

Okay, we thought, *so there's been a break-in.* What we couldn't understand was why Filomena's laptop was still propped upright in its case on the floor, or why her digital camera was still sitting out in the kitchen. As far as we could tell, nothing of value was missing anywhere.

Amanda went into the Italian women's bathroom alone, only

to run back out and grab on to me as though she had seen a ghost. "The shit's not in the toilet anymore!" she said. "What if the intruder's still here and he's locked himself in Meredith's room?"

We didn't know what to do about Meredith's room. Filomena had called back a couple of times and made us appropriately concerned that Meredith had vanished without a trace. So Amanda knocked at the door, gently at first, then ever louder, until she was banging on it for a response. I made a halfhearted attempt to kick it open but wasn't sure it was the right thing to do. We peered through the keyhole, but all we could see was Meredith's brown leather purse sitting on the unmade bed.

We walked back outside hoping to find a vantage point onto her bedroom window, but no ground was high enough.

"Let's try the terrace at the back and see if we can't reach her window that way," Amanda said, and she dashed out onto the deck. By the time I caught up with her, she had one leg over the balustrade and announced she was going to shimmy her way around the house. It was a crazy idea: there were no toeholds, and the ground fell away as much as fifteen feet below us.

I said, "Don't do anything stupid."

Amanda realized it was a nonstarter, pulled her leg back, and gave me a kiss of endearment for talking her out of it.

"Now what do we do?" she asked.

"I don't know," I said. "Let me call my sister, Vanessa. She's in the carabinieri. She'll tell us."

*　*　*

My big sister is someone you don't mess with. Vanessa's not extraordinarily tall and is almost preternaturally slight, but she has the muscle tone of a professional athlete and a tongue so sharp you can cut yourself on it. She's seven years older than me and likes to think of herself as my protector. Honestly, there are times when her refusal to indulge other people's shortcomings, even for a moment, grates on my nerves. But she's also smart and passionate and unburdened by my tendency toward self-doubt and second-guessing. In a crisis, there's nobody better.

Vanessa lived in Rome, where she had a desk job with the carabinieri, the Italian military police. It wasn't what she imagined when, in 2000, she became one of the first women to enter the Italian air force. She beat out everyone, men as well as women, for top place in her year's intake. As she would be the first to tell you, though, Vanessa is no diplomat and refuses to play the game the way Italians expect it to be played. She fell out with her air force superiors over a romantic liaison, joined the navy on the rebound, then mounted a legal battle against a reluctant Ministry of Defense when she wanted to change jobs once more and join the carabinieri. By the time she won that fight, she had spent two years on unpaid administrative leave and was viewed as a troublemaker who needed to be brought down a peg or two.

Vanessa is almost absurdly accomplished: she is a champion show-jumping rider, a certified fighter pilot, and has three university degrees, in archaeology, political science, and international law. When she applied to the carabinieri, she imagined herself flying helicopters or working with a mounted division. Instead, she was assigned to logistics, where her days involved coordinating elevator repairs and making furniture inventories for the force's 375 barracks in the region around Rome.

Since she was so comprehensively desk-bound, I had no difficulty in getting her on the phone right away. I had barely finished describing what we had found at the house when she responded with great urgency. "Leave! Leave right away," she said. "And don't touch anything. If there has been a burglary, you don't want any trace of yourself on the premises. I can't do anything for you from here, but go outside and call the local carabinieri. Let them handle everything—it's not your problem."

I passed the message along to Amanda, and we did exactly as instructed.

* * *

We must have looked like two abandoned waifs as we sat facing the street on a concrete step just above the roadway. Amanda was not wearing nearly enough for the cold weather, just a thin sweater over her T-shirt, and she started to shiver as I dialed the emergency number for the carabinieri. On the first try, the dispatcher said he was busy and told me to call back. Not exactly the response I wanted to hear. When I called back a few minutes later, he was still noticeably impatient.

When I described the break-in and the bloodstains, and he became fixated on the idea that the intruder had cut himself on the glass on the way through Filomena's window. I didn't quite know how to respond to that, and when I hesitated, he growled at me to make sure I was still there.

"So it's a home burglary?" he asked.

"No, nothing's been taken." I didn't know that for sure, of course, and I should have been more careful about my choice of words. At the time, though, I thought I was just performing my civic duty by passing the information along. The only reason I was on the line was because Amanda's Italian was not good enough for her to make the call herself.

"You say there's a locked door," the dispatcher said. "What door is that?"

"One of the tenants', and we don't know where she is. We've tried to call but she's not picking up."

"Okay," he said at length. "I'll send a squad car and we'll look into it."

* * *

Minutes later, too soon—I thought—for anyone to have responded to my call, an imposing man in his late thirties strolled toward us with a sense of purpose that made me nervous. He was in casual clothes and Adidas sneakers. I wasn't sure if he was a member of the carabinieri, inexplicably out of uniform, or someone we needed to steer clear of. I jumped up as he approached, very much on the defensive.

He flashed a badge—I didn't look at it closely—and asked if we were acquainted with a Filomena Romanelli.

"Why?" I asked.

"It's for us to know why," he replied sourly. As I learned later, this was Michele Battistelli, chief investigator for the Polizia Postale, and he was here to trace the abandoned cell phones. His deputy, who had been parking their car, joined him moments later.

I didn't understand at first why they were asking for Filomena, but I did tell them about the mess inside and invited them to take a look. They agreed it was strange that no valuables had been taken. In fact Battistelli, a telecommunications specialist with little experience of burglaries, much less murder, was already formulating a theory that the break-in was staged. No doubt he was thinking of insurance fraud, but the theory would carry over into the murder investigation and prove disastrous for us.

Once Battistelli and his colleague Fabio Marzi started looking around, Filomena's boyfriend, Marco, arrived with his friend, Luca. I didn't know either of them. Minutes after that, while we were all looking at the mess in Filomena's room, Filomena herself showed up with her friend Paola, who was Luca's girlfriend. Filomena confirmed that nothing valuable was gone from her room. Her jewelry was still in the nightstand. After rummaging around—and disturbing the crime scene—she retrieved her cash and designer sunglasses. She later removed her laptop too.

As soon as the police disclosed that Meredith's two cell phones had been thrown over Elisabetta Lana's wall, Filomena felt enough was enough: someone had to open Meredith's door immediately. Battistelli slowed her down just enough to ask if it was normal to find the door locked. Filomena told him no, absolutely not, unless Meredith was away in England. I didn't hear her say this because I was busy repeating the question in English for Amanda. And, unfortunately, I misunderstood Amanda's answer. I thought Amanda said that, yes, Meredith sometimes kept the door closed, even when she was in town. But that was not right; Amanda said exactly the same thing as Filomena. Because of this translation error, Amanda would later be accused of telling lies to throw off the investigation.

Battistelli didn't want to take responsibility for the door. Filomena said that if he wouldn't authorize breaking it, she wanted him to bring in someone who would. "Okay, calm down, there's no need to call anyone," Battistelli shot back. "It's not like we're going to find a body under the couch."

It was not a line he would later care to remember.

Filomena glared at Battistelli and asked Marco and Luca if they'd break down the door instead. Luca needed no further prompting and began shoving and kicking.

The door flew open. I was several people back in the narrow corridor at this point, so I saw nothing. Amanda was farther back still, toward the kitchen, talking to her mother in Seattle. But I certainly registered the horror etched on everyone's face.

Paola screamed. "Blood!" she and the others shouted. "Blood everywhere!" And then: "A foot! A foot!"

I saw Filomena holding her hands up in front of her face and breaking out in great sobs. Marco pulled her back as abruptly as he could. Amanda told her mother about the foot and got off the line. I took her by the arm and escorted her out of the house. The others quickly followed.

Only Luca stayed a few seconds more and later testified he saw Inspector Battistelli venture into the room and lift the blood-soaked duvet that was covering Meredith's body on the floor. Battistelli himself denied doing any such thing, insisting that he knew better than to contaminate a murder scene. Yet, somehow, he felt confident enough on the phone to emergency services to confirm that Meredith was already dead.

The six of us hovered outside while Battistelli and Marzi made their calls. Amanda was in tears, too stunned and fearful to say a word. She and I just held each other in silence. I was too shell-shocked to know what to think; my only impulse was to look out for Amanda, so I concentrated on that. It was better than wondering what had happened to poor Meredith; whatever it was seemed too awful to contemplate. One of the others mentioned seeing blood on the wall and a body laid out in front of an open closet. Amanda picked up only part of this and later said she thought that Meredith had been found *inside* the closet—another misunderstanding later characterized as a deliberate evasion.

Only after the medical emergency team arrived did we learn what we had scarcely allowed ourselves to imagine. Meredith's throat was slashed, a paramedic told Luca, and she had been left to die in a pool of her own blood.

* * *

The carabinieri, like the Polizia Postale before them, got lost on the way to Via della Pergola and had to call Amanda's cell phone for directions. It wasn't an easy place to find because the street signs suggested that Via della Pergola had, at this point, turned into Viale Sant'Angelo, and the one-way traffic system meant there was no going back. The delay had a huge impact in determining our fate because the case was turned over instead to the Perugia city police, who had far less experience than the carabinieri in conducting high-profile criminal investigations and were less likely to assert their independence from the prosecutor's office.

As things spiraled out of control over the next several days, a senior investigator with the carabinieri in Perugia took it upon himself to call my sister and apologize, colleague to colleague. "If we had arrived ten minutes earlier," he told Vanessa, "the case would have been ours. And things would have gone very differently."

* * *

Instead of the carabinieri, we got the Squadra Mobile, the flying squad of the Perugia police, who sent a forensic team kitted out in white protective suits (but no hoods), as well as a handful of detectives, all in plainclothes. At first, I helped Amanda sit down on the same step where we had waited before. She was pale and almost doubled over with anguish. Then we got up so I could give her my green-gray jacket, and we walked toward the crisscross-wooden fence overlooking the ravine. I noticed that a tightly wound woman with jet-black hair—whom I later knew as Monica Napoleoni, the head of the Squadra Mobile's homicide division—was staring at us, her eyes bulging. I couldn't understand what she wanted. At various moments she turned her body away and said something to her colleagues, covering her mouth with her hand so we couldn't read her lips. She shot glances at us while she was talking.

Amanda and I stayed close to comfort each other and to shield ourselves as best we could from the cold. I was so focused I had no idea that television crews were setting up across the street and training their cameras on us. I caressed Amanda's arms and leaned in for a kiss. She was my girlfriend—at least, we were together for the moment—and I desperately wanted to comfort her. The world's media—cajoled by the police and uninterested in the context— would soon play up that kiss, a simple act of human sympathy in a moment of grief and shock, as evidence of the uncontrolled sexual urges of two stone-cold killers.

* * *

Inside the house, the police, later joined by a second forensic team from the Polizia Scientifica in Rome, were making their first assessments. We were privy to none of it. Only later did we learn about the knife wounds on both sides of Meredith's neck, the multiple signs of struggle, the blood-soaked towels under her body, the evidence that her attacker had stripped her almost naked but had not, apparently, attempted any sexual penetration, and the curious trail of shoe prints, all made with a left shoe, and the equally curious trail of footprints, all made with a right foot.

The police asked us questions, just routine stuff to establish our identities and our relationship to Meredith. Filomena had the wherewithal to call one of the lawyers from her office to seek advice on how much to say. Laura, who did not return to Perugia immediately, did the same. I called my family and told them what was going on, but it never occurred to me, or to them, to contact a lawyer. As I saw it, I was just a bystander, a translator for my girlfriend, happy to tell the police whatever they wanted to know.

After some time—it was hard to tell how long—we were told we needed to go to the Questura, Perugia's police headquarters, for more detailed questioning. Amanda and I accepted a ride from Luca and Paola. As we climbed into their car, Paola—who had never met either of us before—asked Amanda how she had reacted when she found the front door open that morning.

Amanda didn't understand the question, so I answered for her, explaining that she'd taken a shower and then come back to my house.

"Really, you took a shower?" Paola said. She was incredulous.

Amanda was still troubled about the toilet that was unflushed one minute and flushed the next, so I mentioned it. Paola and Luca said it could be important and we needed to tell the police right away. So I got out of the car and discussed it with Monica Napoleoni. It was another ill-fated move because Amanda was mistaken— for what reason I do not know. The excrement in the toilet was still there, as the forensics team soon discovered. Maybe it had sunk a little in the bowl as the paper absorbed the water and grew heavier. Or maybe Amanda was just disturbed by the scene and hadn't been thinking clearly when she made that observation—who knows.

As we finally drove off to the Questura, the atmosphere was

frosty. Clearly, Amanda and I hadn't given a good account of ourselves. To break the tension, I quizzed Luca on what he knew, as he seemed better informed than anybody. But everything coming out of my mouth felt clumsy and out of place.

"So she's dead?" I asked.

"Yes."

"Murdered?"

"Yes, someone cut her throat."

"With a knife?"

"No, with a loaf of bread," Luca snapped. "What do you think?"

Amanda, at this point, was crying again. We continued to the Perugia suburbs in silence.

* * *

Around 3:00 p.m., the man responsible for overseeing the investigation, public prosecutor Giuliano Mignini, was given his first glimpse of the crime scene. The head of Perugia's vice squad collected Mignini from his house, where he had just enjoyed lunch with his wife and three teenage daughters, and briefed him on the police's best guesses so far: that Meredith had been sexually assaulted, that the break-in looked staged, that one of Meredith's housemates was saying odd things about the toilet.

Mignini, who was fifty-seven and a lifelong *perugino,* did not have a lot of experience with murder cases, with one striking exception. He had spent the previous five years reinvestigating the drowning of a well-connected local doctor, Francesco Narducci, who was fished out of Lake Trasimeno in 1985. Mignini's theory was that Narducci did not commit suicide, as had long been assumed, but was murdered by members of a satanic death cult. Mignini further theorized that Narducci's death, and the cult, were connected to a string of unsolved serial murders in Tuscany known as the Monster of Florence case—a hypothesis that brought him only ridicule from his Florentine colleagues, who had been trying to track down the Monster for more than thirty years. The case was at least good for generating headlines: Mignini exhumed the corpse, speculated that it was not Narducci's but had been swapped before the funeral for murky reasons connected to a gang of loan sharks, and theorized that Narducci himself had been part of the satanic cult.

By November 2007, Mignini was steeped in accounts of devil-worship rituals, secret Masonic sects, and symbolic portals leading from this earth to the bowels of hell. So when he stepped into Meredith's room, he was alert to things other investigators might have overlooked.

He saw Meredith's Dracula costume from Halloween, including fake teeth and a cape. He saw an open pot of Vaseline on her desk, which in his mind was immediately associated with anal sex. He saw her near-naked body, with her legs splayed open and spots of blood on her chest just above her naked breasts. And he saw the bloody prints with their curious left-shoe, right-foot pattern.

Over time, he would wonder whether Meredith's murder was connected to the same Order of the Red Rose he suspected of being behind the Monster of Florence killings. He knew of a Masonic ritual that involved the removal of one shoe. He also knew about the ceremony of the Rose-Croix, which Masons perform on the Thursday before Easter to initiate new members, but which some Catholics view as a blasphemous imitation of the Passion of Christ. Did that ceremony's use of a Cubic Stone, symbolically mixing blood and water, have anything to do with the sodden, bloodstained bath mat? Was it significant that Meredith's murder took place on a Thursday? Or was it rather, as Mignini argued in a preliminary hearing a year later, that Meredith was destined to be part of a satanic sex sacrifice on Halloween but the ceremony was postponed for twenty-four hours because it clashed with a dinner party thrown by Filomena and Laura?

To an outsider this must sound more like a conspiracy-laden plotline from Umberto Eco than the workings of a public prosecutor's office. I wish I were making it up. But this was the mind-set we were dealing with: a grand, baroque imagination that could never be satisfied with the banalities of a brutal, straightforward murder by a man with a clearly established criminal history. From the beginning, the notion that a burglar broke in, came across Meredith unexpectedly, and killed her in a panic—the simplest and most plausible explanation of the scene at Via della Pergola—could not have been further from the prosecutor's mind.

* * *

The head of the Squadra Mobile, Domenico Giacinto Profazio, raced back to Perugia from his own *ponte dei morti* and quickly concurred, when he arrived in the late afternoon, that breaking in through Filomena's window was too difficult to be plausible. Profazio took a walk around the house and concluded it would have made much more sense for an intruder to clamber over the balcony, the one Amanda had run to, and use a flowerpot or a chair to smash a window. Therefore, Profazio concluded, the murderer or murderers must have come into the house using a key and faked the break-in after Meredith was killed.

The police never wavered from this view for the next four years.

* * *

The night at the Questura seemed to last f___ ___
were put in a waiting room with Meredith's Engli___
around shaking hands and explained that we were the o___
stumbled on the crime scene. But it was hardly the time to start
socializing, and the English girls kept mostly to themselves.

Amanda curled up on me like a koala bear, grabbing hold of my
neck with both arms and resting her body on my lap. We nuzzled,
and at one point she stuck out her tongue at me as a joke.

Police officers passed by regularly and glared at us. *"State com-
posti!"* one shouted. Behave yourselves.

When they told us to sit separately, I responded, "But it's cold."

"This is a Questura," they shot back.

The English girls later said they were appalled by Amanda's behavior, and I admit, it made me a little uneasy too. This was a public
place, in the middle of a murder investigation, and she was acting like
a little girl. She even complained about being hungry and thirsty; the
Questura offered us nothing but a vending machine and we were not
allowed to leave. Days earlier, under very different circumstances, this
quirky, unrestrained behavior had drawn me to her. But here it was embarrassing, and I can understand why Meredith's friends were put off.

In the moment, I didn't say anything because I didn't want to
make Amanda feel worse. The whole purpose of my being there was
to comfort her. So I defended her, even beyond the point where
I felt comfortable or could be said to be looking out for my own
interests. I don't know how to account for that entirely, except to
say I was not thinking straight and badly underestimated the possible consequences of my actions. Amanda did sit on her own peri-
odically to write in her journal; she said she felt like writing a song

bout everything that was going on and—as the Italian papers later reported with relish—"could kill" for a pizza. This was Amanda free-associating, as Amanda the West Coast dreamer was in the habit of doing; she too did not stop to think that someone might later read what she was writing and judge her for it.

I called my father to complain about how long they were making us wait. Papà was only so sympathetic. "Just do what you need to do," he said.

Eventually, Amanda was summoned. She left for so long I fell asleep. Apparently, they tried to question her in Italian first, then brought in an interpreter because they weren't getting anywhere. Amanda ran through everything she could remember about her few weeks in the house and had her fingerprints taken. My own session was much more straightforward: I gave the police my account of the events of the day, they said thank you and let me go.

By the time Amanda was through, it was five thirty in the morning. We headed back to my place—the only place Amanda now had—for a proper meal and some sleep. But we couldn't rest long. The police told us she needed to be back by 11:00 a.m.

* * *

Amanda was called into the Questura again and again, and each time I grew more perplexed. *Why focus on her, and not on Meredith's other friends?* I wondered. She and Amanda were new acquaintances, and there was never any animosity between them. How often could the police ask about their jaunts around Perugia, the meals they shared in the flat, or the way they organized the morning bathroom rota? I just couldn't see what the interest was. I grew frustrated, too, by the way the police seemed to rely on me as a taxi service. I would take Amanda to the Questura in the morning, then pick her up again when she was done. Concentrating on my thesis became increasingly difficult. After the first couple of days, I had to resist the urge to say: If you want her, come and get her yourselves.

What I did not know was that the pool of available interview subjects was narrowing. At least two of Meredith's English friends, Robyn and Amy, had left town, apparently terrified that whoever killed Meredith might come after them next. And a third friend, Sophie Purton, inadvertently poured gas onto the fire of the police's budding sex-game theory. Sophie described a string of men that Amanda had invited back to the house (based on secondhand information from Meredith). Sophie didn't mean they were invited back for sex necessarily, but that was how the police—and the press, once they heard about it—inevitably interpreted it.

Amanda noticed the police's sex obsession right away; they couldn't stop asking her about the Vaseline pot and a vibrator they had found in the bathroom. The vibrator was a joke item, a little rubber bunny rabbit shaped to look like a vibrator and fashioned into a pendant, but the police seemed to find this difficult to accept. What about Meredith's sex life? Amanda knew only that Meredith had left a boyfriend in England and was now involved with one of the men who lived downstairs, a twenty-two-year-old telecommunications student with a carefully sculpted beard and outsize earrings named Giacomo Silenzi. Amanda had helped Meredith out a couple times by giving her a condom from her supply. But Amanda had no idea how, or how often, Meredith had sex and didn't feel comfortable fielding questions about it.

Silenzi had taken extraordinary precautions from the moment he heard about Meredith's murder. When he took the train back to Perugia from his parents' house, he got off one stop early and waited for one of his university professors to meet him. He then sat in the Perugia train station, with the professor, until his parents could make the journey themselves. By the time the police spoke to him, he also had a lawyer. Clearly, Silenzi either suspected the police would pursue a sex angle and felt vulnerable, or was appropriately skeptical of authority. We could have used a dose of that skepticism ourselves.

The day after the discovery of the body, on November 3, Amanda asked if we could go shopping because she'd retrieved nothing from the house, not even underwear, and it was now inaccessible. We first tried an outlet called Timbro, which specializes in fashions for our age group, but it was too expensive. So we moved on to a bright pink teen discount store, Bubble, where she tried on some jeans and eventually settled on a laughably childish thong with a cow motif.

I made a joke in English, saying something along the lines of, "Wow, you're going to look smoking hot in those."

A few days later, this episode would be distorted in the newspapers to make it seem as if the first thing we did after the murder was to buy sexy lingerie—specifically, a G-string—and tell each other how we couldn't wait to try it out. The store owner, who did not speak English, corroborated the story in pursuit of his own brief moment in the spotlight. True, the surveillance video in the store showed us touching and kissing, but that was hardly a crime. I wasn't making out with her in some vulgar or inappropriate way, just comforting her and letting her know I was there for her. Besides, there was nothing remotely sexy about Bubble. A much sexier underwear store was next door, and we didn't set foot in there.

* * *

The police were at last pointed in the right direction by Stefano Bonassi, another of the boys who lived downstairs from Meredith and Amanda, who mentioned Rudy Guede as soon as he was interviewed and described the strange night about a month earlier when Guede slept on the boys' couch.

Guede himself had been behaving strangely. At 2:00 a.m. on the night of the murder, he was spotted dancing at a Perugia club called Domus. The following night he was back, smelling as if he hadn't washed in a while, according to one Italian student acquaintance who was there with him. The news of Meredith's murder had broken just a few hours earlier, and everyone was talking about it. When the dancers were asked to observe a minute's silence, they all complied immediately—except for Guede, who kept right on dancing. That got several people's attention.

The next morning, perhaps in reaction to the ubiquitous banner headlines describing Meredith being slaughtered like a farm animal, he hopped on a train to Milan. And a day after that, he fled to Germany.

* * *

As the days went by—it was now Sunday, November 4, three days after the murder—I realized I had not properly acknowledged my own discomfort with Amanda. I was not scandalized by her, in the way that so many others later said they were, but I shouldn't have allowed her to climb all over me in the Questura, and I should have counseled her quietly not to complain so much. I understood the gallant side of being her boyfriend, but I could have given her better advice and protected myself in the process.

What brought my discomfort to the surface was her old boy-friend, D.J. He kept calling from China to find out how she was, which was understandable, except that she clearly shared an intimacy with him that I was not welcome to intrude on. Amanda would Skype him at five o'clock in the morning and, when he asked, say only that I was half her boyfriend and half not. *So that's the thanks I get,* I couldn't help thinking.

One time when he called, I picked up the phone and told him to try again later because Amanda was in the bathroom. Another time, Amanda put me on the line so D.J. could thank me in person for everything I was doing. The conversation made me extremely uncomfortable. What was I, just the stand-in to get her through her time of difficulty in Italy while he was unavoidably on the other side of the world? I didn't think I was a jealous person, but this was about more than jealousy. Nobody seemed to be considering my feelings at all.

In retrospect, I realize we were all under tremendous pressure. Amanda stayed up until three in the morning one night writing a long e-mail for her friends and family back home to describe everything that had happened. She talked about the "hurricane of emotions and stress" involved in dealing with everything from her grief over Meredith, to the constant barrage of police questions, to the avalanche of practical issues that she, Filomena, and Laura faced as tenants in a house that nobody was likely to be able to enter for weeks or even months. Hours after sending that message, Amanda was back at the Questura—with me tagging along—answering questions about every man she'd met in Perugia since she'd arrived.

She told them, quite openly, about a guy from Rome she went to bed with a few days before meeting me. She had no problem being open about her sex life, and that made her interrogators suspicious. How many men, they wondered, did she plan on getting through during her year in Perugia? The American attitude to sex—the embrace of youthful experimentation as a normal stage on the way to adult maturity—was entirely alien, even abhorrent, to them.

Amanda was getting her period, one more reason for her to feel uncomfortable and moody, and she sent me out to buy tampons and a slice of pizza. As I left the Questura, I noticed that a policewoman had followed me out. She approached surreptitiously, as though not wanting to be seen.

She slipped a business card in my hand and said it was for a lawyer. "Give him a call," she said deliberately. "You're going to need him for sure."

It could not have been a more explicit warning. But I didn't know this woman and I refused to take her seriously. I thought, *What do I have to be worried about?*

I put the card in my wallet and forgot about it. Regrettably, I never saw the policewoman again.

* * *

My family did not share my breezy optimism about the way things were going and worried about the endless time I was spending with the police. Officially, I was a *persona informata dei fatti,* a "person informed of the facts" and helping police with their inquiries, no more. But my father decided he'd call a friend who was a criminal lawyer and ask his opinion.

I'd grown up thinking of Tiziano Tedeschi as an uncle. When I was little, he and my father were almost inseparable, although the closer friendship was now between my father and Tiziano's older brother, Enrico. My father knew Tiziano as a friend, not by reputation. Still, he imagined Tiziano would do everything he could to safeguard my interests.

Papà couldn't help feeling a little disappointed by the response. Tiziano said he put a call into the Questura and there was nothing to worry about. He was told it was all routine.

My sister, Vanessa, made her own separate inquiries and felt much less reassured. The first time she called the Questura, they left her waiting on the line, even though she announced herself as a lieutenant in the carabinieri, and never took her call.

The second time, she had herself put through from the carabinieri's regional switchboard, to make it more official. This time she got through, but only to a junior policeman clearly her inferior. (In Italian law enforcement, protocol on such matters is followed scrupulously.) "Listen," the man told her impatiently, "everything is fine."

"Is there someone I can talk to who is in charge of this case?" Vanessa insisted.

"No, no. It's all routine. Don't worry."

Unlike Tiziano Tedeschi, though, my sister *did* worry. To her, the conversation raised a lot more questions than it answered.

* * *

Amanda was exhausted. She would sprawl out on the chairs in the Questura, complaining of feeling unwell. Her interpreter noticed she was unusually pale and further noticed that her pallor revealed a small red mark on her neck. The police seized on this as possible evidence of injury during the murder, but it was nothing, most likely the residue of a love bite I had given her myself.

Shortly after I returned with pizza on the afternoon of November 4, Monica Napoleoni announced that Amanda, Filomena, and Laura needed to accompany her back to the murder house. They were gone for two or three hours. Later, I learned that Amanda had broken down, shaking and weeping, after she was asked to go through the knife drawer in the kitchen. Napoleoni asked her if anything was missing. Nothing was.

It didn't seem to us that the investigation was going anywhere. What we didn't realize was that they had already decided we were somehow involved and were watching us like hawks for any word or sign or gesture that would corroborate their suspicions. The waiting room where we sat was bugged, and our phones were now tapped too.

That night, still at the Questura, Amanda started asking me the meaning of various Italian swearwords. I gave her the English equivalents of *vaffanculo* (fuck off) and *li mortacci tua* (I spit on your dead ancestors), and we started laughing. It was just a stupid conversation to pass the time. But, to the eavesdropping Perugia police, it added to a mounting body of evidence that something was seriously wrong with us.

Pressure to solve the case was growing by the day. In a city that made a significant part of its living off foreign students, a brutal murder such as Meredith's was hardly good for business. "Perugians," the city's mayor, Renato Rocchi, said, "expect the culprit to be identified quickly and punished in exemplary fashion." The police chief, Arturo De Felice, was getting the message loud and clear. "Every investigative tool at our disposal," he promised, "every resource and area of expertise, has been deployed to get to the bottom of this as soon as possible."

The truth, though, was that the authorities were still clueless about the most important pieces of evidence—in particular, the identity of whoever made the bloody shoe prints and footprints, and the source of the DNA samples found around the house that did not belong to anyone who had come forward so far. If Rudy Guede had not skipped town, he might have been tested, identified, and apprehended by now. Instead, the police could only turn to what they had, the DNA and fingerprint traces in the house that they *could* identify. Laura had an incontrovertible alibi because she had been out of town on the night of the murder. The same went for the boys downstairs. Filomena had not only been with her boyfriend, but with Luca and Paola too. That left Amanda and—since I was always with her when she came to the Questura—me.

What did they have on us? Nothing of substance. But they did find our behavior odd, and we had no real alibi for the night of November 1 except each other, and we did not have lawyers to protect us, and we seemed to have a propensity for saying things without thinking them through. In other words, we were the lowest-hanging fruit, and the police simply reached out and grabbed us.

How could they do that in the absence of hard evidence? Edgardo Giobbi of the Servizio Centrale Operativo, the country's serious-crime squad, essentially gave the game away in a British television documentary that aired six months after Meredith's murder. Giobbi came up to Perugia from Rome to oversee the interrogations, so he knew the sequence of events as well as anybody. He had had it in for Amanda ever since he'd seen her bend down to put on protective footwear at the murder house on November 3 and thought he saw her do a suggestive hip-swivel known in Italy as *la mossa,* "the move."

"The investigation was of an exclusively psychological nature," Giobbi said, "because what enabled us to identify the culprits was, most of all, our observation of their psychological and behavioral reactions while they were being questioned. We didn't rely on any other kind of investigation, but this is what allowed us to finger the culprits in such a short time."

Well, this was at least frank. And staggering too. They arrested us because they didn't like us. Period. Not only did they have no physical evidence, they saw no need for any.

Of course, *something* was required to justify slamming us behind bars. Even in Italy, people don't get arrested for swiveling their hips or kissing outside a house where a murder has just taken place. As November 4 turned into November 5, the police were still scratching around. The bugged room at the Questura wasn't giving them much. (We know this because, if we had given them anything, they would have used it.) The taps on our phones were proving equally frustrating. Some of the investigators, I imagine, thought they would overhear a confession, or some indication of fear or panic. But of course we gave them nothing like that because we had nothing to confess.

What the police did learn from the wiretaps was that Amanda's mother, Edda, was flying in from Seattle and would arrive on Tuesday, November 6. They also heard Amanda talking to her relatives in Germany, who were advising her to take refuge in the American embassy. In short, they could count on her to be vulnerable and alone for just one more day. After that, she might be out of reach, or out of the country. Somewhere along the line, someone decided that if we were to be arrested, it had to happen in the next twenty-four hours.

One real clue, one element of reasonable suspicion, was all they needed to pounce.

And I, inadvertently, gave it to them.

* * *

As November 5 began, we allowed ourselves to wonder if things weren't slowly getting back to normal—the proverbial calm before the storm. There was no call from the Questura. Amanda went to class and wandered over to Le Chic to talk to Patrick. I stayed at home and worked on my thesis.

Then my father called and asked about my pocketknife. Carrying a small knife had been a habit of mine since I was a teenager—not for self-defense, mind you, just as an ornamental thing. I'd use one occasionally to peel apples or carve my name on tree trunks, but mostly I carried them around for the sake of it. Having a knife on me had become automatic, like carrying my wallet or my keys. The one in my pocket that day had been a present from my father.

"You should really leave it at home," Papà advised. "You don't want to get into trouble over it."

I hadn't given the knife a second thought. Now that he mentioned it, I still couldn't see the harm. The blade was barely three inches long and hadn't been opened in weeks. Besides, what kind of idiot killer would bring the murder weapon to the police station?

"Don't worry," I told my father. "I've had my knife on me every day and they haven't even noticed it."

Whoever was listening at the Questura pricked up their ears; I certainly had their attention now.

I got the call at about ten o'clock that night. I was at my friend Riccardo's house for dinner, along with Riccardo's sister and Amanda. The police said they wanted to talk to me. Not Amanda, just me.

"I'm having dinner and I can't come right now," I said.

That annoyed whoever was on the other end of the line. I wasn't taking the request seriously enough. "You need to come in right away," he said.

I told him I would finish eating first. I didn't care how urgent it was; I couldn't be at their beck and call twenty-four hours a day.

* * *

My father called at eleven to wish me good night. By then I'd arrived at the Questura, with Amanda joining me for the ride. After all the times I'd supported her during her interrogations, she felt the least she could do was be there for me.

My father was alarmed. "Are you sure everything is all right? Why are you there yet again?"

"I can't talk now, Papà, but don't worry. Everything's fine."

My words in Italian—*stai tranquillo*—were the last my father would hear from me as a free man.

* * *

The police's tone was aggressive from the start. They wanted to know why Amanda was with me. I said she was my girlfriend and had nowhere else to go. They told her to wait while they took me into an interrogation room.

The questioning was led by two men, a tall, thin policeman I later knew as Marco Chiacchiera, the head of the Squadra Mobile's organized-crime team, and a blond investigator from Edgardo Giobbi's squad in Rome named Daniele Moscatelli. Monica Napoleoni, the Perugia police's top homicide investigator, came and went as the interrogation progressed, as did other officers whose names I learned only much later from the legal files.

"You need to tell us what happened that night," they began.

"Which night?" I asked wearily. I was getting tired of the endless questioning. I don't think they appreciated my attitude.

"The night of November first."

It had been a long week and now it was late. I couldn't focus on which night they were talking about, or what I might have been doing. Hadn't I already told them everything I knew?

"We need you to go over it all again and compare what you have to say with your previous statements. There may be something we've missed."

"I don't remember too well."

"It doesn't matter. Tell us what you can."

I'm recounting this now at a distance of almost four and a half years and I certainly don't claim to remember every word in the order that was spoken. The exchange, as I'm reproducing it here, is based on my memory. I can vividly recall the overall shape and tone and mood of the interrogation, because it scared me half to death and had a catastrophic impact. Some of it is confirmed by the documents the police themselves produced that night and by witness testimony in our trials; some of it has been contested and may well be contested again.

I'd like to be able to give you the full transcript, word by excruciating word. But the police, who were recording absolutely everything else concerning Amanda and me in this period—phone calls, e-mails, private conversations in the Questura—somehow omitted to turn on a single recording device that night. Or so they said. When challenged on this point, Prosecutor Mignini suggested that the Questura was suffering a budget crunch and preferred not to record our interrogations because the transcription costs would have been too steep.

My lawyers, and Amanda's lawyers, subsequently argued that the entire episode was unconstitutional because we had clearly crossed over from "people informed of the facts" to criminal suspects and, under Italian law, needed to be formally notified and provided access to legal counsel. We were vindicated on this point in the Corte di Cassazione, Italy's high court, as I will explain in more detail later. The fact that the night's events were not recorded only heightened the stench of illegality.

I now believe that the only reason they asked me to recount the events of the night of the murder yet again was to catch me out in whatever inconsistencies they could find. They were, quite literally, out to get me, and I didn't appreciate this until it was too late. I told them, again, about the afternoon at Via della Pergola, about smoking a joint—more than I should have volunteered, perhaps—and heading over to my place. I mentioned that Amanda and I gone out shopping, something I had apparently omitted in my previous statements. I couldn't see the importance of this detail, but my interrogators gave me the strangest of looks.

I told them that one day had blended into another in my mind. Perhaps we'd gone shopping the day before. What did I know?

"You need to remember what you did," one of them admonished.

They asked if Amanda had gone out that night, and on the spur of the moment, I couldn't say. Was November 1 a Tuesday or Thursday? I asked. Because I knew she worked at Le Chic on Tuesdays and Thursdays.

I noticed a calendar in the room and asked if I could consult it.

"Don't touch the calendar!" one of them said sharply. The suddenness of this startled me.

Was November 1 the day Amanda spent the evening out and I stayed home? (I was thinking of Halloween.) Or was it the night after that? Somehow I had the two muddled in my head and I couldn't sort them out. As the interrogation continued, I offered both scenarios.

"Watch out," they said, "you are getting yourself in trouble. You're telling us different things. You need to understand the seriousness of the situation."

I thought awhile before answering. "If it was a Thursday, she probably went to work."

"You don't know what she did, do you? Come on, tell us everything."

Napoleoni was in the room for this part of the conversation. Without warning, she turned on me with venom in her voice. "What did you do?" she demanded. "You need to tell us. You don't know what that *cow,* that *whore,* got up to!"

I couldn't believe what was coming out of her mouth. I was only dimly beginning to realize what she and the others were implying. Amanda, the murderer? It seemed too crazy to believe.

Amanda, meanwhile, was waiting for me. And waiting. She had brought some homework into the Questura but was having a hard time concentrating. She was stiff and achy from fatigue and thought she might feel better if she stretched a bit.

She was by an elevator, away from the main waiting area, but she was seen, of course. Ivan Raffo, a young policeman who had come up from Rome, remarked how flexible she was. And Amanda, allowing herself to be charmed in the worst of all circumstances, decided to show him what she could do.

It was a disastrous idea. When I first heard about what happened next, I understood that Amanda, being Amanda, was mostly interested in being open and friendly to the officer. But I also realized she had not been thinking smartly, to say the least. Later, in court, Chief Inspector Rita Ficarra described her shock at walking by and seeing Amanda doing cartwheels and splits. In a police station. In the context of a murder investigation. At least two other senior officers saw her too.

Shortly after, Ficarra and her colleague Lorena Zugarini told Amanda they needed to have a frank conversation. And so began her own long night of the soul.

*   *   *

As my interrogators ratcheted up the pressure, they asked me to empty my pockets. I knew immediately this was not a good development. I pulled out a handkerchief, my wallet, my cell phone, and at last, with all eyes on me, the pocketknife.

One of them picked it up with a piece of cloth and took it swiftly out of the room. I tried to explain that it was something I just carried around with me, but that wouldn't wash. Even I knew things were no longer all right.

"Don't I have the right to a lawyer?" I asked.

They said no.

"Can't I at least call my father?"

"You can't call anyone." They ordered me to put my cell phone on the desk.

People came in and out of the room in a great flurry of activity. At one point, I found myself alone with just one of the policemen. He leaned into me and hissed, "If you try to get up and leave, I'll beat you into a pulp and kill you. I'll leave you in a pool of blood."

The evening was described very differently by the police officers in court. They denied that I ever asked for a lawyer, or that I was put under duress of any kind. Daniele Moscatelli, the cop from Rome, said, "Whatever he wanted, water or whatever, was made fully available to him."

But, I can assure you, I was scared out of my wits, and completely bewildered. I had been brought up to think the police were honest defenders of public safety. My sister was a member of the carabinieri, no less! Now it seemed to me they were behaving more like gangsters.

Then came a sound that chilled my bones: Amanda's voice, yowling for help in the next room. She was screaming in Italian, *"Aiuto! Aiuto!"*

I asked what was going on, and Moscatelli told me there was nothing to worry about. But that was absurd. I could hear police officers yelling, and Amanda sobbing and crying out another three or four times.

What was this? When would it ever end?

* * *

Something was exciting the police more than my pocketknife, and that was the pattern they had detected on the bottom of my shoes. By sheer bad luck, I was wearing Nikes that night, and the pattern of concentric circles on the soles instantly reminded my interrogators of the bloody shoe prints at the scene of the crime, which were made by Nikes too.

I had no idea of any of this. All I knew was, the rest of the interrogation team piled back into the room and told me to take off my shoes.

"Why?" I asked.

"We need them," came the answer.

I did as I was told. "Socks too?"

"No, you can keep your socks on."

The rounds of questioning began all over again: "Tell us what happened! Did Amanda go out on the night of the murder? Why are you holding out on us? You've lost your head *per una vacca*—for a cow!"

They wanted me to sign a statement they had prepared. The first part was a big mash up of the events of October 31 and November 1, most of which, I have to admit, was the result of my own confusion. The account began with the lunch at Via della Pergola, Meredith going out, and the two of us leaving in the later afternoon. But then it described me going home alone and working at the computer while Amanda headed to the center of town.

The statement had my father calling around eleven o'clock, which is what he almost always did, and Amanda returning to my house at around one in the morning.

By the time I read what the police had prepared, it was deep into the night, I was exhausted and scared, and I could no longer think straight. Absurd as it sounds, the statement struck me as accurate enough up to this point. I simply missed the fact that I was—from the investigators' point of view—cutting Amanda loose for the entire evening and depriving her of the only alibi she had.

I objected to just one paragraph. It was a logical continuation of what the police already had me saying, but I missed the connection; I just knew this part was not right. It read, "In my last statement I told you a lot of crap because she [Amanda] talked me into her version of events, and I didn't think about the inconsistencies."

I told my interrogators this part needed to be changed, but they wouldn't back down. Instead, they unexpectedly became much friendlier and said I shouldn't worry about this paragraph. It was just something they needed and it wouldn't affect my position one way or the other. Essentially, they were asking me to trust them. Part of me still wanted to. I wanted to believe this was a world in which the police did their jobs responsibly. And part of me just couldn't wait for the hellish night to be over.

At three thirty, after five hours of relentless interrogation, I signed.

* * *

At this point, Amanda herself had already cracked. As she later told it, her interrogators insisted they had concrete proof she was at the house on Via della Pergola the night Meredith was killed. When she said she had no recollection of this, they threatened her with thirty years in prison and hit her repeatedly on the head. (The police denied threatening her in any way.)

They asked her over and over about the text message she had sent Patrick, her boss at Le Chic, and said it showed she had arranged to meet him even after he told her she didn't need to come into work that night. But this was clearly a distorted interpretation. Yes, she had written *ci vediamo più tardi*—see you later—but in both Italian and English that can simply mean "see you around." The fact that Amanda had added the words *buona serata*—have a good evening—made it abundantly clear she expected no further contact with him that night. But the officers ignored these last two words of her text and later omitted them from the written statement they prepared for her to sign.

For at least an hour, Amanda was interrogated in Italian. The police officers said she seemed to understand the questions well enough, and the statement they produced described her Italian language skills as "adequate"—not an assessment I or the Italian tenants at Via della Pergola would have shared, and not what the police themselves seemed to think the first night we were brought in for questioning. Then, at some point after midnight, an interpreter arrived. Amanda's mood only worsened. She hadn't remembered texting Patrick at all, so she was in no position to parse over the contents of her message. When it was suggested to her she had not only written to him but arranged a meeting, her composure crumbled; she burst into uncontrollable tears, and held her hands up to her ears as if to say, *I don't want to hear any more of this.*

The interpreter, Anna Donnino, tried to calm Amanda and told her how she had once suffered a memory lapse after breaking her leg. Could it be, Donnino suggested, that something similar had happened to Amanda because of the trauma of Meredith's death? In the moment, Amanda appeared to accept this. The police officers kept asking about Patrick, kept insisting Amanda had been at the house. And, by the time she signed a statement at 1:45 a.m., this is what it said:

"I answered [Patrick's] message saying we would meet up right away, so I left and told my boyfriend I had to go to work. . . . Immediately after, I met Patrik [*sic*] at the basketball court on Piazza Grimana and we went to my house together. I don't remember if Meredith was there or if she arrived later. I'm having trouble remembering but Patrik had sex with Meredith—he had a thing for her—but I don't remember too clearly if Meredith was threatened first. I remember confusedly that he was the one who killed her."

Once the police had this spectacular document in hand, they came back to squeeze me and insisted that I sign my own statement. Looking now at the sequence of events, I can see how they used each of us to undermine the other. Once my signature was attached to a document stating that Amanda had gone out for several hours on the night of November 1, they went back and told her I was no longer vouching for her. That, evidently, sent her into a tailspin of fear and confusion—fear of what the police might do to her, fear of what I was saying and what it said about me, and also fear for her own sanity.

As Amanda's questioning continued, Prosecutor Mignini himself decided to take charge. He arrived at the Questura in the dead of night, apparently after being informed that Amanda had "broken," and pressed her for a full confession. Again, Amanda was in floods of tears. Again, she was gesticulating with her hands and bringing them to her head—a detail that seemed particularly fascinating to Mignini, perhaps because hitting oneself in the head is sometimes associated with Masonic initiation rites.

At 5:45 a.m., Amanda signed a second statement detailing what were characterized as "spontaneous" pronouncements of hers. "I am very afraid of Patrik," the statement began—an assertion apparently undermined by the fact that she had gone to see Patrick for a social call just the day before. Again, the narrative had Amanda going with Patrick to her house; again it described Patrick and Meredith having sex.

"At some point," it went on, "I heard Meredith screaming and I was so afraid I blocked my ears. Then I remember nothing more. My head is full of confusion. I don't remember if Meredith screamed or if I heard any banging, but I could imagine what might have gone on."

Unfortunately, the statement also left open the possibility that I was involved. "Not sure if Raffaele was there that night," it said. Amanda, according to the statement, was certain of only one thing:

that she woke up with me the next morning in my bed. The rest was one big question mark.

* * *

When I first found out what Amanda had signed her name to, I was furious. Okay, she was under a lot of pressure, as I had been, but how could she just invent stuff out of nowhere? Why would she drag me into something I had no part of? It soon transpired, of course, that she felt similarly about me. "What I don't understand," she wrote, as soon as she began to retract her statements, "is why Raffaele, who has always been so caring and gentle with me, would lie. . . . What does he have to hide?"

It took us both a long time to understand how we had been manipulated and played against each other. It took me even longer to appreciate that the circumstances of our interrogations were designed expressly to extract statements we would otherwise never have made, and that I shouldn't blame Amanda for going crazy and spouting dangerous nonsense.

Our interrogators resorted to time-honored pressure techniques practiced by less-than-scrupulous law enforcement and intelligence agencies around the world. They brought us in at night, presented us with threats and promises, scared us half senseless, then offered us a way out with a few quick strokes of a pen. The CIA once produced a document about such techniques and essentially itemized all the emotional stages we traveled through that night—confusion, fear, guilt, an irrational dependence on our interrogators, and a sense that the whole world had gone topsy-turvy. As my friend and supporter, Steve Moore, a twenty-five-year FBI veteran, described it from the police perspective: "If you're trying to determine facts and truth, you want your suspect clear, lucid, and awake. If you want to coerce your suspect into saying what you want them to say, you want them disoriented, groggy, and confused."

Even before dawn broke on November 6, the authorities had us where they wanted us. True, neither of us had confessed to murder. But what they had—a web of contradictions, witnesses pitted against each other, and a third suspect on whom to pin the crime—was an acceptable second best.

For me, the night was not yet over. While Amanda endured her face-to-face encounter with Mignini, I was taken to another room and showered with threats and insults.

"You don't know what you've done!" someone said. "Your family will be destroyed. You'll spend the next thirty years in prison."

Or again: "Your poor father, who knows how he will take this. What did he do to deserve a son like you? You need to tell us what happened!"

In retrospect, I'm not sure they were pressing me to confess to a crime. Their more immediate interest was in having me produce more incriminating testimony against Amanda.

"She went out. When did she go out?" I remember being asked.

"I'm not sure she went out," I replied at one point. "I remember something totally different."

"If you can't remember, then it's going to be bad for you. You are creating a lot of problems for yourself."

"I don't know what you're talking about. I never went into Meredith's room. I never even saw the body. So I don't know what you are trying to suggest."

And so it went, around and around and around.

When it became apparent they would get nothing more out of me, I was arrested and handcuffed.

I asked to talk to my family again. I said I needed at least to inform my thesis director where I was. "Where you're going, a degree's not going to do you any good," came the answer.

One of my interrogators opened the door noisily at one point, walked over, and slapped me. "Your father is a fine upstanding person," he said. "He doesn't even deserve a son like you, someone who would stand by a whore like Amanda."

People kept coming and going. Sometimes I was left alone. Sometimes I was shouted at.

And then the morning came.

I was taken to the medical section of the Questura and told to strip. "Take off everything," I was told, "even your underpants."

I had already been shoeless most of the night, but this was a whole new level of humiliation. I was asked about a Japanese manga tattoo covering much of my left shoulder blade—a present I gave myself after passing a brutal programming exam in 2004—and was made to walk around in front of a female doctor.

I felt so ashamed I didn't even look up at her. After a few minutes, she took a pair of scissors and snipped some hair from my head and another sample from my pubic hair. This was done to establish my DNA profile, they said. Of course, they could have swabbed my mouth. Or taken a hair sample with my clothes still on.

As I was escorted to another part of the Questura, I passed a holding cell and heard Amanda inside weeping like a little girl. I could not see her, but the sound carried well enough through a small opening in the door. I asked her quickly about the events of the night, but she was too hysterical to make sense.

I was not taken to an isolation cell of my own—yet. Instead, I was shown into a waiting room and left on a couch for what seemed like a long time. I was alone at last and fell gratefully asleep.

* * *

At some point during my interrogation, I told the officers the best way to find out what I was doing on the night of the murder was to go to my house and check the activity log on my laptop computer. Now the police wanted to take me up on this. I could have insisted on their obtaining a search warrant, but somehow I still had faith that they would switch out of their misguided line of inquiry as soon as I showed them proof of their mistake.

I was taken out to a patrol car, and we raced into central Perugia with sirens blaring. Accompanying me were Chiacchiera and a number of rank-and-file policemen. I was still shoeless, and still in handcuffs, when they made me get out and walk down Corso Garibaldi to my front door. I have no idea if anyone saw me; I was beyond caring about appearances.

As soon as we walked into my apartment, a policeman named Armando Finzi said loudly that the place stank of bleach. That wasn't correct. My cleaning lady had been through the day before and cleaned the tile floor with Lysoform, not bleach. Still, he insisted on mentioning the bleach a couple more times—the clear implication being that I'd needed something powerful to clean up a compromising mess.

Then I watched them pull the place apart. In the kitchen, where I was standing, they went through the trash and sniffed through the cleaning products. When Finzi came across a drawer full of kitchen knives, he called Chiacchiera over immediately. He pulled out the first knife that came to hand, a large chopping knife with an eight-inch blade.

"Will this knife do?" Finzi asked Chiacchiera.

"Yes, yes, it's great," came the answer.

Much later, in court, Finzi made no secret of the fact that this was simply a random pick. He had no reason to select such a knife. He hadn't been given any specifics on the murder weapon from the coroner's report, or anywhere else, and had nothing to go on other than what he called his "investigative intuition."

Before I had time to ponder what the knife seizure meant, Chiacchiera pulled me into the bedroom, where I had a backpack full of books, including some of my beloved Japanese manga comics. Most of these were unremarkable: fantasy stories, futuristic thrillers, run-of-the-mill stuff. But Chiacchiera also found a four-volume set titled *Urotsukidoji,* a series of highly sexualized horror stories with lots of blood, and monsters copulating violently with humans.

He flipped through a volume and demanded, "What is this revolting crap?" He didn't wait for the answer, which was that the series was a collector's item from the 1960s, a present from my friend Gianluigi Ceraso, which I hadn't even taken out of its wrapping. Horror manga was not my thing.

But Chiacchiera didn't want to know. Instead, he threw the book in my face. "You're a real piece of shit, aren't you? Well, we're going to take care of you."

Only belatedly did the police show an interest in my computer. I suggested they turn it off and close the keyboard before carting it off, but they didn't listen. They pulled the plug out of the wall socket and carried it away still open. I'm convinced to this day that the computer could have exonerated me completely, and probably Amanda too, if it had been handled properly. But almost all of that evidence would soon be destroyed.

* * *

65

We traveled back to the Questura. I now had a pair of shoes on, some ASICS Onitsuka Tigers I grabbed from my closet while I had the chance. Somehow, I was optimistic things were about to get a whole lot better. As soon as word of my arrest hits the news, I thought, my father would hire a lawyer and I'd get out of here.

Instead, I had to endure more waiting. At one point I was asked for my computer password. The Questura's computer analysis software only worked with PCs, I was told, not Macs like mine. That should have raised my suspicions, but I gave them the password as instructed. I was exhausted and incapable of thinking straight.

A little later, I had to help the police with a second pocketknife they had found at my place, a Spyderco they had managed to open but could not now close. I showed them how.

The waiting was designed, in part, to give the media time to assemble outside the Questura and capture the first images of us being hauled into police vans and driven off to Capanne prison, about ten miles southwest of town. It was the beginning of the media circus, deliberately orchestrated for maximum effect. I don't have much memory of this "perp walk," only that I was hustled out of the building with the hood of my gray jacket, the one I had lent to Amanda the day after the murder, thrust over my head. Amanda followed behind me, and behind her was Patrick Lumumba, who had been picked up at his house before first light that morning.

After we left, Arturo De Felice, the Perugia police chief, held a triumphalist news conference in which the world was first told that Meredith died as a result of a sex orgy gone wrong. The press corps was so startled they barely asked about the evidence. De Felice alluded to the "sheer level of detail that came out of the investigation, hour by hour, minute by minute." And he acknowledged, once again, the pressure he had felt to solve the case quickly—which the men and women of the Perugia police had now done.

Three culprits, three arrests: case closed.

II

KAFKA ON THE TIBER

Any punishment not rooted in strict necessity is a form of tyranny.

—Montesquieu, quoted by Italy's foremost
legal theorist, Cesare Beccaria

rriving at Capanne prison was like landing on an alien planet. What did I have to do with such a place? I thought of Dante, whom I'd read at school, and his warning on the gates of hell: *Abandon all hope ye who enter here.* Like Dante, I was hoping to be just a fleeting visitor to this underworld. But already I was being treated like a hardened criminal.

The guards made me empty my pockets and pull the laces out of my shoes. I handed over my wallet, my identity card, my bracelets, even my jacket, which went against regulations because it had metal fasteners. All vestiges of normal life, the life of a free citizen, were systematically taken away from me. I was not naked, as I had been in the Questura, but I felt that same helplessness, the same acute vulnerability.

Then came another interminable wait in a holding cell. The guards would bang loudly and unexpectedly on the gates from time to time and shout, "What have you done?"

I did not respond. Instead, I asked to talk to my father, or to a lawyer. They said I could speak to no one.

It grew cold and I had nothing, not even my jacket, to keep me warm. I recognized nobody. Amanda was far away in the women's wing, and I had no idea where Patrick was.

At length I was shown to my cell: a dark, damp, dirty hole with one small window looking out on a vast expanse of reinforced concrete. The bed was a sponge mattress, the toilet caked in grime. I asked if someone was coming to clean; it was an absurd question.

I was a long way from home.

They had put me in solitary confinement. I would stay here until the first court hearing, which by law had to take place within seventy-two hours. After that was a big unknown. Italy has no such thing as bail for criminal defendants. Nor is there any requirement for prosecutors to charge people within a defined time. Often, defendants are set free while the investigation continues. Sometimes, though, they are kept in *custodia cautelare,* or preventive detention, which can mean months or even years behind bars as the investigation marches with painful slowness toward arraignment and trial.

As the hours passed, I noticed spy holes in every corner. So I had no privacy, not even to sit on the toilet. The guards passed by regularly, banging on the bars and shouting as they had earlier. The one blanket I had was not thick enough to keep me from shivering, and the radiator was useless. I had a television, but it did not work. From the next cell, I would hear occasional knocking on the wall and chatter in a foreign language I did not recognize. I guessed it was Arabic.

Looking through the window again, I noticed that the view extended to a guard tower rising up from the concrete. Beyond the tower, I could make out a tiny patch of hillside with a small house on it. The free world, still barely within view.

I stared and stared at that house and allowed myself the briefest of smiles.

* * *

The news of our arrests broke at about 9:30 a.m., about half an hour before we were escorted out of the Questura. By lunchtime, we were all over the news.

My father refused to believe it at first. His older sister, Magda, called him in the late morning and said her husband had seen something on the Internet. "You've got to be joking," he told her. "If Raffaele had been arrested, he would have found a way to let me know."

But of course I was muzzled. The authorities in Perugia eventually got around to calling my family, but they waited so long they might as well have not bothered. Hours earlier, my father's lawyer friend, Tiziano Tedeschi, had the news confirmed by a news reporter calling him for a reaction.

Papà snapped into action right away. He canceled his appointments, called home to ask Mara to prepare a suitcase, and withdrew twenty-five hundred euros from the bank. He asked his younger brother, Giuseppe, who had a high-powered job with the European pharmaceutical giant Bayer, if he wanted to accompany him to Perugia. He did.

By early afternoon the three of them—my father, my uncle, and Tedeschi—were on their way. My father never doubted for an instant that the police had made a mistake. He thought that once they got to Perugia, they would be able to talk it over, clear up the misunderstanding, and have me back at my studies in hours. Vanessa, who spoke to my father en route, agreed that it might work out that way. Often, she said, people got arrested in a sweep in the wake of a major crime, and most were out again within twenty-four hours.

But Vanessa, ever cautious in the face of authority, added a caveat: "Let's just see what reasons they come up with for the arrest."

My father, who reacts every time he senses even a hint of negativity from his daughter, was incensed and unleashed a volley of insults at her. What reasons? In his mind, there couldn't possibly be any.

* * *

That first night in prison, unable to sleep, I wavered between great waves of indignation and a nagging sense of guilt. I knew I had nothing to do with Meredith's murder, but I was furious with myself for having such a foggy memory and I knew it was in part because of the joint I'd smoked on the afternoon of November 1. How many times had my father told me not to smoke? I vowed there and then I would never touch the stuff again.

That said, my poor memory seemed a ridiculous reason to throw me into an isolation cell and accuse me of involvement in the crime. If the problem was with Amanda and the things she might or might not have done outside the house—assuming she left at all—why not focus the investigation on her? I didn't believe for an instant she was capable of murder, but I did have doubts about the crowd she ran in. Maybe she knew something. Maybe there was something she hadn't told me. *But please,* I thought, *leave me out of it.*

* * *

As soon as my father arrived in Perugia with my uncle and Tedeschi, they were told they could not see me. To their astonishment, I had been denied access to legal counsel. They were given a copy of my arrest warrant, but they had no way of discussing it with me, or of comparing my statements with Amanda's or Patrick Lumumba's, which they were not allowed to see.

Italian law allows prosecutors to bar defendants from speaking to their lawyers only in exceptional circumstances, usually in cases involving terrorism or major Mafia crimes. Even then, the prosecutor is required to petition the court in writing to justify such a draconian measure.

A more aggressive lawyer could have raised holy hell to see such a petition without waiting for the first court hearing and then, assuming it was produced, moved immediately to challenge it.

But Tedeschi seemed out of his depth. He was more used to dealing with petty criminals and low-level street thugs in a small provincial town back home. I don't think he'd ever been denied access to a client before, much less dealt with television cameras and front-page headlines. So there was no hell-raising. And I stumbled, unwittingly, into the next trap being laid for me.

* * *

The main evidence Mignini had to take into the preliminary hearing was my Nikes, and he did everything he could to make them as incriminating as possible. Hours after my interrogators ordered me to take the shoes off, they were examined by a forensic team from Foligno. But the Foligno police were relatively cautious: in the official report they produced that same day, they said they could make no more than a partial comparison with the clearest of the prints left in blood in Meredith's room and could comment only on the rough size and shape of the shoe, nothing more. Still, they concluded that my shoes "could have" created the footprints found at the crime scene.

Mignini was not satisfied, no doubt because the finding was couched in all sorts of caveats; the Foligno police stressed that the match was a theoretical possibility only. So the next day Mignini went to the Polizia Scientifica in Rome for a second opinion. They had even less information to go on than the Foligno team because they had only photographs of my shoes, not the shoes themselves. Somehow, though, they came to the much more definitive conclusion that my Nikes were the same make, model, and shoe size as the print on Meredith's floor. No question about it.

They were flat wrong, for reasons that should have been apparent immediately and would become obvious over time. But we weren't shown the report and had no quick way to contradict it. A precedent was also set: this was far from the last time that Mignini would rely on the Polizia Scientifica to dig up incriminating evidence against me at a crucial legal juncture.

* * *

I was told about the preliminary hearing an hour before it began. The guards brought me to the prison's makeshift courtroom in the early afternoon of November 8, and I was relieved to see Tedeschi, even if we had only a few seconds to confer before the judge brought us all to order. His was the first friendly face I'd seen in almost three days.

Tedeschi said it would be best if I said nothing, but I had other ideas. I wasn't happy about the statement the police had made me sign in the Questura, and I knew that the evidence about the shoes had to be wrong because I hadn't worn my Nikes on the day of the murder, or the day after. I was also aware of Amanda's signed statements because a summary of them was included in my arrest warrant. I could not believe what I read. Someone, I felt, needed to be informed she had gone plumb crazy.

So I told Tedeschi I wanted to talk. I had nothing to hide. And he did nothing to persuade me otherwise.

As I learned much later, I was in trouble from the moment I gave my name. I would have been better advised to refuse to recognize the legality of the proceedings; my lawyer could then have insisted on receiving a complete document file and time to prepare before I uttered a sound. As soon as I engaged with Judge Claudia Matteini and confirmed my identity, I was implicitly recognizing the jurisdiction of her court and the procedural validity of everything that went on there.

Tedeschi did challenge Mignini to produce the petition denying me access to counsel, but not until the proceeding was well under way. The prosecutor had no coherent explanation of where the petition was—after several false starts, he said only that he "remembered imparting it"—and the judge herself acknowledged she had not seen it. (To this day, no evidence has emerged of its existence.) But Matteini was remarkably untroubled by this, striking down our challenge without even pausing to consider it. She and Mignini were in lockstep from that point forward, and Tedeschi did nothing to stop them rolling right over me.

It is difficult for me to reread the transcript of that day's hearing without wincing at my performance. I was still working from the premise that the court would listen to me in good faith and that Judge Matteini, as I put it in my journal, had "a good heart." In fact, I only made a bad situation worse.

Even before Judge Matteini had finished reading the complaint against me, I blurted out that I didn't know Patrick Lumumba and that any prints from my shoes found at Via della Pergola could only have been made before November 1. Immediately I ran into trouble because I had in fact met Patrick at his bar, on the night Amanda and I first got together. And I had no idea that the shoe prints in question were made in blood. In no time, I was flailing and suggesting, in response to the judge's pointed questions, that maybe I picked up some of the blood on the floor when I walked around the house on November 2, the day the body was discovered. Even more unwisely, I speculated that someone might have stolen my shoes and committed the murder in them. It just did not occur to me that the shoe print evidence was wrong.

These were far from my only gaffes. Tedeschi complained early on that we were "stumbling around in the dark" because we didn't have access to the full evidence file. But he did nothing to stop me stumbling for close to two hours.

I kept insisting that my father had called at bedtime on November 1, as he did almost every night, when the prosecution knew from the phone records that he had not. Inadvertently, I made small changes in the time Amanda and I returned from our abortive shopping trip into town, and Mignini immediately seized on these, along with everything else, as evidence of "new inconsistencies" in my account.

I felt like a fool describing my extensive knife collection and even described myself as a *testa di cazzo,* a dickhead, for having so many. My judgment and my self-confidence were sinking fast.

Perhaps the worst moment came when I was asked, for the umpteenth time, if Amanda had gone out on the night of the murder. I still had no clarity on this and could not answer the judge's repeated questions without sounding evasive.

"I can't . . . I can't . . . ," I mumbled at one point.

"Yes, no—or I can't remember," she admonished. "Those are your three options."

"I can't remember *exactly.*"

The judge was clearly annoyed. "Listen, sometimes you remember things very well, and other times, when you are challenged, you say you don't remember. I would invite you to be more precise because you need to understand that, with all these contradictions in the face of objective facts like the prints near Meredith's bed, you're not in the best situation."

Not in the best situation? I was in the worst situation imaginable—being falsely accused of murder. If I wasn't handling the questions well, it was because I was out of my depth in every way imaginable. As the great psychologist and Holocaust survivor Viktor Frankl once wrote, "An abnormal reaction to an abnormal situation is normal behavior." Amanda and I had been in a kind of lovers' cocoon all week, and our days and nights blended together in my mind. The shock of Meredith's murder didn't alter that, and may even have made it more difficult to sort everything out once our mundane daily routine was held up to the scrutiny of a criminal investigation. Had we had any prior knowledge of the murder, I imagine we would have had our stories straight and practiced responses at the ready. The judge, though, was not interested in understanding *why* I was having such a hard time, nor was she interested in cutting me any other kind of slack.

I could have been a lot smarter, of course, but the judge and the prosecution had all the tools to catch me out, and I was blindsided by their assertions of "objective fact" that were anything but. My game plan had been to dissociate myself from Amanda and thus deprive them of the argument that I was covering for her because I was in love with her. Accordingly, I told the court I never wanted to see her again. But they didn't let up on me, not for a minute, and only exploited the wedge they had so successfully driven between the two of us.

In his court filings, Mignini described us as unscrupulous, cynical, troubling characters who should not be allowed to walk free pending trial. Amanda, he said, had dragged me into a criminal conspiracy, while I was a person with "particularly sinister habits" who had very possibly supplied the knife that killed Meredith. This wasn't evidence-based prosecution; it was character assassination by any means.

Matteini's final questions were about a blog I had written after my Erasmus year in Germany in which I talked about the joys of experiencing new things abroad, and my sadness that the experience was now over. This seemed easy enough to tackle. She asked what I'd meant when I said, "You can only hope that you'll experience even stronger emotions in future to take you by surprise all over again."

I said I was referring to experiences that help a young person grow and mature, in contrast to "doing exactly the same things and spending time with the same people every day," which I said made life flat and pointless.

What kinds of experiences did I have in mind? the judge persisted.

"Well, for example, being with a woman," I answered. "At the time I was in the Erasmus program I'd never experienced the pleasure of sex. That's one thing I meant when I wrote that."

I thought my answer was innocuous enough. Nobody could fault its honesty. Who could have guessed I was, in fact, providing Matteini with the one thing she felt she lacked: a motive for me to have murdered Meredith Kercher?

* * *

Matteini swallowed the prosecution's story whole. The break-in was staged after the fact, she asserted—just as Mignini had. The murderer or murderers must therefore have got into the house with a set of keys, and Amanda was the only keyholder without a solid alibi for the night in question. Patrick Lumumba had the hots for

Meredith, Matteini theorized, and Amanda and I tagged along to experience something new and different. From my testimony at the hearing, Matteini concluded I was "bored by the same old evenings" and wanted to experience some "strong emotions." (She moved my blog entry from October 2006, the date marked on the document, to October 2007, just weeks before the murder, which bolstered the argument.) She didn't ascribe a specific motive to Amanda, assuming only that she must have felt the same way I did. The bloody footprints "proved" I was present at the scene of the murder, and my three-inch flick knife was "compatible with the possible murder weapon." The house, she wrote, was "smeared with blood everywhere."

Matteini's full-throated language guaranteed banner headlines, but it did not stand up to scrutiny. If the three of us had been in Meredith's room when she died, we would have left traces of ourselves all over the place—DNA, hair, skin, maybe blood. Such a crowded murder scene would have caused far more turmoil than was left in Meredith's room. My knife would have had blood traces on it, and the prosecution knew full well at this stage that it was clean. The description of "blood everywhere" can only have been a misinterpretation of crime-scene photos taken after the forensics teams had painted the house with cyanoacrylate, a chemical used to capture latent prints that makes everything glow pinkish red. In reality, except for the ghastly mess in Meredith's room, there were just a few small bloodstains that a reasonable person could easily have missed.

Even leaving aside the tortured logic of the staged break-in, Matteini had to twist herself into a pretzel to explain how, in her account, Patrick could tell Amanda he was closing his bar so they'd be free to meet, but was somehow seen at his bar later the same night. Presumably, she wrote, he opened back up after the murder to give himself a plausible alibi.

Naturally, Matteini dwelled on the most convenient phrase in Amanda's text message to Patrick, *ci vediamo più tardi*—see you later—while omitting the *buona serata,* which would have made nonsense of her theory that they were arranging a rendezvous. Later in the story, she insisted that we had called the carabinieri only *after* the Polizia Postale showed up. It was, in other words, another piece of staging to look as if we were raising the alarm.

The biggest disaster was that Matteini ordered us kept behind bars for up to a year while the investigation continued. Under Italian law, there can be only three valid reasons to do such a thing: if there are grounds to fear that another crime may be committed, if evidence risks being compromised or contaminated, or if the defendants are deemed a flight risk. Even Matteini did not subscribe to Mignini's arguments on the first two. But, she said, Patrick and Amanda were foreigners and could easily leave the country. And I, as Amanda's boyfriend, might be motivated to run away with her. Apparently, it did not occur to her to confiscate our passports or put us under house arrest.

The ruling came down one day after the hearing. Tedeschi was no longer in town; he said he had business to attend to in Bari and drove back with Giuseppe. I, meanwhile, was back in solitary, staring at the walls and wondering how much longer this insanity would continue. I sat down and wrote a telegram to my father urging him, among other things, to recommend another lawyer. I hadn't talked to Papà in four days, and now I needed him desperately. In the telegram, I recovered much of the lucidity that had eluded me earlier, explaining succinctly that I couldn't remember some specifics about the night of the crime, and that my version and Amanda's differed on whether she had gone out, and for how long.

"The Squadra [Mobile] understands I'm innocent, but now I need to prove it to the magistrate," I wrote. (Clearly I still had some residual faith in the police, even if my experiences should have taught me otherwise.) "I'm in solitary confinement, I am scared and sad. . . . I don't know what to do, everything seems unreal. I'm so sorry, I love you."

My father didn't receive the telegram for days because I sent it to his home in Bisceglie, and he was in Perugia. I was right to think he was the person to lean on in my hour of need. I just had no idea when or how I might hear from him. And neither did he.

* * *

Amanda recovered her lucidity faster than I did. The day we were arrested, she wrote a statement in English that all but retracted what she had signed the night before. "In regards to this 'confession,'" she wrote, "I want to make clear that I'm very doubtful of the verity of my statements because they were made under the pressures of stress, shock and extreme exhaustion." She was still conjuring up images of Patrick as the murderer, but she added, "These things seem unreal to me, like a dream, and I am unsure if they are real things that happened or just dreams in my head."

The next day, she wrote a second, more confident statement: "I DID NOT KILL MY FRIEND . . . But I'm very confused, because the police tell me that they know I was at my house when she was murdered, which I don't remember. They tell me a lot of things I don't remember." Then she gave a substantially more accurate account of the night of November 1 than I was coming up with at the time.

Amanda's statements were given to Mignini before the preliminary hearing, which might explain why Matteini went relatively easy on her and reserved the greatest venom for me.

I didn't get to see Amanda, not even in Matteini's courtroom, because our hearings were conducted one after the other. I became aware that Patrick was being held in the isolation cell next to mine, but I made no attempt to communicate with him. Avoiding any appearance of collusion between us seemed more important than exchanging notes on our experiences.

Very slowly, I was learning.

* * *

The confusion in my head brought back jarring memories of my first big scare about mind-altering substances. It happened during my Erasmus year in Munich, at a party I attended with two girls who were among my closest friends during my time in Germany.

I was drinking beer, but everyone else was ladling out cups of what looked like sangria from a big cocktail bowl. It's funny, given all the media gossip about my being addicted to just about every intoxicating substance on the planet, but I'm not a big drinker at all. Like my father, I don't like feeling out of control, so I usually have just a few sips of beer or wine and steer clear of spirits altogether. That night, my caution was my salvation.

From one moment to the next, the mood in the room changed abruptly. People started pawing and fondling each other, as though they had lost all inhibitions. It was freaky, not sexy at all, and I went looking for my friends to talk about it. But they were as out of it as the rest of the party. The two girls both turned and kissed me on the mouth, one after the other. They had glazed, vacant expressions in their eyes. Some people, I realize, might think this was a fantasy come true. But these weren't the girls I knew—warm, charming, funny, like sisters to each other, and to me. It was as if robots had overtaken their bodies and were now trying to overtake mine.

The next day, I asked the girls what had got into them, and they couldn't say. They remembered nothing.

I have no idea what was in that cocktail, but the episode taught me how swiftly drinks or drugs can change our perceptions and our personalities. Or rather, it *should* have taught me. For some reason, I continued to indulge my occasional marijuana habit, perhaps because it did nothing more harmful than put me to sleep and scramble my short-term memory, which is usually pretty scrambled to begin with.

Now I knew I should have been smarter. I smoked no more than three joints with Amanda in the few days before the murder, but that was three joints too many.

* * *

Because our imprisonment had been officially sanctioned by a judge, we were at last granted a few meager privileges. I was still in solitary, but I was given a working television and allowed to read the newspapers. If I asked for extra blankets, I received them. The ban on contact with our lawyers was lifted, and we were told we could receive family visitors very soon.

Still, I was numbed and bewildered by my surroundings. I had nothing of my own in the cell except the increasingly dirty clothes on my back, and nothing to structure the days except the regular portions of bland, unidentifiable meat and overcooked pasta. I made friends with a young Romanian who seemed friendly enough when I talked to him through the cell walls; he helped me circumvent the interminable system of paying and waiting for basic supplies like soap and garbage bags by giving me some from his own stash. Only later was I told that he was in prison for attempted armed robbery and running a prostitution ring. This was not my world; what was I doing here?

Once I turned on the TV, it didn't take long to discover that the media coverage of the case was almost as mind-blowing as the case itself. Amanda was "Foxy Knoxy," a nickname she had originally been given by her soccer coach when she was seven years old, now twisted into an underhanded commentary on her sexual prowess. In Italian this was rendered as *volpe cattiva,* wicked fox. They also called her *luciferina,* little she-devil, and reported breathlessly on a lifestyle supposedly centered around sex, drugs, alcohol, and outrageous lies. Her outstanding academic record and close-knit friends and family somehow went by the wayside.

Reporters mined the Internet for anything—Facebook entries, blogs, videos—that would bolster the predetermined conclusion that we were guilty. A short story about date rape that Amanda had submitted to a University of Washington creative-writing class was held up as evidence of her warped criminal mind. A Myspace video of her boasting about the number of shots she had downed at a party became an excuse to depict her as an alcohol-fueled harpy. I was described as "crazy," based on a line I'd written in a blog entry, and held up to ridicule for a photograph, taken during a high-spirited moment of fun in my first year in Perugia, in which I was wrapped from head to foot in toilet paper, brandishing a machete in one hand and a bottle of pink alcohol in the other.

None of this was more than standard student nonsense. In the looking-glass world of the media, though, it was tantamount to a criminal indictment.

I knew a lot of the coverage of the case itself was flawed. It was reported, for example, that the police had found bleach receipts at my house, strongly suggesting I had purchased materials to clean up the crime scene. But my cleaning lady didn't use bleach, and the only receipts the police found from November 1 onward were for pizza. I wouldn't have needed to buy bleach, anyway, because I had some left over from my previous cleaning lady. It had sat untouched for months.

Still, I was inclined to believe a lot of what was in the newspapers. Chalk it up to my overprotected childhood, or my naive belief that things, more often than not, are what they seem. In one article, I read with alarm that Amanda had not gone straight home to shower on the morning after the murder, but had met a secret Argentinean boyfriend and gone to a Laundromat to wash a pile of clothes including a pair of blue Nike sneakers. This played havoc with my mind because I had not yet let go of my anger over Amanda's statements in the Questura, and I was beginning to wonder if I could trust her on anything, including her sexual fidelity. Not only did I mistakenly give this story credence, I even asked myself if she might have taken my pocketknife and given it to the son of a bitch who murdered Meredith.

It all seemed so far-fetched, yet I was still working on the premise that *something* had to be off for the police to act the way they did. I, like much of the reading public, simply could not believe that so much could be made out of nothing at all.

* * *

Even before my father received my telegram, he knew he needed to find a second lawyer to back up Tedeschi. If nothing else, we needed someone based in Perugia who could pick up official documents as they became available and develop a relationship with court officials. My family was given a couple of names and decided to go with a recommendation from Vanessa's contact in the local carabinieri, the one who had called her to apologize.

The lawyer's name was Luca Maori, and he introduced himself to my father by pulling up to the piazza outside the public prosecutor's office in a shiny four-wheel-drive BMW 330. He was self-assured, almost cocky, which impressed Papà at first. Maori's father had been an extraordinarily successful lawyer before him, and Luca worked out of a vast, beautifully appointed office with antique furniture and fifteenth-century religious paintings by Mastro Giorgio di Gubbio.

Maori also had a vast country estate, to which he regularly invited my father and other members of my family. He was happy to take the case without payment—as indeed Tedeschi had been before him. In both cases, I came to believe you get what you pay for.

I saw Tedeschi first. He did his best to be reassuring, to sound in control. "Don't worry," he said, "we'll work it all out. On the shoe print we just need to get a proper analysis done." I nodded and smiled, but really I had no faith in him. I had almost no faith in anybody at this point.

Then came Maori. He told me that he too carried pocketknives from time to time. But he didn't seem too interested in connecting with me beyond such superficial niceties. I felt he didn't entirely trust me. His game plan, which became clear over a series of meetings, was to dissociate me as much as possible from Amanda. And that was it. He did not have a clear strategy to undermine the prosecution's evidence on the knife and the shoe print, because—as he indicated to me—he believed there might be something to it.

I didn't feel any sort of progress until I was at last allowed to see my father and uncle and stepmother on November 10. It was an emotional reunion. I was exhausted and demoralized, I stank of piss and sweat and had several days' growth of beard. Still, it felt wonderful to hug them.

They couldn't believe what had happened to me and struggled to hold it together as we talked. "I'll do everything in my power to get you out," my father promised. Years later, I learned that as soon as the guards took me back to my cell, he banged his hands against a wall and wept.

All three of them, my father, Mara, and Giuseppe, were beside themselves with fury at the police—my father called them "animals" and "fucking bastards"—and also at Amanda. How could she say those things? Who was she, really? Did I have any idea? They had a bit of a go at me, saying I'd allowed myself to fall too easily under her spell and had been too unguarded in what I'd said to the police and in court.

I wasn't sure, at that point, that I disagreed. I felt that my lack of caution at the Matteini hearing, the casual way I had said the first things that came into my head, had landed all three of us in prison—me, Amanda, and Patrick. I was having a hard time forgiving myself.

But Papà also gave me some hard information to help structure my thoughts and pull me out from under the miasma. He told me, for instance, that he had texted instead of calling on the night of the murder, and he reminded me about the earlier Will Smith conversation. With his help, I began to separate out the events of October 31 and November 1. Then it occurred to me: Amanda had most probably spent the entire night at my house after all. It was a comforting thought. If she never left, she couldn't have passed my knife, or my shoes, off to someone else. She was just as innocent as me.

I even allowed myself a little optimism: my computer, I decided, would show if I was connected to the Internet that night and, if so, when, and how often. Unless Amanda and I had somehow made love all night long, pausing only to make ourselves dinner and nod off to sleep, the full proof of our innocence would soon be out in the open.

If only it could have been that simple. I did not yet know that the Polizia Postale—supposedly experts in handling technology issues—had seized two of my computers along with Amanda's and Meredith's and somehow wrecked three of the four hard disks while trying to decipher them. The police blamed the problem on an electrical surge, although they could not begin to account for it happening *three times in a row.* The bottom line was that the damaged disks were now deemed unreadable. That left just my MacBook Pro to provide an alibi for the night of the murder. According to the police, it showed no activity from the time we finished watching *Amélie* at 9:10 p.m. until 5:30 the next morning.

That sounded all wrong to me, and my defense team's technical experts would later find reasons to doubt the reliability of this finding. But there would be no easy way out of the mess Amanda and I were now in.

* * *

The next bombshell dropped days later on the evening news. The murder weapon was no longer thought to be my pocketknife, which had tested negative for traces of blood, but rather the outsize stainless-steel kitchen knife Inspector Finzi had pulled out of my drawer so deliberately on the morning of my arrest. The police claimed to have found Amanda's DNA on the handle, and Meredith's on the tip.

I wasn't even capable of following the rest of the report. I was overcome with anxiety, felt my heart leaping out of my chest, keeled over, and passed out.

My first thought when I came to—not that I was thinking straight—was that everything had gone topsy-turvy all over again, that Amanda must have taken the knife from my house and either used it to kill Meredith or given it to the person who did.

Not until the next morning, when Tedeschi came to see me, did I understand that the evidence was nowhere near as damning as it sounded. Would they dare to convict me on the basis of a knife that I knew, and the police knew, was plucked at random because it was big, and shiny, and sitting on the top of the pile in my drawer? The coroner's report, Tedeschi told me, made clear that the murder weapon could not have been anywhere near that big. The Polizia Scientifica had tested the blade for blood and found none.

The police's contention was that Amanda and I had scrubbed the knife clean with bleach before throwing it back in the drawer. Not only did I know that to be false, but it seemed an unlikely scenario from any perspective. Why take the risk of carrying the murder weapon back through the streets of Perugia to my house, instead of just ditching it? Who cleans a murder weapon and puts it back where it belongs for the police to discover and analyze in microscopic detail?

Still, there was something I could not fathom. How did Meredith's DNA end up on my knife when she'd never visited my house? I was feeling so panicky I imagined for a moment that I had used the knife to cook lunch at Via della Pergola and accidentally jabbed Meredith in the hand. Something like that had in fact happened in the week before the murder. My hand slipped and the knife I was using made contact with her skin for the briefest of moments. Meredith was not hurt, I apologized, and that was that. But of course I wasn't using my own knife at the time. There was no possible connection.

As I worked through all that in my head, I was close to panic. My stomach was burning and I felt ready to leap out of my skin. Somehow, I was still looking for reasons to blame myself, however small the oversight or misstep or omission. Did some part of me, despite everything I thought I knew and felt, resemble the *other* Raffaele Sollecito, the spoiled, mysterious, darkly perverted one on the TV? Chalk it up to Catholic guilt, or the deeply disorienting circumstances I found myself in, but whenever I watched the news, I felt I was being stripped away from my true self and flung into some grotesque Big Brother comedy-horror reality show. The normal me seemed to shrink down to nothing and give way instead to the sort of Jekyll-and-Hyde alter ego most people only ever confront in their nightmares. In this alternate reality, a nasty surprise always lurked around the next corner. And the punch line of every joke was reliably the same: me and my hands, soaked in Meredith's blood.

For several days my heart kept fluttering, I kept fainting, and the prison infirmary became concerned enough to write me a prescription for lorazepam.

I took it two or three times, and I suppose it must have worked, because the fainting fits stopped. Still, I didn't like the way the tranquilizer made me permanently drowsy, so I stopped taking it.

I didn't want to sleep through my captivity. If I wanted it to end, I realized, I needed to fight every step of the way.

* * *

My father was not entirely displeased about the kitchen knife, because, as he saw it, plenty of evidence indicated it could not have been the murder weapon. In his perennial optimism, he preferred to hold on to the fact that the police had found nothing *else* at my house despite picking the place clean. If the knife was the best they had, he calculated, we were still in the running to beat the charges.

Papà knew exactly how hard the police had searched, because he had seen them at it with his own eyes, on his first or second day in Perugia. He had stood in the entranceway to my building, as close to my front door as the police cordon would allow, and watched them cart away bath sponges, drainage plugs, detergent bottles—anything that might have been useful in cleaning up after a murder.

While he was there, he had come face-to-face with prosecutor Mignini. Mignini knew who Papà was right away, extended his hand, and, when my father said he was a doctor, asked what his area of specialization was. We later heard that Mignini had asked questions about my father's professional reputation. It was a prescient line of inquiry, because my father was indeed good at what he did. He knew enough science to be attuned to the fine details of forensics, bloodwork and DNA analysis, and would soon become Mignini's toughest and most unforgiving adversary.

* * *

The nuts and bolts of the investigation, the hard evidence, kept yielding good things for us. We were told that my Nikes had tested negative for blood and for Meredith's DNA. So had my car, and everything else I had touched around the time of the murder. Even the mop Amanda and I carried back and forth on the morning of

November 2, an object of particular suspicion, was reported to be clean.

But a smear campaign was also in full swing, and in the media these things were barely noticed. Two days after the papers ran their sensationalist headlines about the knife, they trumpeted what they said was confirmation from Amanda that she was at the house on Via della Pergola when the murder took place. During a conversation with her mother in prison, they reported, Amanda had blurted out, "I was there, I cannot lie about that." She seemed not to realize the conversation was being recorded, and the police picked up on it right away.

As we later learned, her words were completely twisted. The context for the line was Amanda's exasperation that she was being asked to change her story and concede that she wasn't with me on Corso Garibaldi on the night of the murder. So the word *there* did not refer to Via della Pergola at all, but to my flat. "This is so stupid," she said, according to the police's own transcript, "because I can't say anything else. I was there, I can't lie about that, and there's no reason I should."

Her mother had no particular reaction to this. It was in keeping with the rest of the conversation, in which Amanda expressed her frustration that the truth was somehow not good enough for Mignini and her police interrogators.

A few days later, another leak in the press pointed to a similar intent to do her—and me—harm. This time the papers quoted what they said was an extract from her diary. "I don't remember anything," the passage read, "but maybe Raffaele went to Meredith's house, raped and killed her, and then put my fingerprints on the knife back at his house while I was asleep."

Again, this was a malicious distortion. But, again, by the time it was uncovered, the damage was done, and it didn't matter that the truth had been flipped almost entirely on its head. The actual passage, expressing Amanda's consternation about the kitchen-knife allegations, read as follows: "Raffaele and I have used this knife to cook, and it's impossible that Meredith's DNA is on the knife because she's never been to Raffaele's apartment before. So unless Raffaele decided to get up after I fell asleep, grabbed said knife, went over to my house, used it to kill Meredith, came home, cleaned the blood off, rubbed my fingerprints all over it, put it away, then tucked himself into bed, and then pretended really well the next couple of days, well, I just highly doubt all of that."

Such smears not only turned public opinion against us, they also entered our case files and influenced the judges in their rulings. It would take years to set the record straight.

* * *

Even the police realized they were missing a big part of the picture. For all their efforts to pin evidence on Amanda and me, they knew that a lot of the crime-scene forensics did not match. Patrick, meanwhile, was drawing a big blank. Someone else had clearly been in the room when Meredith died, and soon news stories circulated about a "fourth man" still at large. Even before the papers named him, investigators knew exactly who that fourth man was: Rudy Guede.

From the beginning, the police had been intrigued by Stefano Bonassi, one of Amanda's downstairs neighbors, who told them he found his toilet unflushed and full of excrement the night Guede slept over in early October. About a week after our arrest, one of Guede's friends came forward and reported a weird IM exchange in which Guede hinted at a dark secret he could not reveal. The

Squadra Mobile had access to Guede's fingerprints because of his arrest in Milan and checked them against a handprint made in blood on Meredith's pillowcase.

They matched.

On November 19, the police broke into Rudy's flat—just a few steps away from mine—and took a DNA sample from his toothbrush. That resulted in multiple further crime-scene matches. They also visited a friend of Guede's named Giacomo Benedetti and sat in on a three-hour Skype chat with Guede that Benedetti set up. Benedetti's instructions were simple: he was to do everything he could to induce his friend to confess. Benedetti did as he was told and asked Guede every question the police fed to him.

Guede had read news reports about the fingerprint match and was clearly scared. He admitted being in the house when the murder took place but said he'd been on the toilet when he heard screaming coming from Meredith's room. He could describe the attacker only as an Italian man—no specifics—and said he had rushed to Meredith's aid as soon as the man left. That, he said, would account for any traces of him the police might have found in Meredith's room.

Interestingly, Guede said he had cuts on his right hand—which one would expect if he had been holding a knife and Meredith tried to fight him off. He put the time of the murder between 9:00 and 9:20 p.m., which my defense team came to believe was accurate. He said Amanda and Patrick had nothing to do with it. And he acknowledged never having met me in his life.

It was explosive stuff, too explosive to ignore, and the Squadra Mobile discussed how they might send an arrest team to Germany and try to run Guede to ground.

In the end, they didn't have to. Hours after the Skype chat with

Benedetti, German police caught Guede riding a train near Mainz without a ticket. Once they realized who he was, they threw him in jail and began making plans for his extradition.

* * *

I remember watching the news of Guede's arrest on the small-screen TV in my cell and seeing the Perugia police all puffed up with pride about catching him. If anything, I felt happier than they did, because Guede was a complete stranger to me. The relief was palpable. All along I had worried the murderer would turn out to be someone I knew and that I'd be dragged into the plot by association. Now I had one less thing to worry about. Not that I wasn't still wary: so much invented nonsense had been laid at my door I was still half-expecting the authorities to produce more.

And they did. Mignini released Patrick Lumumba and simply replaced him in the official story line with Guede. Now it was Guede whom Amanda and I had supposedly met by the basketball court, Guede whom we had helped carry out the evil deed. Mignini, and Lumumba himself, accused Amanda of substituting one black African man for another in the account she gave in the Questura, all the better to shield Guede from prosecution and make life hell for Patrick. But this was turning reality on its head. The substitution came from the prosecutor's office, not from Amanda.

It was remarkable how closely Mignini and Lumumba agreed on the new story line. Amanda had inserted Patrick into her narrative, they said, because she was about to be fired from her job at Le Chic and wanted revenge, pure and simple. Patrick said he was fed up with her flaunting her sexuality in front of the customers instead of doing her job, and he had reached the end of his patience. "By the end, she hated me," Lumumba told the British newspaper the

Daily Mail. "She's the ultimate actress, able to switch her emotions on and off in an instant. I don't believe a word she says. Everything that comes out of her mouth is a lie."

Lumumba had every right to be angry; he had spent two weeks in lockup for no reason. He had been able to prove that Le Chic stayed open throughout the evening of November 1, producing an eyewitness, a Swiss university professor, who vouched for his presence that night. One would expect his anger to be directed as much toward Mignini, who threw him in prison without checking the facts, as it was toward Amanda. But Lumumba and his strikingly aggressive lawyer, Carlo Pacelli, could find only vicious things to say about Amanda from the moment he got out of jail—even though he had not, in fact, fired her and remained friendly with her for several days after the murder.

By contrast, he never said a single word against Mignini.

* * *

My family was quietly optimistic, in the wake of Patrick's release, that Mignini would soon run out of reasons to keep me behind bars. That optimism soared on November 21, when a lawyer from Luca Maori's office was invited to watch the police conduct another search of Rudy Guede's apartment. On the floor were numerous shoe prints with the same pattern of concentric circles as the ones at the crime scene. These did not, at first sight, appear to be made in blood so much as earth, as though the wearer had gone for a walk in the woods and dragged the dirt in behind him.

Our lawyer, Delfo Berretti, took pictures, and my father showed these to two technical experts. The prints, they said, were an exact match for the ones at Via della Pergola. Now we had concrete evidence to show that the Polizia Scientifica's report had been wrong. Among other things: Rudy Guede wore a size 45 shoe (size 11½ in the United States), and I'm a 42½.

Still, we had a problem. Under Italian law, the defense is not allowed access to the prosecution files until the investigation is formally declared to be over. So, while I could be confident the shoe prints at Via della Pergola were not from my Nikes, I couldn't prove that to a judge using official documents, unless the prosecution was willing to share what it had.

And the prosecution, as we'd come to expect by this point, was not budging an inch.

* * *

The reality of prison life was catching up to me. Regardless of how quickly things were developing in the case, the grim reality was that I was stuck spending almost every hour of every day alone, unable to see or hear anybody else. For long stretches, I would feel a crushing loneliness, a sense that nobody knew I was there and nobody cared. I would stare at the dust and the cockroaches on the floor, up to the single ray of light coming through the window, then back to the floor again, my mind spinning furiously around the events I was having such a hard time bringing into focus.

For the first few days, I yearned only for home, my family, the comfort of a warm bed, my car, my computer. I thought if I had a PlayStation it might even be bearable to wait in my cell while my father worked on getting me released. If only.

Then I started noticing the filth around me and could think only of scrubbing it clean. My family developed a routine to take away my dirty clothes, sheets, and blankets and bring them back freshly laundered on the next visit. Slowly, I recovered an acceptable level of personal hygiene and, with it, some modicum of self-esteem.

After some initial hostility, the staff at the prison treated me decently. One guard talked about the nightmare existences that many prisoners had endured on the outside before they were locked up; she said prison came to some of them almost as a relief. It made me realize just how privileged and cosseted my life had been. After Patrick was released, one of the orderlies who brought my food shouted, "Hey, haven't they let you out of here yet?" Some people, at least, recognized I was innocent.

I received regular visits from a doctor, a psychiatrist, and an educator who asked so many questions I felt sure she had been instructed to extract new indiscretions from me. I smiled and played along, but told her nothing. For two hours a day, I was allowed to leave my cell for a slightly bigger space with a grate in the ceiling opening directly to the sky. This was the exercise room, a ridiculous name for an empty dungeon barely big enough to run around, but I had to make the best of it. I made a point of running every day—until my knees started aching from the hard contact with the concrete floor and I felt obliged to stop before I did myself permanent damage. I also did stretching exercises that I'd learned from kickboxing. One way or another, I was determined to keep working out. It was essential to preserving my sanity.

I also turned to religion. I've never been super-devout, but I do take solace from the Scriptures and spent some time pondering my favorite passages from the Gospels. Wasn't there a line in the Sermon on the Mount in which Jesus blesses the oppressed and those who fall victim to the judgment of others? I would have to ask my cousin Annamaria, who knows the Bible forward and backward.

Over time, I developed a personal, extended prayer I recited every morning. This was a version of a prayer I'd been saying every day since my mother's death, modified to take account of the new horrors unfolding in my life. I took solace in the ritual, which brought me back to my early experience of the Catholic catechism. It became a way for me to feel safe within a deep and private part of myself.

It began with an Ave Maria. Then I would remember all the people in my life who seemed most important: my family, those in difficulty, Amanda and her family, poor Meredith and all those who loved and mourned her. Finally, I prayed for the prosecutors and the judges; I prayed that Jesus would open their minds and roll back the clouds preventing them from seeing the truth. I knew that wasn't likely to happen on its own. Why not pray for a miracle and hope the Lord would somehow intervene?

It wasn't always easy to keep my doubt and anger at bay. Sometimes I would look to Jesus as a source of strength, a higher power beyond the ephemera of each day's battles and anxieties. Other times I found Him as ridiculous as everything else. "You were crucified because you did a lot more for others than you should have," I fumed in my journal one day. "You know what I think? You would have done better to give a little less and live longer. . . . I know you saved us from our sins and all that, but sometimes I wonder if it was worth your while."

Clearly, when I wrote that, I was having a bad day.

* * *

The prosecution's tactics grew nastier, never more so than when Amanda was taken to the prison infirmary the day after Patrick's release and told she had tested positive for HIV.

She was devastated. She wrote in her diary, "I don't want to die. I want to get married and have children. I want to create something good. I want to get old. I want my time. I want my life. Why why why? I can't believe this."

For a week she was tormented with the idea that she would contract AIDS in prison, serving time for a crime she did not commit. But the whole thing was a ruse, designed to frighten her into admitting how many men she had slept with. When asked, she provided a list of her sexual partners, and the contraceptive method she had used with each. Only then was she told the test was a false positive.

To the prosecution, the information must have been a disappointment: seven partners in all, of whom four were boyfriends she had never made a secret of, and three she qualified as one-night stands. Rudy Guede was not on the list, and neither was anyone else who might prove useful in the case. She hadn't been handing herself around like candy at Le Chic, as Patrick now alleged. She'd fooled around with two guys soon after arriving in Italy, neither of them at Patrick's bar, and then she had been with me. Okay, so she was no Mother Teresa. But neither was she the whore of Babylon.

To compound the nastiness, the list was eventually leaked to the media, with the erroneous twist that the seven partners on the list were just the men she'd had since arriving in Perugia. Whatever one thought of Amanda and her free-spirited American attitude toward sex, this callous disregard for her privacy and her feelings was the behavior of savages.

* * *

My sister, Vanessa, had struggled with my plight from the beginning. She was the policewoman in the family; this was her area of expertise. As the days turned into weeks, she began to berate herself for not jumping in the car and driving to Perugia right away. "If I had shown up in uniform," she told herself, and later repeated to me, "my brother probably would not have ended up in prison at all."

She was in a tricky position. She wanted to help, but she did not want to give the impression she was interfering, because it might cause the Perugia authorities to dig in their heels further. Her immediate boss offered to make a call on her behalf; she urged him not to.

As it became apparent I might not be released before trial, her colleagues slowly changed their behavior around her. She was no longer just a fellow officer with a brother in trouble; she was now the sister of a leading defendant in the biggest murder case in the country. Nobody said a word, at first, but she noticed people beginning to keep their distance. They acted a little more formally and joked a little less. These were little things, and if she'd challenged people, they would no doubt have said her imagination was playing tricks. But she found them disturbing all the same.

In late November, she arranged to meet a friend who worked as a top anti-Mafia investigator. The friend did not want to be seen with her anywhere near her carabinieri barracks in Piazza del Popolo, in the heart of Rome, so they met at a bar across the river in a suitably anonymous residential neighborhood.

He gave it to her straight: "They will do everything they can to get rid of you. It won't happen suddenly. It'll be a gradual thing, like a tap dripping. *Goccia a goccia,* drop by drop."

He told her to write down everything she did and everything she witnessed. She should record important conversations. Vanessa would not only have to act by the book at all times, she should be prepared to prove it. Like Caesar's wife, as the Romans like to say: beyond reproach.

Vanessa took the advice to heart and was soon glad she did.

* * *

My last best chance of getting out of prison quickly lay with three judges whose job was to go back over Judge Matteini's ruling and make sure it still held up in the light of everything that had transpired since. They were due to convene at the end of November. My father hired consultants to report on my computer activity on the night of the murder, other consultants to look at the shoe-print evidence, and yet more consultants to go through the coroner's report and assess the likelihood that any of my knives could have produced the fatal wounds.

Papà was spinning like a dervish to clear my name, but not everyone he hired was as helpful as he hoped. One consultant whom he asked to monitor the Polizia Scientifica demanded eight thousand euros up front, only to prove reluctant to make overt criticisms of the police's work, the very thing for which he'd been hired. A forensic expert who also seemed a little too close to the police charged four thousand euros for his retainer with the boast, "I'm expensive, but I'm good." He wasn't. A computer expert recommended by Luca Maori didn't know anything about Macs, only PCs.

And so it went. Later in the case, another disappointing consultant bragged to Papà, "If you give me fifty thousand euros, I'll get your son out of prison." My father couldn't afford to make mistakes, and he quickly learned not to trust what the consultants promised, only what they delivered. At the same time, mistakes were inevitable; he'd never done anything remotely like this in his life, time was pressing, and we weren't getting nearly as much information out of the prosecutor's office as we would have liked. Papà would later blame at least some of the confusion on Maori because his recommendations were often disappointing, and because he seemed altogether too interested in offering himself up for media interviews when, to us, discretion seemed the wiser course.

Still, my father and Maori came up with two solid ideas before the new court hearing. The first was to search the underbrush around the house at Via della Pergola for signs of the murder weapon. The prosecutor's office granted permission for the search, and a team of gardeners from Maori's country estate spent several hours picking through the steep upper stretch of the ravine with the help of thick ropes they used as a dragnet. They came up empty, but the request itself made an important point in my favor: it suggested I was confident about my innocence and wanted only to get to the bottom of the mystery.

The second idea was to ask to see video footage from two security cameras on the route from my house to Amanda's. The first camera was outside a military barracks on Corso Garibaldi, halfway between my front door and Piazza Grimana. The second was a city-operated camera on the corner of Piazza Grimana itself. If Amanda or I had gone to Via della Pergola on the night of November 1, we argued, the cameras would have picked up our trace—possibly in both directions.

Again, the request was as much about appearing innocent as it was about clearing my name. This time, though, we were turned down without explanation.

* * *

In his own preparations for the new court hearing, Mignini came up with what might be termed the Great Mushroom Conspiracy theory. It stemmed from something the coroner found in Meredith's esophagus: a largely undigested piece of food, which one of his assistants said looked like a mushroom. Mignini knew that when Meredith was with her English friends in the early evening of November 1, she ate pizza, ice cream, and apple crumble, but no mushrooms. So where could this extra piece of food, assuming that's what it was, have come from?

Mignini's answer, as he wrote in a brief for the three-judge review panel, was that Meredith and Amanda must have helped themselves to some mushrooms after Meredith returned home. Mignini had learned that both girls were fond of button mushrooms. The police even found some in my refrigerator, which in Mignini's retelling seemed to cast more suspicion on me.

Why could any of this possibly matter? It mattered because Mignini had a problem. The coroner, Luca Lalli, had been unable to ascertain the time of death with any accuracy because he was not granted access to the body until just before 1:00 a.m on November 3, almost twelve hours after it was discovered and more than twenty-four hours after Meredith's murder. (Mignini would eventually concede that making Lalli wait had been a mistake.) Usually, medical examiners take temperature readings to calculate the hour of death, but by the time the Polizia Scientifica had finished going over the crime scene, Meredith's corpse was cold. Lalli did make one significant discovery, however: none of the food that Meredith had eaten in the hours before the murder left her stomach for her upper intestine. That meant, based on normal digestion times, she must have died within two or three hours of her last meal.

This was a problem for the prosecution because Meredith's English friends said they ordered pizza at about 6:00 p.m. That would put the murder at around 9:00 p.m., right around the time Meredith returned home. But at 9:00 p.m. Amanda and I were still at my house watching *Amélie,* according to the police's interpretation of the user logs on my MacBook Pro. How to get around this?

Mignini decided Meredith's last meal had taken place later—the mushroom party—and used that as an argument to buy himself a couple of hours' more time. His brief put the time of death at about 11:00 p.m. Lalli, following Mignini's lead that Meredith's last meal was at 9:00 p.m., later concurred (while at the same time expressing caution about how much was known about the timing of her food intake). The argument was scientifically untenable because what mattered was not the time Meredith *stopped* eating, but rather the time she started. No matter how many mushrooms she put in her mouth after she got home, the digestion of the pizza was already well under way. There were grounds to doubt she had eaten mushrooms at all, because the medical team found only the one fragment, which was never tested or even saved after the autopsy. Similar-looking fragments found in her stomach were clearly apples from the apple crumble; perhaps a piece of her dessert did not go all the way down before she died.

Those arguments, though, would only arise later. For now, the main purpose of the mushroom theory was to keep the court open to the idea that Amanda and I were present at the murder scene.

And it worked.

* * *

The day before the new hearing, I showed Luca Maori a prison diary I'd been keeping so he could assess whether any of it might be useful in court. I had used the diary to try to solidify my memory of the sequence of events. But I'd also jotted down more personal reflections about my accusers, about the prison staff, and about my state of mind. Maori thought it was too risky to keep such a thing in my cell, and I agreed he should take it to his office for safekeeping.

We were still talking when prison guards swooped into the visiting room and ordered Maori to hand over the diary. Maori exploded, saying this was a blatant violation of attorney-client privilege and of my right to privacy. When the guards refused to back down and carried my handwritten pages away, Maori asked the guards to call Mignini's office and demanded the prosecutor's intervention. Mignini agreed and instructed the guards to return the diary. They did as they were told.

It appears, however, that while Maori was on the phone, someone put the diary through a photocopier because the text—minus the last few pages—was leaked to the Tuscan newspaper *La Nazione* and printed ten days later. I can't begin to say how demoralizing and humiliating it was to have my private thoughts and feelings exposed to the world in this way.

And I was not the only target. Shortly after the guards descended on me, they entered Amanda's cell and seized her diaries too. These also found their way into the media, but not for a few months.

The good news was, the authorities found nothing more in our writings that they could twist into incriminating evidence. But the message seemed clear: there was no length to which they would not go to try to make the accusations against us stick.

* * *

The three-judge panel not only ruled against us, they were shockingly dismissive of almost everything my lawyers and I had to say. They looked at photographs of the murder house and decided that Filomena's window was too far off the ground (about thirteen feet) for an intruder to hit reliably with a rock, and certainly too high to clamber up to. "It's a feat even Spider-Man would have had trouble pulling off," the lead judge, Massimo Ricciarelli, wrote with spectacular disdain as he formulated his justification for keeping Amanda and me behind bars.

It should have been obvious from the photographs that there were plentiful toeholds, including a metal grate on the window directly below Filomena's. But Ricciarelli and his colleagues, no Spider-Men themselves, could not imagine anyone reaching the window without a ladder. Since a ladder had not been found, they concluded the murderer or murderers must have gone through the front door. Since the door showed no sign of a break-in, they argued, whoever went in there must have had a key.

This was ass-backward logic: they actually wrote, *because there was no sign of a break-in.* A window was broken and Filomena's room was turned upside down, but, no, there was no sign of a break-in. No sign at all.

The rest of the judges' arguments were equally worrisome. They imagined Meredith's attackers engaging in "frenetic and rapid" sexual penetration, even though the coroner had found no evidence to support this. They said the blood on the bathroom tap was Amanda's—not true; traces of Amanda's DNA (in her own bathroom!) were found mixed with Meredith's blood—and used that to argue for more than one attacker. They placed great significance on an assertion that the sweater Amanda wore on the night of the murder had not been found, when the police's crime-scene photos—which we saw only later—showed she had left it in plain sight on her bed. The judges decided Amanda had indeed confessed to being present at the scene when she told her mother, "I was there." And they said it was "completely irrelevant" what the video cameras on

Corso Garibaldi did or did not show at the time we were alleged to have walked to Via della Pergola to murder Meredith.

Strangely, they put the time of death not at 11:00 p.m., as Mignini had suggested, but at 10:00 p.m. They gave no reasoning for this conclusion.

Amanda and I came in for what was by now a familiar drubbing. The judges said my account of events was "unpardonably implausible." Indeed, I had a "rather complex and worrying personality" prone to all sorts of impulses. Amanda, for her part, was not shy about having "multiple sex partners" and had a "multifaceted personality, detached from reality." Over and above the flight risk if we were released from prison, the judges foresaw a significant danger that we would make up new fantastical scenarios to throw off the investigation. In Amanda's case, they said she might take advantage of her liberty to kill again.

* * *

Because the court's wilder, obviously absurd assertions were entered into the case record, my lawyers and I had to take time and trouble to refute them. The more of them there were, the more difficult and exhausting it became to keep the momentum going in our direction and we started sliding backward. It was like the old Greek myth of Sisyphus, the man condemned for all eternity to push a rock up a mountain but never able to reach the top before the rock tumbled back down again. Every time we thought we were almost there, we would be knocked flat by a new avalanche of judicial bullshit.

Perhaps the most damaging assertion made by the prosecution and upheld by Ricciarelli and his colleagues was that the Polizia Postale had arrived at Via della Pergola *before* I called the carabinieri, not after, and that my emergency call was thus a ruse to make it look as if Amanda and I were raising the alarm when in fact we'd been caught red-handed. Michele Battistelli told investigators that he and Fabio Marzi arrived at 12:35, more than fifteen minutes before phone records showed me making my first emergency call. My lawyers told the review panel this sequence of events was not possible, because Elisabetta Lana was recorded beginning her official statement at police headquarters about the second cell phone at 12:46 and finishing it several minutes later. Battistelli told Filomena and the rest of us that the police had found two cell phones, not just one. Therefore, we argued, he and Marzi may not even have left for Via della Pergola before I'd spoken to the carabinieri.

To which the Ricciarelli court replied: Battistelli *could have* left for Via della Pergola on the basis of the first cell phone only. He *could have* found out about the other one while he was en route, or after he arrived.

The court made no apparent attempt to dig deeper, either through interviews with Battistelli's superiors, or through Battistelli's cell phone records, or by any other means. Had such an investigation taken place, we would have been vindicated. But because the judges decided it *could have* happened the way Battistelli claimed, Amanda and I were deemed too dangerous to set free.

* * *

The review panel cured me of any residual belief in the fair-mindedness of the prosecution or the judiciary. Before the hearing, my lawyers and I reached out to Mignini, whom I had never encountered one-on-one, and urged him to listen to my story away from the adversarial setting of the courtroom. But by the time Mignini came to see me, one day after Ricciarelli's ruling was made public, I was no longer interested.

I could see now that Mignini was not open to changing his ideas midstream. He didn't come for information, only for confirmation of what he already believed. I was becoming aware that, in the Italian criminal justice system, the preventive detention to which Amanda and I were being subjected is frequently used as a pressure tactic to extract confessions. I was now quite sure the authorities were keeping me in solitary confinement to get me to testify against Amanda, if not also against myself. Since I had no such testimony to offer, I did the Italian equivalent of taking the Fifth: I availed myself, as we say, of the right not to respond.

I found some satisfaction in that, but also frustration, because I had at last worked out why Amanda did not leave—could not have left—my house on the night of the murder. She didn't have her own key, so if she'd gone out alone, she would have had to ring the doorbell and ask me to buzz her back in. Even if I'd been stoned or asleep when she rang, I would have remembered that. And it didn't happen.

Realizing this brought me enormous peace of mind because I no longer had to fumble around and curse the confusion in my head. Obviously, I wanted to shout the news to the world. But I also understood that telling Mignini now would have been a gift to him; it would only have bought him time to figure out a way around it.

So I said nothing, and felt good about my silence.

* * *

One thing I felt compelled to do, even though my lawyers would have advised against it, was to reach out to Meredith's family. Even though I had barely known her, I'd been living with the horror of her murder for more than a month and could not begin to imagine what her mother, father, brothers, and sister were going through. Thinking about it helped me put my own predicament in some perspective; it made me grateful I was alive and still able to fight against those who were doing me harm.

I knew the Kerchers had hired an Italian lawyer, Francesco Maresca, whom they picked off a short list provided by the British embassy. I addressed my letter to him, saying how sorry I was for everything that had happened and expressing a wish that the full truth would soon come out.

I was naive enough to believe that Maresca would be sympathetic. I would understand only much later that his professional interest in Amanda and me was the money he could sue our families for. Entertaining the notion that we were innocent did not figure in this mind-set. And so my letter went unanswered.

*   *   *

My family could not believe how the courtroom defeats were piling up and decided something had to change in a hurry.

Although Tiziano Tedeschi spent many evenings with my family discussing the case, my father complained that he never seemed consistently available. Often when they met, Papà said that Tedeschi would interrupt to take personal calls. My father rarely comments on other people's manners, but eventually he felt compelled to ask his friend to turn the phone off.

Tedeschi, meanwhile, had a laundry list of complaints about Luca Maori. He wasn't following proper procedure, Tedeschi said. He was making himself too visible in the media and creating all sorts of legal headaches that could haunt us later.

"Tell him yourself," my father countered. "I can't play referee between my lawyers."

"I have told him, but it makes no difference."

"Well, you need to insist," my father said. "Assert yourself."

It's not clear Tedeschi ever did. He said he felt excluded from the growing relationship between my father and Maori and resentful of the way the family turned to him for solace without letting him run the case as he saw fit.

My father saw things exactly the other way around. He became ever more disillusioned with Tedeschi's performance as a lawyer and interpreted this as a failure of his personal commitment to me and our entire family. Papà approached Tedeschi's brother, Enrico, at one point and asked how things might have worked out better.

"If I had offered to pay him, would he have behaved the same way?" my father asked. "Is the issue that he doesn't have time for us, or that he needs a financial inducement to make the time?"

Enrico, caught between his brother and one of his best friends, said nothing.

My uncle Giuseppe and his wife, Sara, were fed up with both lawyers and inquired into possible replacements. Sara was active in the Alleanza Nazionale, the most conservative party in Silvio Berlusconi's governing coalition, and had friends in high political circles, including a number of members of parliament. Those friends were unanimous in recommending Giulia Bongiorno, a lawyer and politician seen as a rising star in both arenas.

Bongiorno had cut her legal teeth during Italy's most sensational trial of the 1990s. Giulio Andreotti, the grand old man of Italian politics, was brought up on the spectacular charge of collusion with the Sicilian Mafia during his many decades in ministerial office, and Bongiorno was part of the team assigned to defend him. Sure enough, he was acquitted. Not only could Bongiorno handle such a high-profile case, with all the attendant media scrutiny, she also had a reputation as someone able to cut through the verbiage of Italian jurisprudence to formulate coherent, rock-solid arguments. And she knew courtroom procedure better than most judges.

My father was resistant. He felt a continuing kinship with Tedeschi, despite everything, and he couldn't help liking Maori, who was infectiously good company and invited Papà to lavish meals and evenings at the country estate.

My father was not, however, going to sit back and let the professionals handle everything. He developed intense personal relationships with the consultants he hired and came to know the ins and outs of the case better than the lawyers. He was particularly aggrieved when the Ricciarelli court would not accept the evidence showing that the shoe prints at Via della Pergola were made by Rudy Guede. It was time, Papà decided, for the family to do their own detective work.

They started with the Nikes. The shoe prints at Guede's apartment and at the murder scene had eleven concentric circles on the sole, in contrast to the seven circles on mine. My father and his consultants also noticed a small, Y-shaped deformity clearly visible in a number of the shoe prints photographed by the Polizia Scientifica and concluded this was probably a piece of broken glass from Filomena's window that Guede stepped on as he walked across her room.

If they could substantiate that, it would be a big strike against the staged-break-in theory. If the shoe wearer murdered Meredith first and broke the window only subsequently, as Mignini and the judges had argued, that Y-shaped piece of glass would not have shown up in the bloody imprints around the body.

Regrettably, Guede's shoes were not available, presumably because he ditched them; they were not at his apartment and they were not among his possessions when he was arrested in Germany. What my family could do, though, was look for the same size and model Nikes and use them to demonstrate why the shoe prints at Via della Pergola had nothing to do with me.

My father started looking in every shoe shop he could find in Perugia, examining each pair of Nikes for the telltale pattern on the sole. My uncle Giuseppe did the same in and around Bari. The hunt was on.

* * *

A few days after the Ricciarelli court ruling, my sister stepped away from her desk into a corridor and bumped into her boss, along with the head of the medical section and the colonel in overall charge of logistics for the entire carabinieri force. The three of them pretended the encounter was spontaneous, but she understood right away it was anything but. The medical section was on a different floor, and the colonel had traveled from the other side of Rome. Funnily enough, she was the very person they wanted to talk to.

All three offered sympathy for the fact that I was languishing in prison and said they were concerned for Vanessa's well-being. "Why don't you take some time off so you can be with your family?" her boss suggested. The head of the medical section said he could issue a note saying she was under mental stress; that way, she could stay out for weeks, or even months.

Vanessa's guard went up right away. In the carabinieri, psychological problems are automatic grounds to be fired. The force doesn't want mentally unstable people walking around with firearms and powers of arrest. If she agreed to the proposal, she realized her superiors would have a document enabling them to get rid of her whenever they wanted. And she wasn't going to allow that to happen.

"Thank you for the offer," she replied, "but if I want to be with my family, I'll do it on my own time. The best way for me to overcome stress is to keep working."

The three men looked at each other, then back at her, and walked away. Vanessa worried that the thing her anti-Mafia investigator friend had warned her about was now starting in earnest.

* * *

Mignini questioned Amanda again on December 17, and she, unlike me, agreed to answer his questions in the presence of her lawyers. She was more composed now and gave him nothing new to work with. She couldn't have been present at the murder, she insisted, because she'd spent all night with me. When Mignini hammered her about the reasons she had mentioned Patrick's name during her all-night interrogation, she talked about the pressure she'd been under and eventually burst into tears. At that point, her lawyers instructed her to say no more.

One detail Amanda offered was nevertheless used against us. She said that while she and I were lounging about my apartment on the night of the murder, she had read some *Harry Potter*. Soon after, the newspapers claimed this had to be a lie. They printed pictures of a *Harry Potter* book in her bedroom at Via della Pergola and suggested she had inadvertently given away her real whereabouts when Meredith was killed.

This was yet another smear job, which the authorities either encouraged or did nothing to contradict. She had copies of *Harry Potter* at *both* houses, one in German and the other in English, as the police photographs of my apartment and of Amanda's room at Via della Pergola made abundantly clear.

* * *

Amanda and I had had no contact since our arrests, which was becoming an ever greater hardship for me. I would have loved to compare notes on our awful night in the Questura and let her know that, from now on, I had her back. I have no doubt, knowing what I know now, that she would have delivered a similar message to me.

Clearly, though, it was dangerous for us to attempt any communication, much less talk about the case. My lawyers told me that writing to her was out of the question, at least until the investigation was formally over.

It pained me, but I knew they were right. I thought of her, I prayed for her, and I winced when I saw the distorted image of her depicted on television and in the newspapers. Beyond that I could do nothing.

* * *

My father scoured the shops in Perugia without success. Where on earth could Guede have found those shoes? Then, one day, Papà received an excited phone call from his brother, Giuseppe, who was in a branch of the French chain Auchan in Adelfia, in the Bari suburbs.

Giuseppe had found the matching pair of Nikes in a sales rack. They were an old model, which was why they had been so hard to find. It made sense, of course; new Nikes like my Air Force 1s would be too expensive for Guede. His were Outbreak 2s.

"So, should I buy them?" Giuseppe asked.

"*Caspita!* What are you talking about?" My father all but exploded on the other end of the line. "Yes, of course!"

"But they're not exactly the right size. They're forty-four and a half, and Rudy's are forty-five. They don't have any others."

"Buy them anyway!" my father yelled.

So Giuseppe did.

The question now was what to do with them. Papà decided it was time to go public and pitched his story to one of Italy's most prominent news-show hosts, Enrico Mentana. I was all in favor. I couldn't stand the thought of staying in prison a moment longer and was willing to try anything to bring my ordeal to an early end. Why shouldn't the world know that the strongest evidence against me was entirely without foundation?

The rest of the family was more skeptical. "You need to wait until the investigation is officially over," Vanessa said. "Don't say it on TV—keep it for the courtroom so you can surprise them. If you put this out, there's no knowing what they'll do in response. It could be something even worse."

Many times during my imprisonment, Vanessa was the family's answer to Cassandra, the visionary of doom during the Trojan War whose fate was to be routinely disbelieved by those around her. On this occasion Giuseppe agreed with Vanessa, and so did Luca Maori. But my father went ahead with the broadcast regardless. He, like me, could not bear to sit on the information while I languished indefinitely in solitary confinement. He had his technical expert, Francesco Vinci, give Mentana the scientific explanations, and Papà took it upon himself to explain why the case against me was based on erroneous suppositions and outdated information that the prosecutor's office was refusing to discard.

The show, which aired on January 11, 2008, made for great television. But within hours disaster struck, yet again, just as Vanessa had predicted it would.

* * *

That night, the Italian news agencies ran a story that the police had found traces of my DNA on a metal clasp sliced away from Meredith's bra. A few weeks earlier, a forensic team had gone back to the house on Via della Pergola to conduct a new search and recovered a piece of bra that had eluded them the first time around. The small swatch of white cotton had two clasps attached, and it yielded something the police had not been able to establish before: proof positive, or so they said, of my presence at the scene of the crime.

I was suspicious about the timing—it would later transpire the DNA analysis had been done in late December and saved for public airing until this opportune moment—but I also recognized how dangerous this new development was. I knew I had never touched Meredith's bras or gone into her room and had no idea how the Polizia Scientifica had come up with their information. But I also realized that explaining it away would be no easy task. Unlike the kitchen knife, which raised all sorts of questions of plausibility and did not have direct implications for my involvement in the crime, the DNA on the bra clasp suggested I had been in direct, intimate contact with Meredith at the time of her murder, just as the prosecution had been alleging for weeks.

My lawyers offered no comment when the news broke, saying only that they needed to see the evidence. My father would have done better to follow their example. Instead, he tried to control the damage and talked to every reporter who called him. "The most plausible explanation," he said to most of them, "is that the bra had been worn by Amanda as well, and Raffaele touched it when she was wearing it."

There were two problems with this statement. First, it was so speculative and far-fetched it did nothing to diminish the perception that I was guilty. And, second, it showed that my father—my dear, straight-arrow, ever-optimistic, overtrusting father—still couldn't stop assuming that if the police or the prosecutor's office was saying something, it must be so.

The prosecutor's office had no similar inclination to give our family the benefit of the doubt. The Mentana broadcast may have been a strategic error on our part, but it certainly demonstrated that we had the means and the determination to fight back against the barrage of accusations against me. Mignini's office appears to have understood this, and decided never to be caught off guard by us again. Within weeks of the broadcast, my entire family's phones—home, cell, and office—were being tapped around the clock.

* * *

It was open season against us. Two weeks after the bra-clasp bombshell, the newspapers announced the emergence of a *supertestimone*, a "superwitness," deemed reliable by the prosecutor's office, who claimed to have seen Rudy, Amanda, and me together outside the house on Via della Pergola on the evening before the murder.

The witness, described as an Albanian immigrant, was reported to have stopped his car to throw some trash into a garbage bin only to spot Amanda and me arguing. Amanda pulled a large knife out of her handbag, causing the witness to take fright and head back to his car. Before he could take off, he said, Guede stepped out of the shadows and alarmed him even more. He got a good enough look at all of us to recognize our pictures when they appeared in the newspaper weeks later.

We wouldn't find out who this person was for months. We knew right away he was spouting nonsense, not least because he half-admitted it himself. "I realize that after more than two months, my testimony might appear less than credible," he was quoted saying in one newspaper interview. (The story he gave to Mignini was even more fantastic than the newspaper accounts. He said—and later repeated under oath in court—that he'd stopped not to throw out his trash, but because he saw a big black bag in the middle of the road which, on closer inspection, turned out to be Amanda and me.) Such absurdities did not, unfortunately, prevent him from doing the two of us great harm.

A pattern was emerging. Time and again the newspapers, not the prosecutor's office, would announce apparent breaks in the case, all of them negative for us. In some cases, witnesses would be interviewed by journalists before they were formally heard by the prosecution. Even if they later proved unreliable, as many of them did, they played a role in hardening public opinion against us.

Along with the Albanian, we had to contend with a seventy-six-year-old woman by the name of Nara Capezzali, who claimed she had heard a bloodcurdling scream coming from Meredith's house at about 11:00 p.m. on the night of the murder, followed by sounds of people running through the streets.

She too was embraced by the prosecutor's office, even though she was hard of hearing, had a history of mental problems, and lived behind double glazing so thick it was physically impossible for her to have heard the things she said she heard. We dealt with her all the way to the bitter end.

Just once, in the early months of 2008, the authorities let something slip in our favor. Luca Lalli, the coroner, gave a media interview expressing his doubts that Meredith had been raped, thus contradicting the prosecution's contention that we were guilty of sexual violence as well as murder. Lalli said he could now confirm that Guede's fingers had been in the area around Meredith's vagina. But he saw no evidence of penetration, consensual or otherwise, and certainly nothing to suggest that Amanda or I had molested her in any way.

The day Lalli's comments went public, Mignini had him fired. Lalli, Mignini said, had violated the confidentiality of the investigation; it didn't matter what he'd discussed so much as the fact that he'd discussed it at all. Given the way the prosecutor's office was leaking like a sieve when it came to stories casting us in a negative light, this did not strike us as an especially convincing explanation.

* * *

As the prospects for my release dimmed, I decided to finish my undergraduate thesis. I was going crazy with the uncertainty of waiting for something to happen, and graduation, unlike my freedom, was an attainable goal, as well as a reliable validation of who I was. My lawyers brought me books and a computer, which I used to type even though I could not hook up to the Internet from my cell. When I finished, my father lodged a special request with Judge Matteini for my family and professors to come to the prison for my oral presentation and graduation ceremony.

Matteini said yes, but with some strict qualifications. The Polizia Postale would take charge of the computer equipment to make sure it was not misused. There were to be no photographs, and the only family member authorized to attend was my father. My stepmother, Mara, and my sister, Vanessa, were expressly not invited.

Still, it was an emotional day. I was overjoyed to see the five professors on my thesis committee; they were a connection to the real world I had lost almost completely after three months in solitary confinement. My father brought me a new suit and tie and wore a matching outfit himself. I negotiated with the prison authorities to provide soft drinks and little cakes, which everyone downed in a hurry because we were given no time to dawdle.

We met in one of the public rooms used for family visits and interrogations. I used a blackboard there as a projector screen. The police and prison staff were no doubt baffled by my presentation; my thesis was on genetic programming, a way of using computers to mimic the generational changes of Darwinian natural selection and process mountains of data to solve complex problems. Just one of my professors, Alfredo Milani, asked a question; the others seemed unsure if they were allowed to speak.

The professors awarded me top marks for my presentation, and then had to leave immediately. I was not authorized to talk to any of them. My father just had time to give me a hug and tell me how proud he was. "You were brilliant," he said, "even if I didn't understand a word."

Later, he sent all five committee members an anthurium plant, in memory of my mother, who loved the anthurium's flaming red and pink flowers. It was an appropriate symbol of the occasion: an important rite of passage, marked by an abiding grief.

* * *

Within hours, I was unexpectedly transferred to a prison in Terni, fifty miles south of Perugia. In theory, I was being moved to end my time in solitary confinement. Amanda had been out of isolation for some time, and the authorities were finding it increasing difficult to justify keeping me there.

When I arrived, though, I was told no spaces were available in the shared cells; I would be staying in solitary after all. How long for? Nobody could say.

This left me feeling only more bitter. After packing up my things and enduring a bumpy journey inside a cage barely wider than I was, the only noticeable change in my new surroundings was the new roster of guards I needed to get to know. The food was still bland and stirred no appetite in me whatsoever. The exercise regimen was as restricted and uninspiring as it had been at Capanne.

This was a tough period, and it forced me to dig deep just to hold myself together. As my time alone stretched out into weeks and then months, I had to let go of everything that was happening and hold on to other, more permanent, more consoling thoughts: my family and friends, the memory of my mother, the simple pleasures I'd enjoyed with Amanda, the peace that came from knowing that neither of us had done anything wrong.

If they want to kill me this way, I remember thinking, *let them go ahead. I'm happy to have lived life as I did, and to have made the choices I made.*

My thoughts turned frequently to another dark place, perhaps the darkest I have ever seen: the Dachau concentration camp, which I visited during my year abroad in Germany. What struck me was not just the scale of the cruelty perpetrated by the Nazis, but also its jarring incongruities: how prisoners were forced to sing happy songs as they came through the gates for the first time, how workers in the crematorium would not only clear out the bodies but would sometimes see friends hanging by their thumbs from hooks in the ceiling rafters. I was moved, too, by the Jewish memorial erected on the site, an underground tomb encased in stone that was illuminated by a single shaft of light from a hole in the roof.

My experience, of course, was not on the same order of magnitude as the concentration camp inmates'. The torture I went through was strictly psychological. Still, in the darkness of my own cell, I was haunted by memories of my visit. When I took one of my miserably cold showers, I thought of the showers in the concentration camp. When I attended mass, an option at Terni I did not have at Capanne, I thought of the Jewish memorial with its ray of hope beaming down from the heavens. I thought about the forced marches and the hymns of joy the prisoners were made to sing. I thought about the mass slaughter, all those people killed for no reason just as Meredith had been killed for no reason. And I wept for the extraordinary suffering that had preceded mine.

* * *

At the end of February, the prosecutor's office released video footage of the Polizia Scientifica going over the house at Via della Pergola, first on November 2–3 and again on December 18, and we knew we had strong grounds on which to challenge their findings.

The forensic teams wore white Tyvek moon suits, with latex gloves and masks over their mouths and noses. But they often failed to change their gloves after they had touched bloodstains or other important evidence, raising immediate questions about contamination. They crowded into small spaces, bumped into each other, and did not take samples so much as wipe entire surfaces clean. Independent experts we consulted expressed alarm. The police had broken virtually every protocol, they said, and failed to ensure that their results could be verified through replication. We had no opportunity to go in and reanalyze the Polizia Scientifica's findings, because many of the most important spots—including bloodstains on door handles, in the bathroom, on the refrigerator, and so on—had been removed completely.

We also gained some insight into the bra-clasp mystery. On November 2, the day after the murder, the piece of white material with the two metal clasps was photographed on the tile floor directly in front of Meredith's bed. Somehow, though, the Polizia Scientifica did not recover it until December 18, forty-six days later, by which time the room had been turned upside down, Meredith's clothes, bedding, and other possessions had been tossed into great, unwieldy piles, and the missing bra piece had unaccountably shifted under a carpet several feet away near Meredith's desk.

The likelihood of contamination was so great our experts had doubts that a fair-minded court could attribute any significance to a single biological sample found attached to one clasp. How could it be that my DNA was entirely absent from the murder scene except this one tiny trace? With all the coming and going and the scant attention to protocol, it seemed perfectly possible that my DNA was picked up elsewhere in the apartment and transferred, perhaps by a police investigator wearing a dirty glove.

My father was confident enough about the incompetence on display that he decided, once again, to take the evidence public—this time to a local television station in Puglia called Telenorba. Again, the strategy backfired, though for different reasons this time. Many television viewers and critics were shocked to see the police's video footage of Meredith's near-naked corpse, including graphic images of the fatal wounds in her neck. The debate that immediately erupted across the country did not even touch on the Polizia Scientifica's shortcomings; it was all about the shockingly poor taste of broadcasting the footage at all—a decision made by the station, not by my family. Mignini, taking full advantage, later filed suit against us for violation of Meredith's privacy.

We should have been more patient. The findings were promising, but we needed to wait for the government to produce its DNA evidence and see what exactly they had. Then, and only then, could we begin knocking down the most damaging allegations against us.

* * *

My last hope to avoid trial, or at least to get out of prison while I waited, lay with the Corte di Cassazione, Italy's high court, which agreed to hear a last-ditch appeal at the beginning of April. Giuseppe and Sara again said we should give this task to Giulia Bongiorno, and again my father demurred. Luca Maori gave him the name Alfredo Gaito, a Roman lawyer specializing in hearings before the Corte di Cassazione, and Tiziano Tedeschi vouched for Gaito as one of the best in the business.

If he was the best, though, he certainly did not show it to us. He demanded payment up front without offering my family the chance to sound him out. He never came to see me in prison and said nothing to suggest that this assignment excited or moved or infuriated him in any way. We knew the Cassazione would not review the evidence but would examine only the procedural correctness of the decisions made by previous judges. Nobody, though, offered us proper guidance on how best to challenge those decisions.

As it was, Gaito let Tedeschi—a lawyer with little previous experience of the Cassazione—do most of the talking. Our brief was essentially a rehash of the evidentiary points we considered to be in our favor, not a procedural approach at all. Since the Court was not interested in reviewing documents, it was essentially our word against the lower courts', and the lower courts, inevitably, won.

Amanda and I were not present, but we were raked over the coals anyway for our supposedly wayward personalities, our "habitual drug use," and the danger to society the Court said we represented. The one victory we eked out was a finding that we should have been told we were under criminal investigation before our long night of interrogations in the Questura. The statements we produced would not be admissible at trial.

This was not at all the outcome my family had hoped for, and my father vented his fury in all directions. He had imagined that the white marble halls of the Cassazione were far enough from Perugia for clarity to shine through. Mostly he blamed the lawyers. Why was Gaito such a wash? Why hadn't Luca Maori said anything? What did Tedeschi think he was doing?

Giuseppe and Sara had been right all along. It was time for a high-powered lawyer inspiring greater confidence to take on my defense. Given the slowness of the Italian justice system, we might now have to wait up to a year for trial to begin, maybe as long as two years for a conclusion. We could afford to make no more mistakes.

My father not only removed Tedeschi from the case; he never spoke to him again. I was left, once again, facing the darkness of my isolation cell with no end in sight.

III

THE PROTECTED
SECTION

[*Jesus said:*] *"Woe to you, lawyers! For you have taken away the key to knowledge. You did not enter in yourselves, and you hindered those who wanted to enter."*

And as He said these things, the scribes and the Pharisees began to assail Him vehemently, and to cross-examine Him about many things, lying in wait for Him, and seeking to catch Him in something He might say, that they might accuse Him.

—Luke 11:52–54

In May 2008, the authorities in Terni finally moved me out of solitary confinement. I was moved instead into the *sezione protetta,* a special "protected section" reserved largely for rapists, pedophiles, and other sex criminals, along with a smattering of Mafia informants and jailhouse snitches—prisoners seen as such pariahs they could not stay with the general inmate population because they were unlikely to survive.

I was told that the decision to place me there was less about the charges of sexual violence I faced than about my media notoriety. They were, they said, putting me there for my own good.

My own good? The record wasn't too strong so far on things the authorities had done *for my own good.*

I'd been languishing in solitary confinement for six months now, presumably *for my own good* since the authorities had offered no other reason to keep me there. It's difficult to describe just how crazy it can make a person to be deprived of contact with the outside world for twenty-three hours a day. I found it difficult to concentrate on anything for long. I lost my appetite. I struggled to write letters and gave up almost completely on journal entries. I struggled, particularly, to hold on to hope. I felt like a wounded animal, left to whimper in a corner and ignored except for an occasional hard kick to remind me of how little anybody cared. Only the regular visits from my father and my other family members and friends kept me sane; they were the only things I had to look forward to.

Now my despair was compounded by fear. Who knew what fresh horrors were in store? The way I understood it, this was a whole new form of pressure from the authorities. Nothing was said explicitly, but the subtext seemed clear: *If you don't want to tell us what we want to hear, you can take your chances with the perverts and child molesters and transsexuals and see how you like that instead.*

That's what I heard when they said they were putting me in the the protected secton *for my own good.* My only option was to steel myself and figure out a path to survival.

I was put in a cell on my own at first, which was a blessing, and I did my best to keep to myself. The name of the wing was not entirely euphemistic. The guards did keep a close eye on us, and my fear of immediate physical danger subsided quite rapidly. But I had no idea how I was going to find common ground with these people. They were loud and vulgar and mean and alarming. Almost immediately, they bombarded me with their idle, distorted opinions of Meredith's murder to see if they could get a rise out of me.

I didn't ignore them, but neither did I rise to their bait. I said, calmly, that my conscience was clear and waited until they changed the subject.

The experience brought back memories of a trip to Lisbon I took when I was twenty and the night my friend and I went to buy marijuana in the city's red-light district. I remember a street brimming with prostitutes, pimps, and drug pushers; people with scars on their faces and trouble on their minds and who knew what weapons hidden beneath their clothing. I was the idiot tourist with a fanny pack and a camera slung around my neck; I had never felt more vulnerable in my life. I could feel everyone's hard stares as the hustlers and lowlifes sized me up as a potential customer, or an easy mark. I felt profoundly ill at ease and out of place.

I had a similar feeling now about my fellow prisoners. Only this time there was no beating a hasty retreat. These people were my world, for the foreseeable future.

Like some weirdly dysfunctional high school, the protected section had its clans and cliques that vied for the attention of newcomers like me. Two groups were considered outcasts and forced to fend largely for themselves: the pedophiles, mostly old men with strange leers and odd personal hygiene habits, and the transsexuals, who put the rest of us on edge because they flirted and giggled and made flamboyant public displays of their silicone boob jobs. The rest were organized largely by geographical region. The North Africans stuck together, as did the Umbria natives. The *napoletani* (Neapolitans) formed one Southern Italian clique, and the *baresi* (from Bari), the natives of my region, another.

I knew right away that joining any of these groups could spell trouble. They baited each other constantly; violence never seemed far from the surface. The tension was worst at mealtimes, when the prisoners designated as servers were judged by the exact amount of food they slopped on everyone's plate. A little more or less could easily start a fight.

At times the tension was so great you could almost taste it, especially when prisoners got drunk on the wickedly strong hooch they made in their cell basins from basic supplies of apples, sugar, and yeast. (I tried it just once and found it disgusting.) One inmate who called another *figlio di puttana*, son of a whore, had boiling oil thrown in his face. Another aggrieved prisoner smashed the gas bottle he kept in his cell for cooking and came after his target with the broken shards.

To this point in my notably sheltered life, the most violence I'd seen were a few drunken punches thrown at a club. Now I was in the midst of hardened criminals with hair-trigger tempers and feral instincts only heightened by being caged together. This was no place for a self-professed nerd and computer geek; the thought of being attacked by one of these guys, or even being caught in the fray, scared the shit out of me. I was exposed and unprotected in this "protected section" and could only live by my wits.

The guards did their best to break up the fights and were scrupulous about confiscating weapons. But the inmates were usually one step ahead of them. They made knives by sharpening down baby scissors or filing away at spoons. They would hide them in tubs of shaving cream or behind the radiators in their cells. Actually using these weapons was a big risk because being caught meant a trip to solitary confinement and double time for any charges leading to a conviction. But these were volatile people who sometimes acted first and thought better of it later.

The Bari group courted me to join them, as did the Neapolitans, but I said no to them all. Sometimes I would make a joke and say I wanted to be neutral, like Switzerland. Other times I would explain that I was disgusted with my country and was starting a new clique of my own called the United States—the country where most of my public supporters seemed to come from.

I was pleased to discover that I had a talent for keeping trouble at bay. I couldn't flinch or run, because that could give my would-be tormentors the idea I had something to hide and encourage them to go after me all the more. Whenever I was taunted about Amanda, or the knife I had supposedly plunged into Meredith's neck, I had to face down my antagonists, if only to show that I wasn't afraid. I was calm but insistent. My approach reminded me a little of the way my father taught me to react if we came across beavers in the wild; the most important idea to convey was that you weren't worth antagonizing, either because you were unflappable or because you might just fight back.

I thought about a much-misunderstood line from the Bible, when Christ talks about turning the other cheek. People often think that Jesus was encouraging his followers to play the victim and say, "Go ahead, punish me some more, I'll even make it easy for you." But I think that interpretation is absurd, and makes Christianity seem like a religion fit only for masochists. Turning the other cheek *really* means meeting provocation with indifference and just a hint of defiance. It means telling your antagonist, "Do what you must, but you're not going to get what you want, and it might just backfire."

* * *

My sister, Vanessa, had her own daunting environment to deal with. She was the only uniformed woman in a teeming office of about a thousand carabinieri, and while she was used to attracting unwarranted attention, she became aware, over the spring of 2008, that she was being more than just noticed; she was being spied on.

This, as Vanessa saw it, was the start of something that Italians call *mobbing*—essentially, the slow process of making someone's life a living hell. She noticed eyes on her when she walked into the office first thing in the morning, and more eyes on her when she left. One of her few remaining friends confirmed what she already suspected, that people were taking notes on her every move: when she came and went, when she took a coffee break, how long she spent at lunch. Later, she even stumbled across worksheets where her movements were carefully tracked.

Officially, the workday was eight hours, with a half hour for lunch. But officers, including Vanessa's bosses, commonly took off for two or three hours in the middle of the day and then stayed late. They would even put in for overtime for the extra hours.

Before Vanessa felt all eyes on her, she had enjoyed going to the gym for an hour or so in the middle of the day. It was longer than the rules allowed, but she was always back before her superiors and made sure not to leave any pending tasks undone. Now she didn't dare leave at all, even if it meant sitting and staring into space for hours.

Over time, she was given less and less work, even when her bosses were present. She complained to the officer overseeing her, but he was unsympathetic. "Go to the *marescialli*"—the noncommissioned officers—"and ask them for extra work," he said. It was a direct putdown, as the *marescialli* were junior to Vanessa, and her job was to tell them what to do, not the other way around.

* * *

Vanessa is not the only tough nut in the family. My aunt Sara is more than a match for her; she is one of those forceful, gregarious, elegantly turned-out Italian women whose every move lets you know she takes no crap from anyone. Sara has always been a political animal. As a young woman she fell under the spell of Giorgio Almirante, a populist rabble-rouser who took on the mantle of the defeated Italian Fascist Party after World War II and turned it into a grassroots movement to counter what he and his supporters saw as the festering corruption and self-satisfaction of the mainstream parties in Rome. The Movimento Sociale Italiano, as Almirante's group was known, was regarded with deep suspicion, if not outright contempt, in much of the country, which had fought hard and sacrificed much to bury the Fascist movement in the 1940s. But it had a bedrock appeal in the South, which did not enjoy many of the fruits of Italy's postwar boom and felt nostalgic for Mussolini's ambitious public works projects, his commitment to rooting out organized crime, and—something that rarely gets talked about—the galvanizing effect his education and labor policies had on emancipating women in our ultraconservative region.

Sara worked tirelessly as an organizer, and when the movement finally gained mainstream acceptance in the 1990s—changing its name to the Alleanza Nazionale and repudiating the more obviously unacceptable aspects of Mussolini's legacy—she suddenly had a lot of influential friends. Giuseppe Tatarella, godfather to the *other* Raffaele Sollecito (the son of Giuseppe and Sara), was now deputy prime minister and an important vote-wrangler in the Chamber of Deputies, Italy's lower house of parliament. Sara made an unsuccessful run for mayor of Giovinazzo, my hometown, and later served as cultural assessor in Bitonto, a Bari suburb.

The rest of my family is not especially political, but we have all been brought up to admire a strong sense of social order. We like public figures who value personal integrity above the usual Machiavellian intrigues of Italian politics; we like anyone willing to take a stand against obvious injustice. What we like, in other words, are *gente con le palle*, people with balls. Despite the terminology, these people don't have to be men; on the contrary, as both Sara and Vanessa have shown, the people with the biggest balls are often women.

What drove Sara crazy for the first several months of my imprisonment was that she didn't see anyone qualified or willing to show real guts and take charge. Her role models were people like Giovanni Falcone and Paolo Borsellino, two fearless prosecutors who paid with their lives in their unrelenting quest to root out Sicily's top Mafia leaders in the 1980s and early 1990s. *Those* were the sorts of people we needed, Sara felt. The person who should really be running my case was Giulia Bongiorno.

Bongiorno was accomplished and articulate and knew criminal law backward and forward. She hardly lacked for courage; we would later nickname her *la signora trentapalle,* the lady with thirty balls. She was even a member of the same political party as Sara, so they had plenty of connections.

The question was how to recruit her. Bongiorno was not only a full-time member of parliament, she was also about to assume the chairmanship of the parliamentary justice committee. The political risks she ran if she took on my case were considerable. Still, my family thought they should at least give her a try.

Soon after the Corte di Cassazione rejected my appeal, Sara and Vanessa visited Bongiorno's elegantly appointed law office a few minutes' walk from the Italian parliament. They were steered there by another Alleanza Nazionale member, a Sicilian senator with a legal background named Domenico Nania. Once they were in the room, though, there was no talk of political connections; it was all business.

Bongiorno said, "Give me the files and I'll tell you whether or not I want to take this case." She was no-nonsense, straight to the point, and did not waste time on awkward expressions of sympathy that might have sounded forced and insincere.

Would her decision be influenced by how much my family was willing to pay?

"It's not about the price. It's about whether I'm willing to risk my reputation."

And that was that. We waited a couple of weeks while she read through the court documents and made an initial assessment.

And then she came back with her answer. It was a yes.

* * *

The first thing I noticed about Giulia Bongiorno when she came to meet me was that she had little or no bedside manner. She cut a disarming, almost boyish figure with her carefully groomed short hair, her big, round eyes, and rimless glasses. But it was obvious when she spoke that she was a person of consequence. Every word out of her mouth was effortlessly impressive. It was a little jarring, at first, how clipped and detached she was. Some might call her aloof. But, after listening to a lot of meaningless feel-good banter from Tedeschi and Maori and knowing how little good it had done me, I didn't mind. I sensed I could trust her because she would never promise more than she could deliver.

On that first visit we talked through the basics of the case, so she could develop a feel for me and the impression I might make in court. Mostly, though, she wanted to know if I was covering for Amanda in some way.

I told her I was not.

"I believe what you are telling me," she said. "But if you have something to say that you're holding back for any reason, say it, because otherwise it may be too late."

Calmly I repeated, "I have nothing to say."

Then she left. She wrote to me regularly and asked for my input on ideas she was developing. But I didn't have a one-on-one conversation with her again for months.

* * *

My father would arrive like clockwork every Friday. Sometimes he was alone; other times he would bring friends, or other members of the family. He pushed the prison authorities to expand visiting hours as much as possible and was allotted six hours a month instead of the usual four.

He had to reorganize his professional life completely after my arrest. To make sure he could drive to Terni every week, he dropped out of the roster of doctors on call to perform emergency surgeries. Soon he was no longer operating at all. That was a blow, but one he accepted with good grace. He couldn't afford the luxury of stopping work altogether, because the legal bills were mounting and likely to get a lot steeper. But he found that if he volunteered to do house calls rather than receiving patients, he could work a more flexible schedule and earn better money too.

The visiting room at Terni had one peculiarity: a large concrete barrier, about waist-high, separating the two sides. This was specific to the protected section, presumably because they didn't want inmates to have any inappropriate sexual contact with visitors. Having such a barrier was controversial; many in law enforcement and prison management argued that such things were illegal. It meant, above all, that I could not give my father and my other visitors a proper hug. I didn't know how much I could miss the comfort of physical contact until I was denied it.

Papà was glad to see I was doing modestly better and that I felt more or less safe. The food in the special section was slightly more interesting than in solitary, and we could make things of our own on the gas stoves in our cells. But my father and I were both frustrated by the maddeningly slow progress of my case and talked about how best I should pass the time.

My lawyer Luca Maori, who stayed on the case despite the opposition of many members of my family.

Me in court, speaking to my lawyer, Donatella Donati, with two police officers standing guard. My father is in the background, looking at his computer.

Amanda in court, speaking with her attorney, Carlo Dalla Vedova, and several paralegals from his practice.

Via della Pergola, 7. The window immediately to the left of the taped-up front door was Filomena's. The parapet at the far left of the shot is where Rudy Guede most likely threw the rock that broke her window on the night of the murder—a scenario the prosecution and judges in four different courts could not accept.

My attorney Delfo Berretti demonstrates (in August 2008), contrary to the opinion of Judge Massimo Ricciarelli, that it wouldn't take a Spider-Man to clamber up the wall of the murder house to enter Filomena's window.

Public prosecutors Giuliano Mignini (left) and Manuela Comodi (right) display the kitchen knife taken from my apartment to reporters at my trial, September 2009.

My sister, Vanessa, and my father in court, November 2009.

I look with ill-concealed contempt at Monica Napoleoni, the homicide chief of Perugia's Squadra Mobile, during one of the last hearings of my lower-court trial. To the left is Armando Finzi, the policeman who pulled the kitchen knife out of my drawer using only his "investigative instinct."

Giulia Bongiorno, my lead lawyer, in an exchange with chief prosecutor Giuliano Mignini on the day she delivered her closing statement in my first trial, November 2009.

The gates of Capanne prison, outside Perugia, where I spent six months in solitary confinement.

Amanda praying at a crucial juncture in our appeals trial in September 2011, when the prosecution made a last-ditch attempt to maintain the credibility of its deeply flawed DNA evidence.

Prosecutor Mignini looking sour as it becomes apparent that the appeal is not going in his favor, March 2011.

The media frenzy outside the court house on the night of our appeals court aquittal, October 3, 2011.

I receive a rare hug from Giulia Bongiorno as the appeals court sets me free.

My father wiping away a tear with a tie given to him by his own mother as Judge Claudio Pratillo Hellmann orders our release.

Amanda is overwhelmed by the good news as she is escorted out of the courtroom.

My father punches the air for joy. From left to right, Perugia policewoman Lorena Zugarini; my uncle on my mother's side, Michele Palmiotto; my father; his wife, Mara; and my uncle Giuseppe.

Visiting the Getty Museum in Los Angeles, March 2012.

My reunion with Amanda, Seattle, March 2012.

"I think I should enroll in graduate school and continue my studies," I said.

"How are you going to do that without going to class and talking to your professors?"

"I'll try it on my own. You can bring me the books and I can work on my laptop."

And so things transpired. Two Italian universities, Verona and Turin, offered courses I was interested in, and I picked Verona because I thought it would be a more beautiful place to visit, if I was granted the freedom to go there. My father completed the paperwork and paid the fees, and I wrote to my new professors to explain the unusual circumstances and see if anyone might make special accommodations to teach me behind bars. Nobody rushed to volunteer.

* * *

Mignini's office announced in late June that the investigation was formally over, and almost immediately the newspapers were filled with a barrage of negative stories about my family. Even before we'd had time to look over the newly available documents, we were fending off accusations that we'd tried to exploit our political connections to push for my freedom.

Some of the stories said we'd begged Sara's highly placed friends in Rome to apply pressure to the Corte di Cassazione before our hearing in April, or to exploit Bongiorno's prominent position. Others postulated, more wildly, that my family had approached Mafia thugs in Bari and contracted with them to intimidate the Perugia police.

The source for all these stories, we learned to our consternation, were wiretaps the police had placed on my family's phones since

February. This was no small operation: in just a few months they intercepted close to forty thousand calls. Some of the phrases in the news stories were familiar enough; my family *had* let rip about the behavior of the Perugia police and called them pigs, bastards, and *figli di puttana*. And why not? They had every reason to be angry and had no idea that their conversations were being monitored.

But a lot of the other reporting was distorted or wrong, as though designed expressly to cast us in the worst possible light and to discredit any progress we had made in challenging the evidence. Senator Nania went public immediately to deny he had interceded on our behalf with Giulia Bongiorno, conceding only that he had mentioned her name to Sara over the phone. Bongiorno herself pointed out that she had not been hired by my family until after the Corte di Cassazione issued its ruling. These news stories were exactly the kind of political damage Bongiorno had been afraid of, and she was quick to share her alarm with us. The thing that perturbed her most was a report in *Corriere della Sera,* the country's most prestigious newspaper, in which my father was quoted saying, "I want to get Giulia Bongiorno on our side because she can wield political influence on the case."

If my father had really said this, even once, even casually, she warned, she would have had to withdraw as my defense attorney immediately.

Papà said he was quite sure this was a fabrication, but Bongiorno was insistent: "I want to believe you, but you'd better be quite sure."

So we asked to see the intercepts ourselves. They were available, but we had to pay six thousand euros to have them transferred onto audio CDs. The authorities made nothing easy for us.

The transcripts vindicated us entirely and yielded something we were not even expecting: the real-time comments the Perugia police had scribbled to each other as they listened in on our conversations. It was startling reading: incontrovertible evidence, in black and white, that they were out to get us.

Monica Napoleoni, the Squadra Mobile's chief homicide investigator, came out with the choicest lines. She called Mara and Sara *cretine* (idiots) and *vipere* (snakes). Once, when Mara was on the line to my father's sister, Dora, Napoleoni jotted down, *Fanno le stronze come al solito.* They're doing their usual bitch act. Napoleoni's sidekick Lorena Zugarini also got into the swing of things, reacting to one conversation about Mignini and how crazy he seemed to be by writing, all in upper case: "LAUGH AWAY—HE WHO LAUGHS LAST LAUGHS LONGEST."

Some things in the wiretaps had been twisted to the point of absurdity. The story about us hiring Mafia thugs was derived from a house call my father made in the old "casbah" of central Bari. Since it was a rough neighborhood, he didn't want to leave his car unattended, so he asked Sara, who was riding with him, to stay put while he visited his patient. Sara killed time by calling her husband. In the version later fed to the newspapers, Sara supposedly told Giuseppe she was acting as lookout while my father went in to cut a deal with a local Mafia boss. But of course, as the transcripts showed, she said nothing of the kind.

It was galling enough that my family's phones were tapped at all. They were not suspected of any major crimes, the benchmark for ordering wiretaps under Italian law. So why were they being monitored? We never did get an adequate explanation. In the first of many authorization letters that Domenico Giacinto Profazio, the Squadra Mobile chief, addressed to Mignini, he hinted that my father was trying to tamper with the evidence. What he wrote, though, was not that explicit. "Raffaele Sollecito's father is taking steps to lighten the evidentiary burden against his son," he charged, "in such a way as to compromise the outcome of the prosecution at hand."

Certainly, the word *compromise* was pejorative, but otherwise I'm not sure my father would have disagreed: yes, he was working night and day to defend me and was absolutely interested, as a matter of constitutional right, in bringing "the prosecution at hand" to a screeching halt.

To us, Profazio's letter revealed a more profound motive for the wiretaps: the police were nervous about the work we were doing to undermine their investigation and wanted to monitor everything we were doing.

* * *

One pleasant surprise from the investigation files was that the bloody shoe print, the one that had caused us to expend so much energy and motivated so much of the courts' early decision to hold me in pretrial custody, was no longer deemed to be mine. Rudy Guede had come clean in a conversation with Mignini in May and admitted that the shoe belonged to him.

I was not off the hook entirely. The police still insisted that the bloody footprint at the murder scene, the one accompanying the left shoe print that was now identified as Guede's, belonged to me. The scenario this conjured up—of Guede hopping on one foot and me, shoeless, hopping on the other as if in some kind of three-legged race—was obviously absurd and logistically impossible, but no matter. We still had to find a way to counter it.

When my defense team examined the official paperwork, they noticed that the analysis of the footprints—including extensive inquiry into the length and shape of the foot likely to have produced them—had been conducted by two members of the Polizia Scientifica in Rome, working not in their official capacity but as private consultants charging thousands of euros to Mignini's office. One of the analysts, Lorenzo Rinaldi, was a physicist, not a specialist in anatomy, and the other, Pietro Boemia, was a fingerprint technician with no further scientific credentials. That begged the question: if Mignini's office felt it needed to contract the job out to private consultants, why wouldn't it go to people with more pertinent qualifications? The whole thing stank.

We were stunned, too, to discover that some of the most important parts of the evidence were not handed over at all. We were given a document detailing the Polizia Scientifica's conclusions about the DNA evidence on the knife and the bra clasp, but we had none of the raw data, nothing that would enable us to make our own independent evaluation. We put in a request for the data and, when it was rejected, filed another. The DNA evidence was now the bedrock of the case against me. What possible motivation could there be to withhold it?

Something else we were missing was video footage from the surveillance camera in the parking structure across the street from the murder house. We knew the prosecution had this because it was on their evidence list, and we knew it could be significant in settling the question of whether Inspector Battistelli arrived before or after I called the carabinieri on November 2.

But the prosecution was playing hardball, meaning we'd have to appeal the decision to a judge. And that was not now going to happen until after the long Italian summer break.

* * *

Already by June, the heat in the protected section was stifling. We'd soak towels in cold water and hang them over the bars of our windows to try to block out the sun. And we'd fill buckets with water and slop them on the ground, just to keep the temperature down by a degree or two.

With the heat came shorter tempers and constant confrontation, both along the corridor and on the exercise yard. A Lebanese prisoner, Ahmed (I've changed this name, as I have the names of most of my fellow prisoners), was in my face more than the others, forever needling me about Meredith's murder and every last detail he'd read in the newspaper. Ahmed was a smart guy, one of the few with family money, and he knew exactly how to hit me where it hurt most.

"Hey, you know what I'm going to do with Giulia Bongiorno?" he said one day. "I'm going to fuck her up the ass!" Everyone who heard collapsed in laughter. He'd go after my family, tease me about Amanda, whatever it took to provoke a reaction. I'd get back at him the same way, making fun of the fact that his family was so rich, calling him a spoiled kid, even giving him a hard time because he'd been adopted.

I was not proud of doing this, but it was a way to survive. Sometimes, I felt that prison stripped us of our humanity and reduced us to attack dogs, good only for turning on each other at the slightest provocation. Was this how I was going to spend the next thirty years of my life? The thought was too awful to contemplate.

I did make some friends, if that's the right word. Early on, a man not too much older than me named Filippo Greco let me know that he was a fan of comic books and Japanese manga. So we talked about that and got along well enough to become cellmates. He told me about an ex-girlfriend and their complicated breakup, and sympathized with everything I was going through. Really, he sounded so normal I almost forgot that he was in here because he had raped someone.

Filippo and I were solid for a couple of months. Then, one day, he flew into a rage with his food server, whom he suspected of talking trash behind his back. Filippo reached through the slot in his cell door and grabbed the ladle out of the server's hands. He whacked him in the head, shouting *"figlio di puttana!"* and telling him he hadn't wanted soup for lunch in the first place. The server dropped his tureen, soup went everywhere, and both of them ended up in solitary confinement.

* * *

I focused on my studies and on going to the exercise room each morning and afternoon. *Exercise room* is probably too grand a term, as it did not contain any actual equipment. We'd lie down using two stools for support and do stretches. Or we'd lash big bottles of water on each end of a broomstick and use them for weight training. In another room, we had a Ping-Pong table, foosball and a chessboard.

I wrote a lot of letters, to my family and to a growing number of supporters from Giovinazzo, my hometown, and the wide world. When July 9 rolled around, I couldn't help remembering Amanda's birthday, and I decided it was time to break my silence with her—lawyers and family be damned. I wanted her to know I was thinking of her.

So I sent her roses. And began what would turn into a long correspondence in which we talked about music, or books—everyday things that seemed more comforting than the craziness around us.

It seemed easy to slip back into communication with her, not least because her Italian had improved enormously and we now had a comfortable common language. Neither of us harbored any ill will for what had been said in public. We knew, without having to articulate it explicitly, that we had each other's backs. Every time she wrote, she signed off *ti voglio bene,* the Italian way of saying "I love you."

The roses I sent made the papers—of course they did—and gave my lawyers and family palpitations. They warned me in no uncertain terms never to discuss the case with Amanda and said sending presents could only attract unwanted publicity. Vanessa laid into me about that. Papà was more understanding, saying that the most important thing for me was to have moral support. While the correspondence with Amanda made him nervous, he trusted me not to do anything stupid.

I talked about Amanda with Filippo, my cellmate, and he listened, just as I had listened to his problems. One day, though, he told me he was bisexual, and his eyes started to brighten visibly when he looked at me. Then he burst into tears and tried to caress my face.

It was more pathetic than threatening, but it was definitely a deal-breaker. I moved in with another cellmate just as soon as I could.

* * *

In late August, my defense team was at last granted access to the murder house and had a chance to assess how much of a Spider-Man Rudy Guede would have had to be to break Filomena's window and climb up the exterior wall.

The first thing they observed was that an intruder had no need to throw the rock from the grassy slope thirteen feet below the window. A gravel driveway leading from the street to the front door of the girls' apartment included an open area a little to the left that overlooked the ravine. This area was at the same elevation as Filomena's window, separated only by a six-foot gap where the ground fell away sharply on the other side of a wooden fence. So Guede, or any other intruder, would not have had to hurl a rock in the air or clamber up with it; he merely needed to lob it about one-third of the distance required for a free throw in basketball, his favorite sport.

What about scaling the wall itself? Delfo Berretti, from Luca Maori's office, decided he would have a go, removing only his work jacket before hitching himself up onto the iron grate covering one of the boys' bedroom windows directly below Filomena's. As photos taken that day show, Berretti had no trouble maneuvering himself into a position where he could have reached into Filomena's broken window, opened it, and swung himself up to climb in. An iron nail was in the brick wall halfway between the two windows—the prosecution would later make a big deal of this—but Berretti didn't even need it to pull himself up.

Again, I was struck by how capricious the courts had been. Judge Ricciarelli was so sure the wall was unscalable he used it as a reason to keep me in solitary confinement, when a little elementary checking would have told him his assumption was wrong. How many months or years of my life would his nonchalance end up costing?

My father hired a telecommunications expert to help resolve a few other mysteries from the night of the murder. The prosecution had given no adequate explanation for a series of calls registered on Meredith's English cell phone after she'd returned from her friends' house around 9:00 p.m., and many of them seemed baffling, assuming they were made—as the prosecution argued—by Meredith herself. We believed Meredith was dead by the time of the last two calls, and our expert Bruno Pellero intended to help us prove that.

Meredith's last confirmed call was to her family in England at

8:56 p.m. Nobody answered. Since she was in close contact with her ailing mother, she might ordinarily have been expected to try again, but she never did. Almost exactly an hour later, someone started calling Meredith's voice-mail service but did not stay on the line long enough to get through. Two minutes after that, another call was made to the first number in Meredith's contacts list, her bank in England, but the caller did not include the international dialing code.

These abortive calls seemed to be the handiwork of someone, most likely Meredith's attacker, messing around with her phone. How could we establish that for sure? Pellero, an effortlessly brilliant telecommunications expert from Genoa, figured it out by matching up the phone records with the cell transmission towers where the signal for the calls had been picked up. He made his way from the house on Via della Pergola to the spot where it seemed most likely that the phones were tossed into Elisabetta Lana's garden, stopping every few seconds and testing to see which transmission tower area he was in. He discovered that the odd calls around 10:00 p.m. were almost certainly not made at the murder house, but rather in the Parco San Angelo, an open area right across the street from Lana's garden wall. Pellero talked to Elisabetta Lana and conducted a thorough inspection of her garden to try to pinpoint the exact spot from which the phones had been thrown.

To his surprise, she told him the Squadra Mobile had done exactly the same thing in the first few weeks after the murder. They had even tossed oranges from the street to try to simulate the trajectory of the discarded phones. It was quite likely, in other words, that they too understood that the cell transmission tower for the 10:00 p.m. phone calls did not match the house on Via della Pergola.

This aspect of the Squadra Mobile's work was not in the case records. If they had found what Pellero and my family thought they had, it would have contradicted Mignini's evolving theory of the crime. But their work, if it existed, simply vanished.

* * *

My neighbor in the protected section was, like me, a headline maker. His name was Roberto Spaccino, and he'd been all over the newspapers following the murder of his pregnant wife, Barbara, about five months before Meredith died. According to his prosecutors, Spaccino had beaten Barbara for years and cheated on her right and left with the female customers of a small chain of Laundromats he operated. Spaccino, however, claimed an alibi. He said he'd paid a late-night visit to one of his Laundromats, only to find the house turned upside down on his return and his wife bludgeoned to death. Their two sons were still peacefully asleep in their beds.

I didn't know what to make of the story, but Spaccino could not have been friendlier. We commiserated about our cases and the fact that both of our prosecution teams were convinced we had staged break-ins to cover our tracks.

Over time, I found the details of his story to be less than believable, but I kept that strictly to myself. He took a protective interest in me and kept me away from some of the crazier pedophiles and rapists. Compared to the rest of the block, Spaccino was almost normal.

* * *

The pretrial hearings that began in mid-September gave my legal team its first look at the woman who posed the greatest obstacle to my exoneration, Dr. Patrizia Stefanoni of the Polizia Scientifica's crime lab in Rome. She was the one who appeared to be holding out on handing over the DNA evidence. And the pretrial judge, Paolo Micheli, initially supported her position.

When we pointed out that we could hardly prepare for a cross-examination without seeing the documents on which Stefanoni's work was based, Judge Micheli relented, if only a little. We received her conclusions, but not the data demonstrating how she got there.

It was becoming obvious the prosecution had something to hide, and while we were troubled by the refusal to hand over the most important evidence in the case, we had to presume that sooner or later we'd get hold of it. Even in her initial questioning by the judge, Dr. Stefanoni was forced to admit that her sample sizes were alarmingly small, that her results could not all be reproduced (something even she said was a standard scientific requirement), that there was some vagueness about where exactly on the kitchen knife she'd found Meredith's DNA, and that she'd found traces of several people's DNA on the bra clasp, not just mine. She also acknowledged that a contaminated or improperly analyzed DNA sample could, in theory, lead to an incorrect identification.

Whenever Stefanoni was put on the spot, she would either take off on flights of extraordinary wordiness or else resort to monosyllables. We also noticed she had a habit of twirling her finger through the ends of her long, black hair. She was a nervous witness, which was good for us.

For the mass media, the pretrial hearings had little to do with the evidence; they were an opportunity to photograph Amanda and me for the first time since our arrests. I chose not to show up at all the first day, partly because I didn't want to be hounded by photographers, and partly because I was still afraid that Amanda would do or say something stupid. I'd be brought up to Perugia from Terni in a maddeningly tight cage in the back of a van and was feeling vulnerable because I was back in solitary for the duration of the hearings.

Not that the newspapers cared. They were interested mostly in Amanda, her demure white blouse, her minimalist makeup, and her natural good looks. Never mind whether we were guilty or innocent, present or absent; the story line insisted we were *belli e dannati,* the beautiful and the damned. When I smiled at her and blew her kisses at the second hearing, the newspapers were full of it, and it did us only harm.

* * *

The hearings stretched out over more than a month and gave us a few reasons to be hopeful. The Albanian superwitness, a man named Hekuran Kokomani, showed up in court wearing a baseball cap and a hoodie concealing most of his face. When my lawyers cross-examined him, he fell apart in spectacular fashion. He couldn't remember what time or even what day he supposedly saw me with Amanda and Guede in Via della Pergola, and he said it had been stormy—an observation contradicted by weather data for both October 31 and November 1. He said Amanda had a gap between her front teeth, prompting great hilarity when, at the judge's request, she smiled to prove him wrong.

We also managed to obtain the parking lot video footage after proving to the court—from the prosecution's own documentation—that it existed and was in their possession. In the long run this would be helpful, but Mignini managed to use it against us by pointing out that the car carrying the Polizia Postale arrived at 12:35, according to the time stamp on the tape. This was fifteen minutes before I called the carabinieri; only later would we work out that the time stamp was wrong.

Judge Micheli issued his ruling at the end of October. On the plus side, he found Guede guilty of murder and sentenced him to thirty years behind bars in an accelerated trial requested by Guede himself. Judge Micheli also accepted our evidence that it wouldn't have been that difficult to throw a rock through Filomena's window and climb the wall.

But, Spider-Man or no Spider-Man, he still didn't believe Guede got into the house that way. He argued that Filomena's window was too exposed and that any intruder would have run too great a risk of discovery by climbing through it. Therefore, he concluded, Amanda and I must have let him in. There seemed to be no shaking the authorities out of their conviction that the break-in was staged.

To our astonishment, Judge Micheli broadly accepted Dr. Stefanoni's testimony, despite the many doubts he'd raised in questioning her. (My father later laid much of the blame on our consultant, Vincenzo Pascali, who was upbraided by the judge for failing to follow court protocol and confusing what was already a complicated issue.) Micheli said he couldn't accept that *both* the kitchen knife and the bra clasp had been contaminated, because they had been collected in entirely different places. And that was that. The upshot: Amanda and I were ordered to stand trial, and to remain in custody until it was over.

Another judge, another crushing disappointment.

* * *

Despite prevailing, the prosecution couldn't help being stung by Kokomani's embarrassing performance, and they took one line in Judge Micheli's ruling particularly to heart. Without Kokomani's testimony, Micheli said, nothing indicated that Guede, Amanda, and I had known each other before the night of the murder. "The assumption that there was a criminal conspiracy remains fatally unsupported by actual evidence," he wrote. With the clock ticking down to the start of our trial and the prosecution still wedded to the idea that Meredith's murder had been some sort of ritual slaughter, the pressure was on to find some of that evidence.

On November 20, an unemployed university researcher named Fabio Gioffredi made a providential appearance in the prosecutor's office and provided what Mignini was looking for. Two nights before the murder—which is to say, more than a year earlier—Gioffredi said he had seen Amanda, Meredith, Guede, and me outside the house on Via della Pergola. He had glimpsed us for just an instant. Still, the moment lodged in his mind because he had just had a minor car accident; he scraped another vehicle as he pulled out of a parking space down the street.

Oddly, Gioffredi had no memory of the details of the other car. There was no police report on the accident and no insurance claim. Gioffredi said he gave his phone number to the owner of the other car, but never heard from him and never paid any money for the damage. In other words, there was no independent record of the incident. Still, he was sure he remembered Amanda, whom he did not know, wearing a long red coat with large buttons (which she did not possess). He said that the rest of us, whom he did not know either, were in dark clothing.

My family's reaction to Gioffredi was that he was just another *pestamerda,* an annoyance much like Kokomani, whom we could swat away with relative ease. It didn't take long for one of the computer consultants hired by my father to establish that, at the exact time Gioffredi said I was meeting Amanda and Meredith and

Guede, I was in fact at home, on my computer, reading and taking notes on a complicated genetic-programming paper I was reading for my thesis.

Then something very strange happened. My father found it impossible to get through to Luca Maori's law office. Papà had been in almost daily contact because Maori's assistants, Donatella Donati and Marco Brusco, were cataloging and analyzing all the trial materials as they came in. Now Papà could not get them to return his calls.

At length he went to Perugia to confront Maori directly. Nobody greeted him as he entered the office; he had the sense everyone was shrinking away from him. What was going on? He marched right up to Maori and demanded an explanation.

"It looks bad, very bad," Maori told him. "This Gioffredi is a credible guy and I don't know that we can counter him."

My father was incredulous. The man charged with taking on my defense was not only freezing him out; Maori plainly believed I might actually be guilty.

All of us knew from the beginning that Maori had doubts about taking on the case. We chalked it up to his uncertainty about Amanda, which my family understood and largely shared. To be fair, the issue was not just whether I was innocent. The longer the case went on and the more rulings went against me, the greater the risk to Maori's reputation and career in Perugia. Still, we had to wonder, if he had this little faith in me, why had he gotten involved at all?

Papà told him about the data from my computer, but still Maori was skeptical. "Why don't you let me see it?" he asked.

My father didn't have the data with him, but he said his brother, Giuseppe, could fax it over. The atmosphere in Maori's office was thick with mistrust and pent-up emotion as they waited for the fax to arrive. Five minutes, ten minutes passed. My father got on the phone with my brother; something seemed to be wrong with his fax machine. Then Maori's machine started acting up. Time continued to tick by, and Maori grew ever frostier.

Finally, the pages started to come through. Maori read them, nodded, and picked up the phone to speak to Donati and Brusco. Clearly he was telling them it was okay to talk to the Sollecitos again. Maori's coldness vanished in an instant, replaced by his habitual charm. He wanted my father to believe everything was back to normal, as though the entire episode had simply not occurred.

My father, though, was apoplectic. He said nothing, but he knew he could never fully trust Luca Maori again.

* * *

The prosecution, undeterred by its previous announcement that the investigation was over, spent much of November digging up other witnesses to testify against us, and leaking the most damaging parts to the newspapers. One witness we had already heard from in the pretrial hearings; he was a homeless heroin addict named Antonio Curatolo, who claimed to have seen Amanda and me lurking near Piazza Grimana on the night of the murder, looking as if we were waiting for someone. We didn't take him seriously at first because he also remembered seeing buses waiting to take people to discotheques, and on November 1 there had been no such bus service because it was a holiday. But Judge Micheli, for some reason, found him credible, and Mignini would later use him to substantiate the theory that the murder occurred closer to midnight than to 9:00 p.m.

Another enduringly troublesome witness was Marco Quintavalle, the owner of a convenience store a few steps from my house, who had been interviewed by police several times in the immediate aftermath of the murder and asked if he remembered me buying bleach. He did not, describing me as a quiet, polite regular customer. Now, more than a year later, he suddenly remembered that he had seen Amanda come into his shop early in the morning of November 2 to purchase cleaning materials. At least, he thought it was Amanda. He was riddled with uncertainty, and his receipts from that morning showed no evidence of purchases, incriminating or otherwise. Still, the prosecution jumped all over him and later put him on the stand to bolster the argument that Amanda and I had spent that morning wiping the murder scene clean of our traces—but not, curiously, Guede's. It was one of their more dishonest, not to mention absurd, arguments, because any forensics expert could have told them such a thing was physically impossible. Still, it was all they had, and they single-mindedly stuck to it.

Investigators also delved into my past. Two members of the Squadra Mobile traveled to Giovinazzo and, according to several people they encountered, asked leading questions at my old school about a nonexistent episode in which I supposedly attacked a fellow student with a pair of scissors. They learned I had once been written up for possession of a tiny quantity of cannabis, an episode that was later blown up to suggest I was a drug pusher and maybe also an addict.

Most shockingly, they started making inquiries into my mother's death in an attempt to cast suspicion on my family history. My mother, Vincenza Palmiotto, died of a heart attack in June 2005, as the certificate issued by the coroner's office and signed by her doctor made abundantly clear. Still, the two officers saw fit to speculate that she had fallen into a deep depression in the years following the divorce from my father. She was so despondent about Papà's upcoming marriage to Mara, they claimed, that she "could have" been pushed to commit suicide.

The point of such an outrageous and unfounded inquiry was, presumably, to insinuate that mental instability ran in my family. Suicide, murder—what's the difference? How could they sink so low as to drag my beautiful mother into their smear campaign? Really, the Perugia police are lucky I'm as even-tempered as I am, because nothing moves a Southern Italian to murderous rage more quickly than insulting the name of his dead mother. I can be grateful, I suppose, that she did not live to see the sick, twisted lengths the police were prepared to go to pin Meredith's murder on me. This blow was as low as they dared to stoop, and I will never forgive them for it.

* * *

I thought about my mother every day in prison. Sometimes I saw her as my protector. Sometimes I thought of her untimely death the same way I thought about my imprisonment, as an illustration of how unjust and cruel life can be.

I grew up as loved as any child could wish to be, but I was also in the shadow of two parents who bickered and fought until the day my father decided he could no longer stand it and left. I was eight years old. My mother had planned for nothing than to be a faithful wife and mother, and the divorce left her devastated. For the rest of her life, she showed no interest in other men and never took a job. With Vanessa almost out of the house, I became her abiding preoccupation. She mothered me to pieces, to the point where people wondered if I could ever go out into the world and survive without her.

At times, it was stifling. She and my father continued to fight, even over the bills we had to pay. By the time I was eleven or twelve, my mother was afraid to confront Papà directly and used me instead as her messenger, her go-between. I hated playing the role and retreated ever further into a fantasy world of comic books and video games, because they seemed simpler and more comprehensible than the emotional chaos around me.

I was a diffident, socially awkward kid. My childhood passion was the Japanese comic strip *Sailor Moon,* about a shy, fourteen-year-old girl whose magical powers turn her into a benign avenger, a champion of justice who, with her talking cat, reliably defeats the forces of evil. Believe me, there were times in prison I wanted to invoke Sailor Moon and defeat a few evil forces of my own.

When I finished high school, I needed to get away, so I applied for university in Perugia, where I had the opportunity to live cheaply at a residential college set up specially for the children of doctors. My father, who understood why I wanted to leave, thought it would be a smoother transition than launching out on my own. My mother, on the other hand, was anxious for me to stay close to home and talked me into applying to the University of Bari. My mind, though, was made up: when Perugia accepted me, it was time to cut my old ties and try life in a different part of Italy.

I didn't regret the choice for an instant. The college had a midnight curfew but relatively few other rules. I made friends easily and enjoyed having a buffer from the *perugini,* the locals who tended to be reserved and a little cold, especially toward Southerners. My college roommates played pranks on each other. We dressed up in crazy costumes and had water-pistol fights; usual student stuff. Once, we heard a rumor that one of my fellow residents had a porn movie showing a woman having sex with a pig, so we watched it, just for laughs, and were mildly disappointed that the pig was merely cross-

cut into the footage. The college's administrators issued a mild repri-
mand when they found out about this. (The prosecution later seized
on it as evidence that I was some sort of porn addict.)

The reports of my drug addiction were similarly exaggerated.
When I was seventeen or eighteen, I did experiment briefly with
ecstasy, poppers, and, on one occasion, cocaine. But I was way too
timid to push my luck with any of them, and I stopped almost as
soon as I started. I knew they were dangerous and, as with alcohol,
I had an instinctive aversion to feeling out of control.

I did, however, develop an occasional pot-smoking habit, as did
many of my friends. I didn't dislike the relaxing feeling that washed
over me when I smoked. It was another escape from the stresses of
daily life. But it was hardly a regular thing. I was held back both by
my own inhibitions and by constant admonitions from my father.
I knew, even without his reminding me, that it was bad to lose that
degree of sensory perception, even for a few hours.

The one time I was caught, by an undercover carabiniere in a
nightclub, I wasn't even the one with marijuana. My friend Gabriele
had it. I was worried he was over the legal limit for personal use, so
I talked our other friend Gennaro into claiming joint responsibility
with him. That way, the amount would be divided in three. The policeman realized what I was doing and wrote me up mostly because
he was angry that I was making it harder to take punitive action
against Gabriele.

By the time June 2005 rolled around, I was studying hard for
my final exams and looking forward to my father's wedding to Mara.
They'd been together for ten years so it was a much-postponed celebration. I knew my mother was taking it hard—that much the police got right—and I knew too that she was struggling to look after
her own mother, who had been diagnosed with bone cancer. I didn't

see her that often now that I was in Perugia, but we talked by phone several times a day, just as I later did with my father. She'd been complaining of not feeling herself, which I attributed to the situation, not her personal health. And she'd been particularly obsessive about calling, even though she knew I was busy with my exams; I felt she was monitoring my every move. She would call to ask if I'd drunk a glass of water, and I usually just had. An hour or so later, she'd call again to ask if I'd been to the bathroom. And I usually just had. It was uncanny how she always knew.

One morning, I received an alarming call from my godfather, Vito Barbone. "Come home," he said. "Come right away. Your mother's not at all well. She needs you." That was as much as he was prepared to say.

I knew right away it was ominous news, so I let my professors know I'd have to postpone my exams, ran around to borrow some cash, and drove like a maniac to Giovinazzo.

When I arrived at the house, notices with my mother's name were on the door—the custom in my part of Italy to mark someone's passing. I ran upstairs in a blind panic, demanding to see her. I found her body already lying in an open casket.

Beyond the shock, I was overcome with rage at my family for neglecting my mother to the point where she could die alone at the age of fifty-five. Wasn't anyone paying attention? Didn't anybody care? I said there and then I didn't want anybody with the last name Sollecito attending the funeral because the whole family had covered themselves in shame.

I meant what I said, and the Sollecitos abided by my wishes. Vanessa and I were the exceptions, of course; we accompanied the casket into the church. But everyone on my father's side of the family stayed out of the ceremony. My father's wedding was postponed for several months.

When I thought back on all this from my prison cell, I realized that part of my anger came from guilt and embarrassment that I had not done more myself. I needed to blame someone for her sudden death, so I lashed out, forgetting my own part in it. I had lost a mother for no good reason, just as I had now lost my freedom for no good reason. It would require all my forbearance to come to terms with that, to work through my pain and loss and come out stronger.

At least my second loss was not as definitive. My freedom, unlike my mother, was something I could still hope to regain.

*   *   *

Once it became clear I was standing trial, even Vanessa's bosses stopped pretending there wasn't a problem. They felt sure I was guilty and said so openly in front of her.

"How do you know the prosecution isn't a sham?" she countered.

"That's not an attitude worthy of someone wearing the uniform of the carabinieri," they admonished.

Her other colleagues, the ones who had no professional need to speak to her, ceased communication altogether. When she went for coffee, she went alone. She started losing weight, shrinking down to 105 pounds from more than 125, until her uniform sagged visibly and she felt she was quite literally disappearing.

Vanessa liked to wear civilian clothes to work and change in a bathroom some distance from her office once she arrived. One morning, her superior called her cell phone and told her that, in future, she needed to clear this with him.

She felt she was being treated like a toddler. "Sir," she said, "I'll go to the bathroom when I want."

"You can't talk to me that way," he responded. "You must do as I say."

"All right, but I need to see a written order if I'm going to comply."

Her superior relented. Shortly before Christmas, though, he called Vanessa back into his office and ordered her to hand over her service pistol.

She was stunned. The only instances she knew of where officers surrendered their weapon was when they were recuperating from an illness or an injury for an extended period—or when they were fired. Vanessa was sure the request was illegal, but she did not know how to lodge a protest, except to insist that she sign a form documenting what was happening. She knew already this would all have to be thrashed out in court.

Shortly afterward, Vanessa was transferred out of the logistics office altogether and sent across town to a department handling computer equipment and weapons inventories. For a while, this came as a relief. She was put in charge of organizing the Lazio region's entire armory, and there was plenty to do. But she noticed, after a few weeks, that the time sheets she submitted were being challenged and corrected in red pen. Even more bizarrely, the corrections were being made at her old office in Piazza del Popolo, even though she wasn't reporting there anymore. When she asked why she was being treated this way, she was told, "With you, it's different."

When my father heard about her troubles, he advised her to keep a low profile, to say the right things to her superiors, and to make more of an effort to be one of the boys.

Vanessa said that was impossible. "I'm not going to start going to work outings and licking asses. I've never done it before, so they'll realize it's just an act anyway."

Her defiance, she knew, was working against her. But if she was going down, she preferred to go down fighting, not bowing and scraping pathetically before the people who were ruining her life. She had too much dignity for that.

* * *

As my trial date neared, Giuseppe, Sara, and Vanessa argued that we should kick Maori off the defense team. Vanessa was particularly adamant because she'd approached Maori a few weeks earlier for advice on how to protect the inheritance she shared with me from our mother and make sure the court could not freeze or garnish our joint assets. As she recounted the episode, Maori had recommended signing over the assets to him, at which point she said a curt thank-you, turned around, and walked out. (Maori remembered the conversation differently, saying he had advised her to keep the assets as they were.)

My father did not share the others' outrage. He did not trust Maori any more than they did, but he had a longer game plan in mind. He knew he needed people in Perugia to do the legwork, and Donati and Brusco had been outstanding; starting from scratch with a different team seemed too daunting. Then there was the question of how we were perceived. Getting rid of one of my lead lawyers on the eve of the trial would smack of desperation, as though I were frantically shuffling pieces around to conceal my underlying guilt. Bongiorno urged us not to do it. So Papà decided that we would just put up with Maori and hope for the best.

I was pushing for another sort of change, a single trial team to defend Amanda and me together. I was told right away that this was out of the question, but I don't think my logic was wrong. The only way either of us would get out of this situation, I reasoned, was if we stuck together. If the prosecution drove a wedge between us, we would more than likely both be doomed.

Eventually, as each piece of the evidence weakened and crumbled, Bongiorno would come to agree with this assessment. But Amanda had her own team of high-powered lawyers—a prominent, multilingual Roman attorney specializing mostly in civil cases, Carlo Dalla Vedova, and a Perugian local counsel, Luciano Ghirga—who didn't want to take any chances on me, just as my lawyers didn't want to take any chances on her.

So our legal defenses remained separate, even as our fates remained closely intertwined.

* * *

My lawyers and I went into court confident that we had at least done our homework, and that we had a coherent answer to every hypothesis we expected the prosecution to put forward. We knew the science favored a time of death close to 9:00 p.m., when Amanda and I were still watching *Amélie,* and we sensed the prosecution was weakest in its assertion that the murder must have happened later that night. Curatolo, the homeless witness, didn't seem much of a reason to place us in Piazza Grimana in the late evening. Likewise, Nara Capezzali, the old woman who claimed to have heard a scream through her double-glazed windows, seemed easy enough to refute.

We were relishing another gift that the videotape evidence from the parking lot had yielded: a car that broke down as it left the lot at about ten thirty on the night of the murder and sat for almost an hour until a tow truck came and dragged it away. The three occupants of the car, plus the tow-truck driver, could testify that no-body came or went from the house on Via della Pergola for at least an hour, knocking Mignini's previous estimate of an eleven o'clock murder flat on its face.

Still, we had no certainty about the single most important part of the case, the evidence pointing to my DNA in Meredith's room. Stefanoni and Mignini were holding out on that information, and we needed to pry it from them quickly before more damage was done. The shots would ultimately be called by the judge, and we hadn't had a lot of luck with judges so far.

Giulia Bongiorno understood exactly what was at stake as we set to work. "We need to knock down the validity of that DNA trace on the bra clasp," she said. "Otherwise it's not going to end well for us."

* * *

On January 16, 2009, with photographers snapping our every move, we filed into the Sala degli Affreschi, the Hall of Frescoes, inside Perugia's fifteenth-century courthouse and waited for Judge Giancarlo Massei to take his place beneath a large, gaudy crucifix and formally open the proceedings. I couldn't help smiling at Amanda because I was pleased to see her. And she smiled back.

Italian trials operate quite unlike their counterparts in Britain or the United States because the judge holds an unusual amount of power over the outcome. There is no jury in any recognizable sense. Rather, cases are decided by the judge, his deputy, and six "popular judges," self-selecting members of the public, chosen by lottery, who are invited to contradict the robed professionals if they dare but, in practice, rarely do. They are not sequestered, if only because Italian trials, punctuated by long breaks between hearings, can last a year or longer. Nor are they under any obligation to steer clear of media coverage, or other information they might obtain outside the courtroom; they are free to form opinions any way they choose.

In lower-court trials, popular judges need only have completed middle school, so they are not exactly picked for their critical-thinking skills. One popular judge in our case, a school secretary named Anna Maria Artegiani, made her presence felt mostly by falling asleep during the sessions. (She later wrote a book describing what an honor it was to have been part of the judicial process.) Of the other lay judges, only one, a professional lawyer, seemed to pay any discernible attention.

Another peculiarity of the Italian system is that criminal cases are heard at the same time as civil actions arising from them. So, in addition to the prosecutors, Amanda and I had to contend with lawyers for the Kerchers, Patrick Lumumba, and Rudy Guede, all of whom had a vested interest in our guilt. Francesco Maresca, representing the Kerchers, and Carlo Pacelli, representing Lumumba, were suing us for damages, while Valter Biscotti, representing Guede, was playing more of a zero-sum game: the guiltier we were, the easier it would be for him to argue that his client was a bit player, not the main antagonist, and so push for a reduction of Guede's sentence on appeal.

Not only did all this make the lawyers' bench lopsided in the prosecution's favor; it also meant that evidence deemed inadmissible in the criminal case could potentially be heard by the court anyway. One of Judge Massei's first decisions—an inauspicious indication of which way he was leaning—was to allow the civil lawyers to discuss the "confessions" Amanda and I had made in the Questura, even though the Corte di Cassazione had thrown them out in our criminal proceeding.

That first hearing was largely procedural and passed in a blur of camera flashes. My strongest memory was of seeing the deputy judge, Beatrice Cristiani, with tears in her eyes as she looked at me, shaking her head as if to say, *What are you doing here? How could you have squandered your family's good name and your future—for this?*

* * *

The prosecution attempted to derail us with the very first witness. (It was now February 6, three weeks after the opening hearing.) Filippo Bartolozzi was the commander of the Polizia Postale who took Elisabetta Lana's statements after she found Meredith's cell phones, and he came right out of the gate saying he had sent Inspector Battistelli to Via della Pergola after the discovery of the first cell phone, shortly before noon, not after the discovery of the second. The distinction was important because it lent credence to the prosecution's contention that I called the carabinieri only *after* the Polizia Postale arrived at the house, to cover my tracks.

Bartolozzi was substantiating what the courts had previously only guessed at, so his testimony was potentially dangerous. He said he was a stickler for precision and was sure of the time he sent the patrol because he always checked the clock on his computer. Luckily, he crumbled as soon as Bongiorno began her cross-examination. If he was such a stickler for precision, she wondered, why had he written in a contemporaneous police report that he dispatched Battistelli and his colleague only after learning about the *second* cell phone?

"Yes, yes, fine," he acknowledged after scrambling about for an answer, "but the only reason I put the discovery of the two cell phones together and mentioned the patrol being dispatched afterward was to make the narrative smoother."

Bongiorno shot back, "But it hardly *makes the narrative smoother* to say that you sent the men out on patrol after the second cell phone was found, if in fact you sent them out after the first one."

Bartolozzi had no answer for that. One prosecution witness down, eighty-seven more to go.

* * *

As that first day of testimony progressed, Mignini and his deputy Manuela Comodi continued with the same theme, insinuating that the arrival of the Polizia Postale had taken me by surprise and that I had gone back inside the house to make a surreptitious call to the carabinieri following their arrival.

The whole notion seemed so absurd that I did something Italian court protocol permits defendants to do more or less at any time: I approached the bench and made an unscheduled statement in my own defense. I pointed out that Battistelli had entered the house at my express invitation, because Amanda and I were alarmed by what we had seen there. He didn't ask to come in and had no authority to do so on his own. "If I'd had something to hide or had been caught unawares, I would never have let him enter," I argued. "I would have given him the information he wanted outside the house."

I also reminded the court that I had made an initial attempt of my own to kick down Meredith's door. Why would I have done that if I was one of the murderers who had locked the door in the first place?

When I had finished, Bongiorno leaned over to commend me for my remarks, which we had planned together. But the hearing continued, without comment from the judge or rebuttal from the prosecution. It was, I later reflected, as if I'd said nothing at all.

This was not a unique occurrence; it was a frustration throughout the trial, for both Amanda and me. No matter how much we demanded to be heard, no matter how much we sought to refute the grotesque cartoon images of ourselves and give calm, reasoned presentations of the truth, we never escaped the feeling that our words were tolerated rather than listened to; that the court was fundamentally uninterested in what we had to say.

* * *

A week later, Meredith's English friends took the stand and testified with such uniform consistency it was hard to think of them as distinct individuals. Robyn Butterworth, Amy Frost, and Sophie Purton all said that Meredith had been unhappy with Amanda's standards of hygiene, particularly her forgetfulness about flushing the toilet. It sounded almost as if they were reading from a prepared script. Meredith, they agreed, had found Amanda a little too forward for keeping her condoms and what looked like a vibrator in their shared bathroom. And, they said, Amanda had acted weirdly in the Questura.

That was it. They mentioned nothing positive about the relationship. No word on Meredith and Amanda's socializing together, or attending Perugia's annual chocolate festival, or going to the concert on the night Amanda and I met. If either Meredith's or Amanda's computer had survived the police examination, there might have been photographs, e-mails, and other evidence to point to a more meaningful interaction. Instead, the girls' testimony only served to drive them apart.

Butterworth said that, in the Questura, Amanda had "shown no emotion." Frost testified that she never saw Amanda cry. Purton said, "As soon as I saw her, I approached her for a hug. But I seem to remember she didn't respond. She seemed rather cold." All three remembered Amanda saying she'd seen Meredith's body in the closet, a line Mignini milked to suggest some sort of dishonesty. At no time was it suggested Amanda had misunderstood something she had overheard in Italian—not even when, in a delicious irony, her lawyer, Carlo Dalla Vedova, felt compelled to correct the court interpreter's translations of the girls' English.

The next day—we actually had back-to-back hearings for once—Amanda arrived in court wearing a T-shirt with the words ALL YOU NEED IS LOVE emblazoned in huge pink letters, to mark Valentine's Day. It seemed she wanted to find a way to defuse the English girls' ill will toward her, but it didn't work. Not only was her dress widely deemed to be frivolous and inappropriate, she was criticized further for her housecleaning habits by Laura and Filomena.

At a certain point Amanda hit her limit and burst into tears. And then she addressed the court. "Listening to all these witnesses . . . I am truly and sincerely sorry to hear so much exaggeration after all this time about the cleaning," she said. "Yes, I talked to the girls, but it was never a source of conflict. On the contrary, I always got along well with them."

Her words, once again, seemed to tumble into a void.

* * *

Amanda's family came to court one day with a large number of wristbands on which they had printed the slogan FREE AMANDA AND RAFFAELE. They also produced an Italian version (marred, unfortunately, by a grammatical error) that said LIBERO AMANDA E RAFFAELE, and a handful more, for those members of my family uncomfortable about our fates being too closely intertwined, saying LIBERO RAFFAELE.

I gratefully put one of the English ones on my wrist as a proclamation of my innocence and a symbol of defiance. I wore it back to my cell at night and left it on when I slept. I would touch it for comfort, or when I grew anxious. I played with it and pulled at it and spun it around my wrist until it was frayed and discolored and dirty. But I did not take it off again for almost three years.

*   *   *

We encountered another unexpected obstacle at the end of February, when a police officer named Stefano Gubbiotti cast more confusion on the question of when the Polizia Postale arrived at Via della Pergola. He had reviewed the surveillance footage from the parking lot and noticed the car arriving at 12:36, according to the video time stamp in the corner of the tape. However, he added, the clock on the camera was running ten minutes fast, so the car really arrived at 12:26—almost half an hour before I called the carabinieri.

On the spur of the moment, my lawyers did not know how to respond. Over time, they realized Gubbiotti had the timing exactly reversed. The clock on the camera was ten minutes *slow,* so Battistelli and Marzi did not show up until 12:45. Even then, the parking lot footage showed their car hesitating, starting to move into the lot and then pulling back out. What appears to have happened is that they found parking somewhere else, and Battistelli got out of the car to approach the house on foot, which is when Amanda and I saw him. According to this chronology, he couldn't have shown up at the house much before 1:00 p.m., just as we'd remembered it.

How did we know the clock was slow and not fast? Watching more of the videotape, we saw that the time stamp marking the arrival of the carabinieri was 1:22 p.m. But the carabinieri cannot have arrived then, because at 1:29 p.m., according to the phone records, they called Amanda to ask for directions. They must have arrived somewhere around 1:32 or slightly later—meaning that the clock was lagging about ten or twelve minutes.

Unfortunately, we lost the chance to challenge Gubbiotti on this directly, and the suspicion that Amanda and I had lied about our contact with the carabinieri lingered all the way to the end of the trial.

* * *

One of the reasons our hearings were so spread out was that Mignini was fighting his own, separate legal battle to fend off criminal charges of prosecutorial misconduct. He and a police inspector working on the Monster of Florence case stood accused of intimidating public officials and journalists by opening legal proceedings against them and tapping their phones without proper justification.

To Mignini, the case smacked of professional jealousy because the prosecutors in Florence resented his intrusion on a murder mystery they had struggled for so long to resolve. But Mignini's behavior had already attracted international condemnation, never more so than when he threw the journalist most indefatigably devoted to following the Monster case, Mario Spezi, into jail for three weeks. Spezi had ridiculed Mignini's theories about Francesco Narducci, the Perugian doctor whom Mignini suspected of being part of a satanic cult connected to the killings. In response, Mignini accused Spezi himself of involvement in Narducci's murder—even though the death had been ruled a suicide. It was a staggering power play, and the international Committee to Protect Journalists was soon on the case. Spezi was not initially told why he was being arrested and, like me, was denied access to a lawyer for days. Even Mignini, though, could not press murder charges without proving first that a murder had taken place, and Spezi was eventually let out.

I firmly believe that our trial was, among other things, a grand diversion intended to keep media attention away from Mignini's legal battle in Florence and to provide him with the high-profile court victory he desperately needed to restore his reputation. Already in the pretrial hearing, Mignini had shown signs of hypersensitivity about his critics, in particular the handful of English-speaking investigators and reporters who had questioned his case against us early on. He issued an explicit warning that anyone hoping he would back off the Meredith Kercher case or resign should think again. "Nobody has left their post, and nobody will," he said. "Let that be clear, in Perugia and beyond."

Just as he had in the Monster of Florence case, Mignini used every tool at his disposal against his critics and adversaries. He spied on my family and tapped their phones. He went after Amanda not just for murder, but also for defaming Patrick Lumumba—whom she had implicated under duress and at the police's suggestion. He opened or threatened about a dozen other legal cases against his critics in Italy and beyond. He charged Amanda's parents with criminal defamation for repeating the accusation that she had been hit in the head while in custody. And he sued or threatened to sue an assortment of reporters, writers, and newspapers, either because they said negative things about him or the police directly or because they quoted others saying such things.

Mignini's volley of lawsuits had an unmistakable chilling effect, especially on the Italian press, and played a clear role in tipping public opinion against us. We weren't the only ones mounting the fight of our lives in court, and it was difficult not to interpret this legal onslaught as part of Mignini's campaign to beat back the abuse-of-office charges. His approach seemed singularly vindictive. Not only did we have to sit in prison while the murder trial dragged on; it seemed he wanted to throw our friends and supporters—anyone who voiced a sympathetic opinion in public—into prison right alongside us.

* * *

In March 2009, in a break between court hearings, I traveled to Verona to sit the first exams of my master's degree. It was an attempt to maintain some semblance of normality and to give myself something else to focus on. Preparing for the exams, though, was no easy task, and not just because I was studying by myself. The journey itself was a nightmare.

As on my trips to Perugia, I was cuffed and confined in a tiny holding cell in the back of a van with lousy suspension. A guard sat with me, blocking any view I might have out the window. For this longer trip, we took some extraordinarily circuitous route, picking up other prisoners along the way in cities I couldn't name. Nobody told me what was going on.

The journey lasted eight hours, and when I arrived, I felt green from top to toe, as if I had been tossed through a spin dryer. Once in Verona, I was shown to a filthy isolation cell with cockroaches scuttling across the floor and pornographic pictures on the walls. This was my home for several days. The exams were over in a day, but I had to wait for the next transport to take me back down to Terni. I complained, about all of it, only to get into trouble for complaining.

Being back in solitary confinement messed with my head, and I grew increasingly insecure about my ability to carry the course load on my own. I passed this preliminary set of exams—a singular satisfaction—but had doubts about how much longer I could go on without professors to guide me or classes to attend. My studies, which had always driven me and given me great pleasure, were turn-ing into yet another object of dread.

*   *   *

My family rode the roller coaster of the trial with a characteristic mix of innate optimism and quiet foreboding. They were forever asking themselves if they could do more, investigate further, or reach out to more people. My aunt Sara was particularly adept at throwing great mountains of information together into slick, easy-to-use Power-Point presentations. We nicknamed her *la signora hard disk.*

Almost everyone came to court at every hearing, with one nec-essary exception: Vanessa, who had been advised not to deepen her troubles at work by making a public spectacle of herself at trial. As a uniformed police official, she had a professional obligation not to appear on television or express personal opinions in the media. Giuseppe thought she should have gone ahead anyway. If the televi-sion cameras picked up the fact that there was a carabinieri officer in the family, he argued, it might give television viewers a clue that law enforcement in Italy was not a monolith and that not everyone was siding with the Perugian police.

Certainly, staying away did nothing for Vanessa's crumbling ca-reer, because in April 2009, three months into my trial, she was fired.

The final act of her humiliation began in January, when she was informed she would have to take a professional exam to maintain her place in the force—even though she already had tenure. Much of the testing was psychological. Vanessa trained for it by going through old MMPI tests, the ones most commonly used by the CIA and the US military, and passed with flying colors.

Then came the final hurdle, the *colloquio attitudinale,* a discussion with her superiors about the way she approached her work. She was ushered into a room where two captains grilled her intensely, notably about me. She said it felt like an inquisition.

When they asked about my murder case, she got right to the point. "If you've decided to get rid of me," she said, "at least spare me the questions."

They denied they had any such intent but did not appreciate the tone. "You're doing your job," they acknowledged, "but not with a state of mind worthy of the carabinieri."

A number of times, Vanessa had been singled out for special assignments, for example on security details for visiting foreign dignitaries, and had often received praise for her contributions. She argued that she would not get picked for such jobs if something was wrong with either her performance or her attitude.

But the captains persisted. "A carabinieri officer should never let anything in his or her personal life affect his mood." Ever since my arrest, they noted, her relationship with her superiors had not been good.

Vanessa was indignant. How could her brother's imprisonment not affect her? Was she not human? How was she supposed to foster good relations with her superiors when they were systemically freezing her out?

She was right to think that the argument was futile. Within an hour of the conversation, she was handed a letter informing her that she was being dismissed from the force because her attitude was not commensurate with her position. There was no further explanation. Later, Vanessa obtained her performance appraisals and saw that in the last two she had been marked "below average," again without supporting documentation. She tried to appeal her dismissal to the Ministry of Defense, but she could not even get her letter delivered to the appropriate office.

The morning after she was fired, in despair, Vanessa slipped in her bathroom and bruised her tailbone badly enough to warrant a visit to the doctor. The doctor sent her to a military hospital for X-rays and other tests, and she was given a note excusing her from work for thirty days. She had only five more days in the office, so that was more than enough to ensure she wouldn't have to face her superiors again.

The carabinieri were not content to let matters rest there. Five months later, she was notified that she was under criminal investigation for faking an injury and defrauding the carabinieri by continuing to draw a salary without doing the work expected of her. The notification even cited one of the phone calls intercepted by the Perugia police a year earlier, in which my sister had—incautiously, for sure—fantasized about breaking a finger so she could get out of uniform, switch to a civilian desk job, and throw herself into my defense without restriction.

This new investigation went nowhere because the first judge who heard the case declared the alleged crime to be "impossible"—in the sense that Vanessa had already been fired, so there was nothing and nobody to defraud, even leaving aside the fact that more than one doctor had confirmed and documented her bathroom injuries.

The accusation alone had a chilling effect on me, however, because Vanessa understood she could only get into worse trouble if she started making public statements on my behalf. So she continued to stay away from my trial and kept entirely silent.

* * *

That spring, I struck up an unlikely friendship with a former member of the Naples underworld named Luciano Aviello. Like a lot of the mafiosi in the protected section, Aviello was an informant who needed to be kept away from the general prison population and, especially, from former associates who might want to kill him for cooperating with the police. He was in solitary confinement, but I was authorized to visit him—for reasons I did not entirely understand at first. I agreed because I had nothing better to do with my time, and because I was too naive to see I was being set up.

I realized it soon enough, though, when the subject turned to my trial. "You should tell them you've been protecting Amanda," Aviello suggested. "If you do that, I'm sure you'll get a reduced sentence."

I responded that I wasn't protecting anyone, and if they wanted to keep me in prison for life because I was not willing to say otherwise, then so be it.

Aviello believed me and respected me for refusing to bend. He wasn't a friend in the ordinary sense of the word; he would be sweet at times and then fly into theatrical fits of rage. But he did stick by me. After a while, he admitted that he'd been in touch with the Squadra Mobile in Perugia, and they had asked him to get me to say something incriminating. When he told them he'd had no luck, they asked him to sign a statement saying that I had talked about protecting Amanda anyway. He refused.

I can't be sure if the police did pressure him as he described, because I have only his account to go on. But I do know he did one interesting thing seemingly designed to get the Squadra Mobile off his back once and for all: he came out with a manifestly ridiculous story that his brother Antonio had come home one night covered in blood and admitted he had killed Meredith Kercher.

This story came as a total surprise to me; Aviello and I never discussed it. I would have loved to thank him in person for the way he threw the police effort into confusion, but our relationship ended rather abruptly. I stopped visiting him as soon as I knew he had been in touch with the Squadra Mobile, because I understood that our continuing relationship was dangerous—to both of us. Soon after, he was transferred out of Terni; I can only assume this was because his presence there no longer served any useful purpose to the authorities. Much later, I sent him a present, an embroidered handkerchief, to express my gratitude.

*   *   *

On May 8, the prosecution hit a technical glitch. Manuela Comodi, Mignini's deputy, could not get her computer to play a video of the forensics team finding the bra clasp. The judge suggested a ten-minute break so Comodi could get things working, but she kept flailing. I stepped in. I was, after all, a computer expert, and it seemed only natural to take the DVD and format it correctly on one of my defense team's computers.

I'd been looking forward to this day in court for some time because I was outraged by the way the clasp had been recovered a month and a half after the murder, and outraged too that Monica Napoleoni was in the room when the Polizia Scientifica made their discovery. She had no place being there; the only logical explanation, I felt, was that she knew about the clasp in advance and was directing traffic to make sure it was found.

My thinking was, let them play the tape. And if it's thanks to me, it will bolster the impression that I'm unafraid of the evidence.

Unfortunately, nobody else felt that way. Bongiorno was astounded that the prosecution had come to me for help at all; the whole thing struck her as inappropriate from start to finish. In the media, I was ridiculed for what was deemed to be extraordinary naïveté, and I earned no credit whatsoever with the prosecution or the judge.

*　*　*

Two weeks later, my lawyers had another crack at Dr. Stefanoni and pried a lot more information out of her. Over two days of testimony, she acknowledged that the laboratory where she worked was not certified to do DNA analysis, although she claimed this made no difference to the quality of her results. She admitted that the amount of DNA recovered from both the bra clasp and the tip of the kitchen knife was extremely small—so small that she could not do a complete reading of my DNA. What she obtained is known in technical parlance as a "low copy number," a warning from the machine that the result may not be reliable.

Stefanoni further acknowledged that the DNA she claimed to be picking up could not be associated with a specific time period, so there was no way of knowing for sure if my DNA—assuming it was there at all—became attached to the bra clasp on the night of the murder, or weeks later as a result of evidence gatherers moving back and forth in the apartment.

Stefanoni was at a loss to explain how the bra clasp, which had been photographed on the floor near Meredith's body on November 2, could have found its way under a rug near Meredith's desk on December 18 without being contaminated more or less by definition. The phrase she came out with was *"È traslato."* It made its way over there. But the words in Italian also carry the connotation of miracles and religious apparitions. When the Catholic Church talks about saints appearing in two places at once, or the house of the Virgin Mary flying from the Holy Land across the Adriatic, it uses the same term.

One other strange thing: Amanda and I were on trial for sexual assault, yet Stefanoni confirmed that a stain on Meredith's pillow-case that looked a lot like semen was never tested in her lab. She made all sorts of excuses about how testing it might compromise the lab's ability to use the pillowcase for other things. The semen might well be old, she added, the result of Meredith's consensual sexual relations with Giacomo Silenzi.

This seemed extraordinary to my defense team, so much so that we asked for—and obtained—permission to inspect the pillowcase ourselves and soon discovered signs of semen on one of Guede's shoe prints. How could the prosecution have missed this? If the semen was fresh when Guede stepped on it, that meant it *must* have been produced on the night of the murder. We thought long and hard about demanding a full analysis, but we did not trust the Polizia Scientifica as far as we could spit and were deathly afraid they might choose to construe that the semen was mine. So we held back.

As it was, Stefanoni's testimony was an unmitigated disaster for the prosecution, in this and every other respect. We could now make a compelling case for access to the data underlying her DNA results, because the results themselves raised so many questions. Over the next month, my consultants and lawyers prepared a brief to present to the court, knowing that Judge Massei's response could determine the outcome of the entire trial. If the DNA evidence collapsed, the court would have nothing else to tie me to the crime scene.

* * *

Meanwhile, we had to worry about Amanda taking the stand. Her lawyers decided that the best way to refute the stories about her wayward personality was to have the court take a good, hard look at her up close. But my lawyers were deeply concerned she would put her foot in her mouth, in ways that might prove enduringly harmful to both of us. If she deviated even one iota from the version of events we now broadly agreed on, it could mean a life sentence for both of us.

In fact, she performed magnificently. Judge Massei let Patrick's bulldog lawyer, Carlo Pacelli, have at her first, and Pacelli was so aggressive that Amanda's lawyers complained he was grilling her like the Inquisition. Pacelli wasted no time in raising the coerced statements Amanda had made during her long night in the Questura—statements the prosecution was barred from using, but he, as a civil lawyer suing for damages, was authorized to bring up.

It could have been a bloodbath, but Amanda pushed back, explaining calmly how she had been pressured both verbally and physically during her interrogation, repeatedly told she was a "stupid liar" and given respite only after she tentatively agreed, at the police officers' suggestion, that Patrick could have been responsible for the murder.

"Under pressure," she said, "I imagined lots of different things . . . including the suggestion that she [Meredith] had been raped."

"Was it the police who suggested that you say this?" Pacelli asked.

"Yes."

"And to make you say these things, they beat you?"

"Yes."

Amanda proved equally tenacious with Mignini and Comodi, and they responded by filing a new charge against her—slandering the police—based on her own sworn testimony. This characteristically nasty maneuver demonstrated, to me, that she'd given them nothing else to work with.

I was proud of her. She was soberly dressed, with her hair in a ponytail, spoke clearly and simply (mostly through an interpreter), and held her ground despite being obviously tense and exhausted, with black rings around her eyes. Even the newspapers gave her credit for her assured, unflappable tone.

A fair court, I felt, couldn't help believing her. But we didn't know, yet, how fair Judge Massei intended to be.

* * *

I lived through the trial in constant anxiety. Soon after it began, I developed such acute digestive problems it was difficult to keep anything down. I lost weight steadily until I was positively skeletal. The doctors prescribed all sorts of things—simethicone (usually given to colicky infants), laxatives, antiflatulence pills—but nothing worked until I hit upon another baby product, soluble barley. It was the only thing that reliably agreed with me.

My life in prison had no consistency because of the constant transports to and from Perugia. When I got there, I would often find excrement and old scraps of food embedded in the cell floor, which required hours to remove. I tried to study, but the second round of exams I took in Verona was simply beyond me and I failed them all. If I couldn't find a professor to help me, I could not continue.

I also tried to stay focused on the trial itself. But I found myself lapsing into depression, anger, and sheer consternation at my situation. How much longer would all this go on? It became ever harder to see it ending at all.

"O Almighty God," I scribbled in my journal one day, "thank You for putting me to the test every day and, as proof of Your omnipotence, sending me idiots who don't know what they are doing or what they are saying, to remind me I am just a miserable human being compared with You. Sooner or later they will pay for their misdeeds and for the suffering they have caused. May Your name be praised. Amen."

For several months from the end of 2008 to the spring of 2009, those of us in the protected section enjoyed several hours of relative freedom each day—"office hours," as they were called—when our cell doors were left open and we could roam the corridors at will. That privilege came to an abrupt end after a fight broke out between Ahmed, the Lebanese who didn't like me, and a Southern Italian wife-beater named Beppe Fontanelli. There were rumors that Beppe had been talking to the prison authorities—presumably about the rest of us—in a bid to get his sentence reduced. When Ahmed found out, he stormed into Beppe's cell and lashed out. They'd both been drinking the section's homemade hooch, which they called "vodka."

It wasn't pretty; I heard the whole thing from three or four cells away. Beppe was hit in the head with a gas bottle and screamed, *"Fate tutti schifo!"* You're all disgusting! Then he broke Ahmed's nose, grabbed his finger, and tore off the tip with his teeth.

I did my best to stay calm. This was a gangland vendetta, I rationalized, and had nothing to do with me.

Having the cell doors closed most of the day certainly made the section feel safer, even if it was more claustrophobic. And I had some protective friends. Some time before the fight, I had shared a cell with another mafioso, a Neapolitan drug trafficker I knew just as Gennaro. He made me cakes and told stories of his life on the streets. I also struck up a friendship with a gangster named Vittorio Vespa, who sang Neapolitan songs through my keyhole. "Ask for a song," he would say, "and I'll sing it." Vespa would then sing what he wanted regardless, and we would both laugh.

These weren't bad people to have looking out for me.

One solace was a new passion I discovered for painting; I threw myself into it and spent weeks at a time working on reproductions of famous artworks or copies of Japanese manga images. It was a great way to empty my mind of all its troubles and focus on something creative.

Another solace was a blossoming correspondence with Amanda. Not only did we smile at each other in court, we sent each other music and magazines and books—which the prison authorities permitted as long as they were all paid for—and exchanged frequent letters. It was a way for each of us to break the tension of the trial. Amanda wrote to me about all sorts of mundane things, everything from the new music she was discovering to her efforts to be better at "girly" things and turn out more formally in court. She also let me know that she had my back, just as I had hers. *Io lo so che non sono sola, anche quando sono sola,* she wrote in Italian at the end of one letter. I know I'm not alone, even when I'm alone. And then her familiar sign-off: *Ti voglio bene.* I love you.

I liked hearing from her so much I asked for permission to phone her from time to time. My lawyers thought this was a terrible idea, as the line was bound to be tapped and anything we said could be used against us in ways we might not even be able to imagine. My family was similarly unimpressed. *"Sei coglione!"* my sister, Vanessa, railed at me. You're an idiot!

The prison authorities granted my request, but for the phone calls to happen, Amanda needed to give her consent too. She never did; most likely she was was listening to her lawyers a little more carefully than I was listening to mine.

* * *

At the end of July, just before a monthlong summer vacation, the court granted our request to see Dr. Stefanoni's underlying data. When we reconvened in September, my consultants came out swinging. Not only had the DNA test on the kitchen knife come back "too low," Dr. Stefanoni had overridden the machine to force it to come up with a result on a single, irreproducible sample. Recognized scientific protocols should have told her that no reliable result was possible.

The test on the bra clasp, meanwhile, had also come back "too low" and presented an incomplete genetic profile, meaning that the identification of my DNA was far from confirmed. Adriano Tagliabracci, the specialist we hired from the University of Le Marche in Ancona (whose DNA lab is, unlike Stefanoni's, certified by the International Society for Forensic Genetics), told the court the identification she obtained was common to three to four people out of every thousand. So in Perugia, a city of 160,000, the identification— even assuming it was not compromised by contamination at the scene—would potentially apply to five or six hundred people.

The prosecution, in response, accused Dr. Tagliabracci of trying to smear the good name of government crime-lab workers so courts would stop using them and turn to private labs like his instead. It was a curious argument. They also produced the kitchen knife itself, parading it around the courtroom like a holy relic inside a clear plastic box, stamped HANDLE WITH CARE in English for the benefit for the foreign press. They did not mention, of course, that the way the knife had originally traveled from my kitchen to the Polizia Scientifica lab in Rome broke recognized chain-of-custody rules. As the prosecution's own paperwork showed, it was not put in a sealed evidence bag but was placed in an envelope and mailed inside an ordinary box.

The defense found plenty of other problems with the knife. One of Amanda's expert witnesses, Carlo Torre, explained that it was way too long to be the murder weapon. Meredith's skin around the wound showed signs of bruising, suggesting that whatever knife was used was plunged all the way in. The length of the wound was eight centimeters, far shorter than the seventeen-centimeter blade on my kitchen knife. Still, the government insisted the knife was "not incompatible" with the murder weapon.

Amanda's lawyer, Carlo Dalla Vedova, asked the government's own expert witness, Giancarlo Umani Ronchi, just how loose the definition of "not incompatible" was. "Aren't you saying, Professor, that any knife with the same basic characteristics, which is to say with a single blade that cuts on one side only, would meet the same standard of 'non-incompatibility'?"

Umani Ronchi replied, "Basically, yes."

Umani Ronchi also drew inadvertent attention to the problem of Meredith's last meal and the time of death when he argued that the coroner might have made a mistake during the autopsy. Perhaps the reason no food was found in Meredith's upper intestine, he said, was that Dr. Lalli, the coroner, forgot to place a tie at either end of the duodenum, allowing whatever food was inside to slip down to Meredith's lower intestinal tract before it could be detected. The argument was dubious to begin with because human intestines are long and convoluted and it is difficult to see how half-digested food could simply slip through. But the argument was also wrong: video of the autopsy showed Dr. Lalli had in fact tied each end of the upper intestine, just as Umani Ronchi said he should have.

By early October, we were ready to petition the court for an independent analysis of the prosecution's most important data: the DNA evidence, the autopsy results including the estimated time of death, and the computer analysis that had burned through three computers and potentially compromised a fourth. We didn't bother to ask for a review of the footprint analysis by Rinaldi and Boemia because we had demonstrated some elementary measuring errors and felt confident that would suffice. But we did ask for tests on Nara Capezzali's double-glazed windows to settle once and for all the question of whether she could have heard Meredith screaming.

It was all for naught. After two hours of deliberation, Judge Massei emerged from his chambers and decided he had enough information already. "The consultants [for each side] have brought an abundance of data to the court's attention, which makes further analysis unnecessary," he said in his written ruling.

It was perhaps the most shocking moment of the trial. The court was not interested in digging further into the scientific truth behind Stefanoni's DNA tests, or the rest of the evidence we were contesting. Massei said he was content to have the arguments on either side and simply evaluate them himself. What that meant, in effect, was that he was calling an abrupt cease-fire in the war of attrition we were successfully waging against the prosecution's case.

More bluntly, Massei had taken Mignini's side, and we were going down.

* * *

Not everyone wanted to recognize the gravity of the situation right away. Amanda, for one, remained optimistic. "It's only one part of the battle," she told me as we walked out of the hearing. "We have so much more in our favor." Most of our lawyers sought to put a similarly positive spin on things.

But not Bongiorno. She was incapable of pussyfooting around, and while I was not happy about her message, I was grateful she had the courage to deliver it. "They want Amanda," she told me gravely, "and that means they're going to ask for a life sentence for both of you. They're going to argue that the bra clasp ties you to the murder scene, and they'll get to Amanda that way because you both say you were together that night."

Bongiorno asked, one last time, if I had anything to say that could put some distance between Amanda and me. I had heard that same question in different forms from everyone—my family, the police, and all my lawyers. Was I absolutely sure I wanted to vouch for Amanda's whereabouts on the night Meredith died, even if it meant tossing my life away after hers?

I was adamant: "I have nothing to add to what I've already said. If we want to fight this battle, we have to do it my way, and that means establishing Amanda's innocence as much as mine. There is no other way."

Bongiorno listened and said no more. But, she also believed me. As she later confided, she wanted me to understand that arguing for Amanda's innocence alongside my own made her task more challenging. Now, though, she was beginning to conclude that she had no choice.

My father was all over the place. He knew exactly how bad the news was, but he wanted to shield me as best he could. "Whatever happens, don't worry," he told me. "There's always the appeal. The work we've done won't go to waste."

Vanessa, characteristically, was much blunter. She'd started coming to the court hearings following the dismissal of her criminal complaint and couldn't help noticing the atmospherics: the confidence in Mignini's demeanor, the way he took Stefanoni and Napoleoni out to lunch, the warmth he showed to the Squadra Mobile members as he put a paternal arm around them.

"Raffaele's going to be convicted. I can feel it," she announced. She said this not to be a killjoy, but because she cared passionately about me, and it broke her heart to think the struggle for my freedom would probably continue for years longer. My father was furious—not because she was wrong, but because she voiced her thoughts out loud.

* * *

Mignini and Comodi strode into court for closing statements as though they owned the place. Mignini made a point of mentioning that he had known both Judge Massei and his deputy, Judge Cristiani, for years and congratulated them on the way they'd handled the hearings. My family found that particularly nauseating, the closest thing to an open admission that the judges and the prosecution were part of the same chummy fraternity. According to Mignini, anyone who agreed with him—his fellow lawyers or the media—was admirably objective, while anyone who criticized him deserved condemnation for attempting to delegitimize the proceedings.

Still, Mignini's swagger belied a considerable insecurity, which became more obvious as he kept talking. First, he abandoned his sex-orgy-gone-wrong theory entirely. The new motive, as he expressed it, was that Amanda hated Meredith—for being too strait-laced, for having too many English friends, for criticizing Amanda when she forgot to flush the toilet. Mignini didn't postulate any motivation for me whatsoever, saying only that I was Amanda's inseparable *fidanzatino,* her "little boyfriend," who presumably would do whatever she asked. Was this really Mignini's idea of why people kill each other? Over an unflushed toilet?

Second, Mignini unexpectedly changed his tune about the murder weapon. He still insisted that my kitchen knife had inflicted the fatal wound, but allowed that it was too big for some of the other incisions. He suggested, instead, that I had brought along one of my pocketknives to initiate the attack on Meredith—a theory for which he did not have a shred of evidence. This switch in story lines sounded alarming at the time because it placed me at the center of the action, but in retrospect it was obviously a sign of prosecutorial weakness.

Mignini had to scrabble around to explain how Amanda, Guede, and I could have formulated a murder plan together without any obvious indication that we knew each other. Guede, he postulated, *could have* offered himself as our drug pusher. I *could have* been taking acid and cocaine as well as marijuana: "It's difficult to say for sure." Mignini's speech became so bogged down with *might haves* and *could haves* and *perhaps*es and arguments of plausibility and compatibility and non-incompatibility that it was unclear how many hard facts he was relying on. He acknowledged that his entire reconstruction of the crime was *ovviamente ipotetica*—obviously hypothetical. One startling admission he made would prove useful to us later on. If the break-in had not been staged, he said, "the two defendants would have to be innocent. . . . The break-in would be attributable to an outsider acting without help from either of them." Our point exactly. Mignini's line appeared to be a tacit admission that he had no other solid evidence to go on.

To maximize our role in the crime, the prosecution felt obliged to minimize Guede's, to the point where they seemed to be taking his side. Mignini referred to him as "poor Rudy"; Comodi, in her own summation, described him as a "poor, disaffected young man" who had been deprived of the usual social protections and thus had valid reasons for going off the rails, unlike Amanda and me. Guede, she said, had not supplied the murder weapon. He had not staged a break-in. He had not chosen to attack the police or the investigators. Unlike us, he had shown signs of remorse, even pity as he brought towels from the bathroom to soak up Meredith's blood.

This was an outrageous argument from start to finish. How were Amanda and I supposed to show remorse for a crime we had not committed? How could Guede, whom the authorities themselves believed deserving of a thirty-year prison sentence, be characterized as a victim of circumstance?

Comodi didn't pause to justify her arguments; she merely kept on making them. She called me impassive and cold, willing to do absolutely anything to win the approval of others. Amanda, she said, was narcissistic, manipulative, and aggressive, incapable of empathy or emotional warmth, and focused so completely on satisfying her immediate needs she didn't care what anybody else thought.

After hours of this, Amanda jumped up to make another im-promptu statement. She couldn't bear to listen without defending herself, which she did with all the calm she could muster. "Meredith was my friend, and I didn't hate her," she said. "The idea of taking revenge on someone who was always kind to me is absurd. . . . All the things that have been said are pure fantasy. It's not the truth, not the way things were at all."

I said nothing. It seemed such a farce. Judge Massei, who looked a little like Woody Allen, kept looking at me as one might at a badly behaved child. What possible argument could I come up with to diminish the feeling we were being played for fools?

Arguments were not all that Comodi had up her sleeve. She and her team had concocted a twenty-three-minute video in which animated figures took on the roles of Meredith, Guede, Amanda, and me and played out the murder scene as the prosecution had presented it. The prosecution claimed that the video was not evidence per se, just a visual guide for the court. But to me and my lawyers it looked like a monstrous exercise in giving a bogus veneer of credibility to wild theories that the prosecution couldn't begin to prove. The characters on-screen didn't even look like us; they were avatars playing out a video-game projection of the prosecutors' fevered imaginations. Later, we learned that the prosecutor's office spent a staggering 182,000 euros on this nonsense. Nobody spends that kind of money on a visual guide; it was a blatant attempt to push for a guilty verdict by any and all means.

After considerable protest from our side, Judge Massei agreed not to allow the film to be reproduced by the news media in any form. Even he understood that the images would stick in the public's mind more vividly than the actual evidence. But he also denied a request that our lawyers be allowed to take away a copy to study so they could challenge it in their own closing statements.

It was a movie destined to be shown just once. Unfortunately, it had the desired effect.

* * *

Bongiorno was brilliant, as we expected her to be. She showed up the nonsense of Guede's being my accomplice when we didn't know each other. She showed up the nonsense of my nonexistent motive for murder, saying I had been portrayed by the prosecution as a "bafflingly silent afterthought" to the whole story. She ridiculed the introduction of the kitchen knife based on Inspector Finzi's "instinct" and ridiculed, too, the last-minute introduction of an unidentified second knife at the scene of the crime. She noted that the prosecution and the courts had been mistaken about attributing the bloody Nike shoe prints to me and expressed similar skepticism about the bra clasp. If I had really left my DNA on the clasp, she said, I would have had to be a human dragonfly, darting in and out and betraying no other sign of my presence in Meredith's room.

She was engaging, to the point, and absolutely devastating to the prosecution. But we had no idea at this stage if anything she said would make the slightest difference.

* * *

The judges and their retainers retired for just ten hours before returning with a decision. While we waited, through the evening and into darkest night, the entire Squadra Mobile lined up in full uniform as though anticipating a victory parade. The atmosphere was downright sinister. My uncle Giuseppe was so afraid of breaking down if the judgment went the way we feared that he stayed in his hotel. Vanessa surveyed the scene and called him to say she was sure we would lose.

She was right. Judge Massei convicted us as charged, on all counts. Mara, my stepmother, yelled out, *"Forza, Raffaele!"* Keep your strength up. But her voice sounded strangled, her protective instinct toward me masking her despair. Amanda broke into helpless streams of tears, grabbed her lawyer, Luciano Ghirga's, arm, and moaned, "No, no!"

My stomach was churning and my head felt ready to burst, but I betrayed no outward sign of emotion. I didn't want to give my tormentors that satisfaction.

The only glimmer of good news was that Massei did not give us life sentences, as Mignini had requested. Instead, he gave us twenty-five and twenty-six years (one more for Amanda than for me). It was a mind-bogglingly long time to contemplate behind bars, but it was a softening of sorts, which Bongiorno immediately took as an admission that the case was flawed. Later, we would learn that Judge Massei had taken note, however weakly, of all the points she made in her closing statement. They were the only things that held him back from giving Mignini everything he wanted.

To everyone's surprise—not least her assistants'—Bongiorno gave me a hug in the few moments before the police escorted me away. She said, "Don't worry, we'll work to make sure things go differently on appeal." In the darkest moment of my life, I was pleasantly surprised to note that I still trusted her.

What even Bongiorno couldn't sugarcoat was the length of time we'd now have to wait for the next round. It could take a year, maybe longer, for an appeal to begin, then another six to twelve months for the second trial. We'd have to go through the whole thing again—with Mignini and Comodi and all the witnesses, and the civil-suit lawyers sniping at us, and the press parsing our every smile and wink and facial contortion. It was too much even to think about.

Bongiorno told the media that for her this was not just a conviction. It felt like "the painful deferral of an acquittal that is bound to come." I didn't dare believe this could all still come out right, but the word *painful* was spot-on.

For the next several days, I slept and slept, first at Capanne and then back in Terni. I didn't even want to think about what had just happened, much less pick up the pieces and move on.

I felt helpless and afraid and incapable of anything.

IV

JUSTICE

How do judges not feel tormented by the idea that, because of their mistakes, innocent people languish in prison their whole lives? A magistrate I know answered this way. It may be that half of the sentences handed down are unjust, he said, and therefore half of those in prison are innocent; but by the same reasoning half of those acquitted and set free are in fact guilty and should be in prison. Instead of worrying about individual cases, it's important to look at the bigger picture and understand that every error is compensated by another in the opposite direction. So the scales of justice are in balance and we judges can sleep easy at night.

—Piero Calamandrei, *Elogio dei giudici*
(In Praise of Judges), 1935

One thing about being convicted of murder: you certainly find out who your friends are.

Amanda enjoyed an outpouring of support from investigators and law enforcement veterans, and from politicians on both sides of the Atlantic who thought they could do some good by intervening. Rocco Girlanda, an Italian member of parliament and president of the Italy-USA Foundation, paid her a visit at Capanne within days of the sentence and declared that she was nothing like the conniving harpy depicted in court. Maria Cantwell, a US senator from Amanda's home state of Washington, issued a statement saying the trial had not only failed to prove Amanda's guilt beyond a reasonable doubt, but also suffered from flaws in the Italian justice system itself—the lack of an adequate jury system, the "harsh treatment" to which Amanda had been subjected, and the fact that the prosecutor was himself facing charges of misconduct, yet had not been removed from the case.

My first reaction to all this was, *What about me?* How come all the attention was on Amanda? That I too had been sentenced to a quarter of a century behind bars seemed to pass most people by. Not that I didn't have friends and supporters of my own; of course I did. I had dozens of them, in my hometown, across Italy, and across the world, and I was grateful to them all. Many reached out to me precisely because they felt I was being unjustly ignored.

As I watched the continuing media coverage, though, I began to feel relieved that nobody was launching a political campaign on my behalf. The sentiments in support of Amanda provoked an immediate backlash, with the leading Italian newspaper *Corriere della Sera* asking in scathing terms if perhaps the Marines weren't about to land in Perugia to pull Amanda out from behind enemy lines. It also suggested, none too subtly, that the US government might want to close its military detention center at Guantánamo Bay before giving any international lectures on fair treatment of prisoners.

I felt sure that Mignini and his colleagues were not remotely swayed by Cantwell's intervention, or by Girlanda's awkward public fantasies about Amanda's innocence, or by reports that Hillary Clinton was taking a personal interest in the case. On the contrary, the prosecutors made it clear on several occasions that they regarded the public campaign on Amanda's behalf as an intolerable intrusion on the workings of the Italian justice system. The press reports just made them dig in their heels.

The next piece of bad news came down within three weeks of our being found guilty. Rudy Guede's sentence, we learned, had been cut down on appeal from thirty years to sixteen.

The thinking of the appeals court was that if Amanda and I were guilty, then Guede couldn't serve a sentence greater than ours. If I had supplied the knife and Amanda had wielded it, as Mignini and Comodi postulated and Judge Massei and his colleagues apparently accepted, we needed to receive the stiffer punishment.

I didn't think I could feel any worse, but this was an extra slap in the face and it knocked me flat. Not only were Amanda and I the victims of a grotesque miscarriage of justice, but Meredith's real killer, the person everybody should have been afraid of, was inching closer to freedom. It wasn't just outrageous; it was a menace to public safety.

My father said it best. "I'm sixty years old," he told a television reporter, his head shaking in disbelief, "and still I don't understand anything about the way justice is administered in Italy."

* * *

I have just two notes in my diary from late December 2009, that miserable end to a miserable year. The first was the Russian phrase for *Merry Christmas*. I was, after all, in the gulag. And the second, a more hopeful one, was a line from a Shakespeare sonnet: *For thy sweet love remember'd such wealth brings . . .*

I wasn't thinking of Amanda so much as everyone who was rooting for me. The only way I could imagine surviving was by holding on to that emotional bond and having faith that it would see me through to whatever conclusion this story would eventually reach.

* * *

My family felt that they were solidly behind me, but their support was far from cohesive. Actually, they were in an ugly mood, and the atmosphere grew only uglier over the following days and weeks. They spared me at the time, but I found out later they were at each other's throats, looking for reasons to blame each other, or the lawyers, or whomever they could lunge at, for the calamity that had struck us all. Vanessa said the air was so thick with recrimination and anguish that it was almost impossible to breathe; as soon as the holidays were over, she raced back to Rome.

First, though, she chimed in with Giuseppe and Sara to insist that Luca Maori had to go. My father, as usual, resisted, and so did

Giulia Bongiorno. Both of them, in their different ways, were optimistic that the lower-court verdict was a temporary setback, and that, if we kept pursuing the same course, we'd be in good shape for the appeal. This lawyerly way of thinking drove some of the other family members mad. What were we supposed to do in the meantime? Did we have to just sit and wait, *for years,* until the justice system finally saw the light?

I know my father shared this impatience; he would have done anything to spare me even an extra day behind bars. But, under Bongiorno's influence, he was perhaps more realistic than the others. Maori wasn't that involved in the case anymore; Bongiorno was in charge of my appeal, and my father was more steeped in the minutiae of the case than Maori or anyone else. I think the decision had a personal dimension as well. Papà couldn't help liking Maori, despite everything, and the same was true of Bongiorno. She had learned, early on in their association, that Maori owned an apartment just a few steps away from the parliament building in Rome, and she was now living in it as his tenant. I don't think for an instant that she put her personal convenience ahead of my legal interests. But it emphasized how the team dynamic had been set, for better or worse, and provided an additional reason to keep things the way they were.

For my part, I wasn't nearly as concerned about Maori, whom I'd long ago dismissed as a lightweight, as I was about some of the other members of the family, especially my aunt Magda and her husband, Enrico, who kept on at me about Amanda and said it was time to cut myself loose from her because I hardly knew her and had no idea what she might have done—or could still do. It was the same old refrain I'd heard many times before. Coming from them, it hurt more than it could have from any lawyer. I was infatuated, they insisted, and my infatuation had done quite enough damage. Did I really want to remain behind bars until I was an old man?

Hearing this made me so angry I wanted to punch a wall. Bongiorno understood that the only way to get either of us out of prison was to get us both out; she'd said as much in her closing statement at trial and went out of her way to defend Amanda, who wasn't even her client, as vehemently as she defended me.

If Bongiorno understood the stakes, why couldn't my own relatives?

*　*　*

The turning of the year was a particularly depressing time. I thought of the parties, the family celebrations, all the toasting that was going on far away from my four stone walls. In prison, every year is like the last. Nothing changes. There's nothing to look forward to and nothing to celebrate. The worst year of my life had come to a close, and the year to come promised to be equally grim, if not worse.

I remember reflecting on whether anything, really, could have been different. Had I missed an opportunity to escape this miserable fate? I wasn't at all sure that I had. Maybe, just maybe, if I'd lied or compromised with the truth, I could have cut some deal and worked it to my advantage. But I also knew I could never have lived with myself if I had done so. I reread some lines from my journal I'd written sometime earlier and they seemed especially apt now: "Is there such a thing as a man who can feel remorse for something he has not done? I don't think so. Is there such a thing as a man who would lie to save his own skin? Certainly, but I am not that man."

I knew I was doing the right thing by sticking to my guns and telling the truth. I can't pretend, though, that it was easy. "It's horrible to be treated like a terminal patient when that's not what you are," I wrote in another journal entry. "We are all afraid of what we cannot control and whose outcome we cannot know. I keep feeling that fear, and I still have no idea how to shake it."

* * *

On January 22, 2010, Mignini was convicted on abuse-of-office charges and sentenced to sixteen months in prison, six more than even the prosecutor had requested. The judge in his case later wrote that Mignini and his codefendant, Michele Giuttari of the Florence police, had taken advantage of their positions to blackmail people and either order wiretaps or open investigations into their perceived enemies for reasons that had nothing to do with the business of criminal investigation. Mignini was upbraided for failing to accept any limits to his behavior, and for finding criminal intent "in the slightest hint of anything that might be susceptible to critical interpretation." That certainly sounded familiar from our experience.

There remained, however, a crucial difference between Mignini the convicted criminal and Amanda and me. He was never placed in preventive custody. That meant, under the rules of Italian criminal procedure, he didn't need to worry about jail time until his case had been heard all the way up the Corte di Cassazione, a process that would take years and supersede any dealings we would have with him.

In the meantime, the law recognized him as innocent until proven guilty; nothing and nobody could prevent him from continuing his duties as prosecutor, if he so chose. And he so chose. We were, after all, his passport to professional rehabilitation, and he showed no sign of letting up on us, even for an instant.

* * *

Vanessa was barely surviving in Rome. She was doing odd jobs—waitressing, working as a personal trainer—while she and her lawyers pressed the carabinieri to reverse their decision and take her back. She was buffeted on all sides. One romantic relationship that had buoyed her for a while came to a crashing halt because of the case against me; Vanessa was tight-lipped on the subject, but apparently her partner didn't feel safe lying in bed and thinking about me knifing someone to death without warning. If I could do such a thing, then what might Vanessa, who shared my DNA, be capable of? Vanessa couldn't believe what she was hearing and ended the relationship immediately.

"Really, Raff, how can I trust anybody?" she said. The only creature in the world she could count on absolutely was Ulisse, a stray cat she had found in a neighborhood park just a couple of months before my arrest. "He's never scratched me. All he does is caress and lick me," she would marvel. "No human in my life loves me so much. He's the most stable force in my life."

My sister's bad luck struck again toward the end of January 2010. She was riding her moped to a friend's house for dinner when a bus knocked her flat on a busy stretch of highway running through the ancient city walls near the church of San Giovanni in Laterano. It was dark and rainy, and the driver did not see her. She and her moped skidded beneath the bus, and she managed to pull her head clear just a fraction of a second before the wheels thundered by. Her right hand lagged behind, and the rear tire ran right over it.

At first she tried to convince herself she was fine. The shock numbed her nerve endings and she felt nothing. But before long terrible shooting pains started running up her forearm and she yowled in agony. By the time she arrived at the hospital, her fingers had swollen badly; all of them except the thumb were broken. When the nurses announced they would have to cut off her rings, Vanessa screamed even louder than she had from the pain and told them it was out of the question. She was wearing the engagement ring my father gave my mother, which she had worn ever since Mamma's death. Nothing, she said, could be allowed to damage that ring. And so the nurses pulled it off, inch by agonizing inch, along the great welts that were forming and the crunch of mangled bone.

I don't know where my sister gets her strength and determination, but she has enough for an entire army.

For a long time it appeared Vanessa would not regain use of her hand. Most painful of all was the nerve damage, which made it intolerable for her to endure vibrations or movement of any kind. My father wanted her to go home to Bari for treatment, but she knew she could not bear a journey that long. So she stayed in Rome for the long weeks and months of her rehabilitation. Vanessa had two operations and had to fight to prevent the doctors from amputating the worst-affected finger, her ring finger. Eventually, she persuaded them to operate for a third time and insert metal splints to compensate for the loss of any workable bone structure. Her physical therapy was so painful she had to take morphine to get through it. But Vanessa would not let up. Over time, she regained partial use of her fingers and even adapted her riding technique to ensure she could hold a pair of reins and get on a horse again.

The accident spelled the end of the road for her in Rome. If she'd still been with the carabinieri, she would have been pensioned off with lifelong disability payments or transferred to a comfortable desk job at the Ministry of Defense. Now she had nothing. The carabinieri would never take her back, no matter how many lawsuits she might win, because she was no longer physically capable of serving.

I felt boundlessly sad and helpless. This was not my fault, but it had come about as a direct result of the hell that my life and the lives of those around me had become. *"Oddio,"* I said to Vanessa when she was finally able to visit later that spring. "Dear God—what else can happen to us?"

* * *

We received the sentencing report in early March 2010. I doubt an Italian court has ever published 427 pages quite this shameful, illogical, or flat-out ridiculous. It was not exactly a surprise to be ripped to shreds by Judge Massei (when he cared to remember that I existed), or to see him endorse Patrizia Stefanoni's forensic results, or to read yet another account minimizing Rudy Guede's actions and responsibilities. What I did not expect was to laugh out loud at the sheer absurdity of his arguments.

The biggest surprise, which my lawyers saw as a huge benefit moving toward the appeal, was that Massei did not accept Mignini's theory of the crime. Massei had clearly paid attention to Giulia Bongiorno when she said I could not have planned a murder with Guede because I did not know him. So, instead of endorsing the premeditated crime conjured up by the prosecution, Massei imagined a spontaneous one. Amanda had not, in his telling, stoked the flames of hatred in her heart over an unflushed toilet, or otherwise marked Meredith for death over a period of days or weeks. Rather, the whole tragedy came about because Rudy Guede needed to take a shit on a cold night.

Bear with me, because the judge's reasoning is every bit as crazy as it sounds. First, he claimed that Amanda and I spent the evening of November 1 at Via della Pergola. We were, he said, making love in Amanda's room while Meredith was minding her own business in hers. What evidence did he have for this? Precisely none. "But," he noted, "there is nothing to confirm that Amanda and Raffaele were anywhere else late that evening." Massei appeared to have forgotten it is incumbent on the prosecution to prove its case, not simply to say there is no evidence to the contrary. But let's leave that to one side for a moment; the story gets better.

Rudy Guede, in his account, was wandering the streets of Perugia when he realized he needed to go to the bathroom. Or decided he wanted to spend time with Amanda and me (even though he did not know me). Or was looking for a place to sleep (even though he had an apartment of his own just a few minutes' walk away). Whatever the precise reason—Massei said there was no way of knowing for sure—he rings the doorbell of the girls' apartment. *And Amanda and I, even though we are busy having sex, decide we have to pause to pull on our clothes and let him in.* Did we think it would be rude not to open the door to him, even though it was eleven o'clock at night and we barely knew him? Was there some reason why Meredith, whose bedroom door was still open in the judge's account, would not answer instead? Massei's report is entirely silent on the mechanics of this.

In any case, Rudy comes in, goes to the bathroom, and takes a dump. We, meanwhile, go back to our lovemaking. Rudy supposedly finds this a turn-on, to the point where he forgets to flush, comes out of the bathroom, and decides he wants to get it on with someone. "Lured by the atmosphere of sexual solicitation and giving way to his own concupiscence," Massei writes in painfully precious terminology, he barges into Meredith's room to see if she's willing.

She's not. Soon, she's fighting him off and yelling. That gets our attention. But, instead of stepping in to defend Meredith, we take

Rudy's side. We have, after all, been smoking pot—what other spur to irrational violence do two otherwise blameless college students need? Amanda produces my kitchen knife, which she just happens to be carrying around in her handbag, I pull out a pocketknife, one thing leads to another, and the next thing you know, Meredith is dead. "This Court," Massei concludes, "can only take note of the choice made to engage in extreme evil." That, for him, was our motivation: *extreme evil.* Even Mignini had tried harder than that.

What is perhaps most extraordinary about Massei's scenario is that it was not based on anything heard in court. It was his own imagination at work, from start to finish. Nothing in the Italian justice system *prevents* judges from taking off on such flights of fancy, but it certainly doesn't look good. Such sentencing reports effectively say, I don't like the way the evidence has been presented, so I'll come up with my own version, *which I'll pluck out of thin air if I have to.* Naturally, Massei's report begged question after question, some of which he attempted to answer, however tentatively. Why, for example, would Amanda have had my kitchen knife in her handbag if we weren't planning on using it? "It's possible, even probable, given Raffaele Sollecito's relationship with knives," he wrote, "that Amanda was persuaded by her boyfriend to carry around such a knife for her own security so, if necessary, she could flash it at ill-intentioned persons encountered in the night." Why such an enormous knife? Do people really carry around large chopping knives for self-protection? Amanda's bag, the judge noted, was very spacious; he contented himself with the observation that the knife could at least fit. My lawyers later objected that such a knife would inevitably rip the bag's lining to shreds, and Amanda's lining was intact. It appears that Massei did not think of that.

The knife posed all sorts of problems for the judge. Why, if it was the murder weapon, had no blood been found on it? "Just because the blood test came back negative," Massei answered, "does not mean there was no blood there." This was the sort of argument the US government used, none too successfully, when weapons of mass destruction failed to show up in Iraq; it was the notion, famously espoused by Donald Rumsfeld, that "absence of evidence is not evidence of absence." Why stop incriminating Amanda and me just because nothing substantiated our guilt? There *could have* been blood on the tip that nobody spotted. We *could have* been at Via della Pergola even though no physical evidence supported that contention. Meredith *could have* been sexually assaulted, because the gynecological exam did not categorically exclude it.

We had to wonder, was this dispassionate jurisprudence, or were these arguments of convenience concocted to justify a predetermined conclusion?

Time and again Massei's reasoning got knotted up on points that seemed to defy logic, and he would pull out some extraordinarily convoluted argument to free himself from trouble. Yes, he wrote, Rudy Guede *had* thrown rocks through windows and staged break-ins in the weeks leading up to the murder. But the circumstances at Via della Pergola were *completely different* because Guede knew the occupants and would surely do nothing as violent as smashing a window in a house belonging to his friends. So a real burglary was out of the question. And Guede could not have staged a burglary either—because the staging would immediately draw attention to his standard operating procedure in a string of previous incidents.

It took a moment to absorb this in its full circular ridiculousness.

Or again, if Amanda and I had committed the murder, why did

we lurk around the house for the police to find us? Because, Massei said, we knew the authorities would want to question us sooner or later, so we decided we might as well make it easy for them. *Right. As first-time violent criminals always do.* (My otherwise impeccably sober appeals brief later called this argument "mind-boggling.") Why, if I was trying to further the idea that there had been a break-in, did I tell the carabinieri that nothing had been taken? Massei had to expend several paragraphs explaining this away. Because, he said, I wanted to establish some credibility with law enforcement and I knew, since I'd staged the break-in, that nothing had in fact been taken and I didn't want to get caught in a lie.

Huh? I had to read that one several times too. It was nonsense even on its own terms. Meredith's money, credit cards, and cell phones *were* stolen, as the police later established. If I'd committed the murder, wouldn't I know these were gone? Massei chose not to go anywhere near that subject.

Rather, he went on a mean-spirited tear against Amanda and me over the tiniest details, much as Mignini and Comodi had done before him. If we knew on the night of the murder that we were going to Gubbio the following morning, he asked, wouldn't Amanda logically have taken a change of clothes to my house and showered there? Wouldn't that have saved time? (He appeared to forget she was expecting to go to work that night.) Why would she take a mop to my house when I had cleaning supplies of my own and needed only to wipe up a small amount of water? How come she slept in until ten or ten thirty when she was, by nature, a morning person? Didn't we want to take full advantage of the day?

These questions all pointed to an exaggerated form of moral disapproval: because we didn't go to bed punctually and rise early, because we dawdled on our way to Gubbio—a mere forty-five-minute drive from Perugia—and didn't mind walking back and forth between our apartments to gather our things, we must somehow be degenerate people. More likely, in the judge's view, we simply lied about it all. We lied and we smoked a joint and we had sex. What other proof of murder did a court of law need?

* * *

Even Massei understood that he needed to address the issue at the heart of the case, the DNA evidence, and he did so at great length, reproducing every argument he and his colleagues had heard over months of testimony. In the end, though, he ducked the whole question of which side the science favored. Instead of determining whether Stefanoni's methodology and results had met acceptable standards, he focused on her *intentions*. Nothing, he said, suggested that she had prejudged the situation or was looking for results to confirm the identities of the suspects already in custody. Because her *intentions* as an honest working professional were good, her results must also be good. "From a strictly logical point of view," he wrote, "there is no reason why Dr. Stefanoni would have wanted to manipulate the results from the [DNA] machine to seek out indications that one or other of the defendants was guilty."

With that, he dismissed the entire controversy.

As it turned out, Massei may not have been entirely correct to say there was no evidence that DNA results were used to fit a predetermined story line. Giuliano Mignini, of all people, had given a television interview a couple of months earlier in which he stated quite openly that he was looking for a certain result from the kitchen-knife analysis.

Mignini was asked by a special correspondent for the show *L'altra metà del crimine* (The Other Half of the Crime) how he could be so sure my knife was the murder weapon when the DNA readings had come back "too low" and did not appear to conform to international standards. Mignini stuttered and danced around the question before replying in gloriously convoluted Italian, *"Ho ottenuto di farlo risultare."* I managed to get it to come out right.

His answer didn't take refuge in science, or in Dr. Stefanoni's judgment. He seemed willing to take full ownership of the conclusions reached at the Polizia Scientifica lab in Rome.

* * *

Life in the protected section had two relatively bright spots that spring. The first was that an old professor of mine from Perugia, Alfredo Milani, agreed to come to Terni as often as twice a week to tutor me. He obtained special permission to come outside of normal visiting hours, so it didn't affect how often my friends and family could see me. And Milani was spectacular. We would go to the prison library, away from the protected section and away from the visiting room with its big concrete barrier, and work for hours at a time. Milani liked to bring material on a CD-ROM so I could upload it directly to my laptop, but this made the prison authorities nervous and he was told he needed to obtain written permission. Sometimes he had permission; sometimes he brought a CD anyway, even if it meant risking confiscation.

Milani was more than a teacher. He was a true friend, who always asked after my well-being and brought me presents, most memorably a Rubik's Cube. He guessed, correctly, that it would be a good distraction to while away the hours. It took me three months to solve the riddle of that cube, something that engaged the attention of my father because he remembered that a Rubik's Cube was part of the plot of *The Pursuit of Happyness,* the film he saw on the night of Meredith's murder. Such are the coincidences of my life.

The other bright spot was that I was put to work in the library to update the catalog and set up a computerized lending system. Not only did this get me away from the rapists and the perverts for a few hours each day; it was also a sign, I think, that the prison administrators were looking out for me and maybe even felt sorry for the bind I was in. It was a welcome relief from the numbing monotony of the protected section and gave me a structure and a purpose for each workday other than endless immersion in my legal case. When I asked for help with the library work, they gave me an assistant from the ordinary section of the prison, a thoroughly engaging local scam artist named Carlo Merluzzi, who, when he wasn't cataloging with me, played chess and teased me about my relationship with Amanda.

"Stop writing to her all the time!" he would insist. "Don't you have anything else to do?"

She was hardly my only correspondent; I was writing to dozens of family members and supporters all the time. True, Amanda and I *were* regularly exchanging letters and books and music CDs, but that seemed only healthy to me; we were enduring the same unjust punishment and we were helping each other through it. Amanda sent me a number of Kafka novels, including *The Trial,* which hit home in ways most students who read it in college can scarcely imagine. I sent her an Italian novel by Anna Marchesini entitled *Il terrazzino dei gerani timidi* (The Balcony of the Timid Geraniums), about a young girl coming to grips with a mystifying adult world.

The central character was a little like me—introverted and living in her own poetic imagination.

My family, as usual, didn't understand why I was in such close touch with Amanda. When they visited, our conversations were fraught with tension and frustration, which quickly got me down. Since my new cellmate, Gaetano Raucci, was a psychiatrist, I had an opportunity to talk the situation over with a professional.

Raucci was an odd bird, not immediately approachable. He and his wife had gone through a bitter divorce, during which she had accused him of molesting their infant daughter. He was found not guilty in the lower court, but then sentenced to prison on appeal. I could never figure out whether I thought him guilty or innocent, but he was, understandably, an angry guy. He'd watch current-affairs programs on TV and vent for hours about Italy's political leaders. Or he'd tie himself up in knots over his favorite soccer team, Inter Milan.

When it came to my family, though, his wisdom shone through. I shouldn't act too defensively, he said; it was a mistake to adopt a posture of knee-jerk opposition to them. If I wanted them to listen to my point of view, I should offer something, even a symbolic gesture, to soften them up. Following Raucci's advice, I made coffee for family visitors and brought cups to each of them, with the right amount of milk or sugar. They were no less hostile on the subject of Amanda, but at least they gave me the time of day. And, for a while at least, I kept my cool.

* * *

My family was not beating up on Amanda entirely without cause. What I did not know at the time, because they preferred not to fill me in, was that they were exploring what it would take for the prosecution to soften or drop the case against me. The advice they received was almost unanimous: the more I distanced myself from Amanda, the better. The legal community in Perugia was full of holes and leaks, and my family learned all sorts of things about the opinions being bandied about behind the scenes, including discussions within the prosecutor's office. The bottom line: Mignini, they were told, was not all that interested in me except as a gateway to Amanda. He might indeed be willing to acknowledge I was innocent, but only if I gave him something in exchange, either by incriminating Amanda directly or by no longer vouching for her.

I'm glad my family did not include me in these discussions because I would have lost it completely. First, my uncle Giuseppe approached a lawyer in private practice in Perugia—with half an idea in his head that this new attorney could replace Maori—and asked what I could do to mitigate my dauntingly long sentence. The lawyer said I should accept a plea deal and confess to some of the lesser charges. I could, for instance, agree that I had helped clean up the murder scene but otherwise played no part in it. "He'd get a sentence of six to twelve years," the lawyer said, "but because he has no priors the sentence would be suspended and he'd serve no more jail time."

To their credit, my family knew I would never go for this. It made even them uncomfortable to contemplate me pleading guilty to something I had not done. It was, as my sister, Vanessa, put it, "not morally possible."

The next line of inquiry was through a different lawyer, who was on close terms with Mignini and was even invited to the baptism of Mignini's youngest child that summer. (Among the other guests at the baptism was Francesco Maresca, the Kerchers' lawyer, who had long since aligned himself with Mignini in court.) This lawyer said he believed I was innocent, but he was also convinced that Amanda was guilty. He gave my family the strong impression that Mignini felt the same way. If true—and there was no way to confirm that—it was a clamorous revelation. How could a prosecutor believe in the innocence of a defendant and at the same time ask the courts to sentence him to life imprisonment? The lawyer offered to intercede with Mignini, but made no firm promises. He wasn't willing to plead my cause, he said, but he would listen to anything the prosecutor had to offer.

Over the late spring and summer of 2010, my father used this lawyer as a back channel and maneuvered negotiations to a point where they believed Mignini and Comodi would be willing to meet with Giulia Bongiorno and hear what she had to say. When Papà presented this to Bongiorno, however, she was horrified and said she might have to drop the case altogether because the back channel was a serious violation of the rules of procedure. A private lawyer has no business talking to a prosecutor about a case, she explained, unless he is acting with the express permission of the defendant. It would be bad enough if the lawyer doing this was on my defense team; for an outside party to undertake such discussions not only risked landing me in deeper legal trouble, it also warranted disciplinary action from the Ordine degli Avvocati, the Italian equivalent of the Bar Association.

My father was mortified. He had no idea how dangerous a game he had been playing and wrote a letter to Bongiorno begging her to forgive him and stay on the case. He was at fault, he said, and it would be wrong to punish her client by withdrawing her services when I didn't even know about the back channel, much less approve it. To his relief, Bongiorno relented.

My family, though, did not. Whenever they came to visit they would suggest some form of compromise with the truth. Mostly they asked why I couldn't say I was asleep on the night of the murder and had no idea what Amanda got up to. Vanessa, one of the most vocal advocates of this line of defense, later acknowledged that they had all "hammered my balls" over it. And it didn't work. I became hostile and defensive; they would accuse me of losing my head over Amanda; and so the merry dance would go round and around until we were all furious and exhausted.

I had little peace even from some of my more casual visitors. In early October, I received the first of two visits from the bishop of Bari, Don Luigi Martella, whose niece was a big supporter of mine. He too wanted to know why I would throw away my life to "save" Amanda's. I explained, once again, that I was not acting out of some amorous obsession but because I knew her to be innocent. To be fair, Don Luigi was very responsive, and we talked at length about how difficult it was to accept suffering for something I had not done. I should take strength from Christ's example, he said; sometimes the acceptance of suffering is what gives a person's life meaning. I appreciated that, and I also appreciated him looking around the prison and saying, "This is not your house." I derived a lot of strength and encouragement from that remark.

A few days later, I finally plucked up the courage to tell my family I wasn't going to take their hammering anymore. I wrote a letter to my aunt Magda—but intended for all of them—in which I made clear I wasn't going to abandon Amanda, especially since she was growing more despondent with every passing month about the chances of regaining her freedom. "I'm really fond of her, *zia*," I wrote, "and I don't know what I'm supposed to do and how I'm supposed to do it. Unfortunately I've understood that Papà, Vanessa, you, *zia* Sara, and many others in the family do not have any sympathy for her, because I've been told over and over that her behavior has been one of the causes of the trouble I'm in. You don't know how deeply this position of yours upsets me. For more than three years I've had to fight against it, against the thinking of my own family."

Rereading the letter now, I'm proud of what I wrote because it expressed all the indignation I felt at the time and drew a clear line in the sand. There were some things I just wasn't prepared to do, and my family needed to understand that in unambiguous, uncompromising terms.

"Have you ever asked yourself," I went on, "why I am sometimes reluctant to write to you unless you write first and ask me to respond? It's for this reason. I no longer have the strength to put up with your desire to blame Amanda for things she is not responsible for and does not deserve. I hope you'll understand and send this message to the other members of the family. Papà told me a little while ago that he thought I was doing all this because she doesn't love me anymore and I'm desperate. In other words, that I'm frantically trying to get her attention even though she's ignoring me.

"Well, that's not the way it is. First, she is not ignoring me; the affection and the desire to help each other are mutual. Secondly it's of no consequence to me whether she loves me or not, seeing as there's nothing I can do about it in this situation. I'll resolve that issue by myself once we get out of here, and you can rest assured I won't go crying to anyone if I end up disappointed."

Then came the crux of the matter: "Amanda and I are one now."

Io ed Amanda siamo una cosa sola adesso.

This was my manifesto. "Whoever mistreats her, mistreats me," I said. "Whoever speaks ill of her does the same to me. Whoever thinks bad things about her does so to me as well. These are not just words. It's the truth. Jesus said the same thing on behalf of all human beings who are faithful to the Word of God. More humbly, I am saying the same thing about a girl for whom I feel an immense affection, whom I consider more than a sister and closer to me than if she were of my own blood, my own DNA, my own flesh."

I think they finally got the message.

My father, who had been less vehement than some of the others but was nevertheless part of the general anti-Amanda chorus, wrote a letter back saying he would always be on my side, no matter what, and that he had nothing to do with the attempts to get me to change my testimony.

His concern, he said, had been mostly about the letters I'd been exchanging with Amanda, because he was afraid the police or the prosecutors might intercept them and misuse them as evidence against us. Now, though, he had the grace to back down, which I appreciated. As he put it, what was the point of distancing myself from Amanda at this juncture, three years after our arrest and close to a year since our conviction in Judge Massei's court?

I had made many mistakes over the course of my long and painful misadventure. But my determination to stick by Amanda, and by what I knew to be the truth, was one thing I knew I had exactly right. Nothing in the world—not the people I cared about most, and certainly not the threat of further punishment for a crime I did not commit—could induce me to change my mind.

* * *

I never felt at home in prison—how could I?—but I did slowly get used to its strange rhythms and peculiarities. Where once I was appalled by the jokes and the not-so-subtle threats my fellow inmates made at each other's expense, I found myself beginning to join in. One of the most pathetic figures in the section was a man convicted of raping a number of wheelchair-bound women. He was short and stubby and covered in tattoos, and we knew him only by his last name, Pozzi. Mostly, we steered well clear, but one day one of the transsexuals decided to jump on a food trolley and have himself wheeled past Pozzi as a sexual offering. "Don't worry," the transsexual said, "I can't move my legs!"

Another contemptible inmate was an old man with no teeth who had brutally raped a ten-year-old boy in his basement and stuck a broomstick up his anus. We never let him forget it. "Hey," people would call out when he passed, "do you have a broom I could borrow?" I even did it myself once. Not my proudest moment.

I had the creepy feeling, when I thought on it, that I was slowly turning into one of them.

* * *

The appeals court took eight months to read through the files before convening its first session at the end of November 2010. It was difficult to imagine any judge looking at our case objectively, because we'd had our hopes raised and crushed so many times. On the other hand, we knew that Italian appeals courts tend to reverse rulings, if only to leave all options open for the Corte di Cassazione—hence the much-observed (and, to me, absolutely hair-raising) maxim that in Italy, 50 percent of all criminal court decisions are routinely wrong.

Our hopes rested largely on our request for an independent assessment of the forensic evidence. Not only were we confident that such an assessment would turn out in our favor; if the appeals court granted us such a review, it would be a strong early indication that our judges were, finally, fair-minded people. What were the chances of that? The presiding judge, Claudio Pratillo Hellmann, was originally from Padua, in the north of Italy, and his deputy, Massimo Zanetti, was from Viterbo, outside Rome. So they weren't lifelong members of the Perugia establishment. Beyond that, the "popular judges" were a little better educated than the ones we had under Judge Massei because the rules governing appeals hearings called for a high school diploma as the minimum qualification. Was that a guarantee of anything? At this point, who knew?

At the second hearing, on December 10, Judge Zanetti offered a lengthy review of the case and immediately raised our hopes that the court intended to look at the evidence afresh. "We have to start from the one objective fact that is certain and beyond dispute," he said, "that on November 2, 2007, shortly after 1 p.m., the corpse of the English student Meredith Kercher was found at Via della Pergola, 7." The prosecution was furious at what it saw as a cavalier dismissal of other evidence it had worked so hard to establish and later argued that the court had been biased from the outset. But Zanetti's point was simply that he and Judge Hellmann would not make assumptions or indulge anyone's theories without hard evidence. Only in the context of a trial as flawed as ours could that be viewed as a controversial statement.

Later that same day, Amanda got up and made an impassioned plea on behalf of both of us. It was by far the longest speech she had delivered in court, and she did it entirely in Italian, which she now spoke fluently. My lawyers, and especially Bongiorno, did not want me to say a word, so all I could do was listen and root for her in silence as she made the case that we were both victims of a terrible miscarriage of justice.

She started with Meredith, her friend, who she said had been kind, intelligent, and always willing to help out when asked. "Meredith's death was a terrible shock for me. She was a new friend, a reference point for me in Perugia. . . . I always felt an affinity for her, and immediately after she was killed, I felt how terribly vulnerable I was too." Amanda described how she leaned on me for emotional support, and also on the authorities, whom she trusted to get to the bottom of the crime. "It took me a long time to accept the reality that I was being accused and unjustly redefined as a person. I am not the person the prosecution insists that I am, at all. They would have you believe I'm a dangerous, diabolical, jealous, uncaring, and violent girl. Their whole case rests on that. But I'm not that girl and never have been."

Amanda was indeed calm, considerate, and understated, the antithesis of the she-devil depicted in the tabloids. "I stand before you more intimidated than ever. Not because I'm afraid or because I'm a fearful person by nature, but because I have already seen the justice system fail me. The truth about me and Raffaele has not yet been recognized, and we are paying with our lives for a crime we did not commit. . . . I am innocent, Raffaele is innocent. We didn't kill Meredith."

The judges were rapt. For the first time since the beginning of our nightmare, I dared to believe that someone was listening to us.

* * *

My hunch was correct. Eight days later, Judge Hellmann issued the order we had been yearning for: he appointed two independent experts from La Sapienza University in Rome to review the DNA samples found on the kitchen knife and the bra clasp, "to establish whose genetic profiles may be found there or, alternately, to explain why such an attribution is not possible."

Amanda started taking deep breaths and gulping, as though holding back the urge to yell for joy. Her mother and stepfather wept openly with relief. I was beaming from ear to ear; I couldn't quite believe I was hearing right. I saw the happiness on the faces of my family and thought, *Finally, we are turning a corner.* My heart was in my throat.

My father seemed to be keeping his composure, but he too was awash with emotion. As he and Mara left the courtroom, Mara overheard Manuela Comodi in the next room shouting *"Incompetenti!"* at nobody in particular. Then, as they stepped into the elevator and the doors closed behind them, Papà burst into tears—something he'd done maybe half a dozen times in his life. He told me later he'd been close to crying a week earlier when Zanetti made his statement about the court starting from scratch. Now he let it all out; three years of anxiety and consternation and constant defeat finally countered by some real glimmer of hope. When he stepped out of the elevator, he was too undone to face the television cameras and, uncharacteristically, marched away without comment.

It wasn't over yet, of course. We still had to go through the appeals trial, piece by painstaking piece. But we knew now that we were going to get a fair hearing. Finally.

* * *

Back in the prison library, Carlo had no doubts: I was on my way out. "You know," he said, "if the independent analysis goes well and you are released, you'll have to let go of the whole Amanda thing. There's no point thinking about her. You'll just need to move on."

I said he'd misunderstood. I wasn't interested in getting back together with her. I was just allowing myself to imagine us set free; maybe I would get a chance to see her face-to-face before she left the country. We'd gone through a lot together, and the only times we'd set eyes on each other in the past three years had been in court.

"Come on," Carlo said, "you're still crazy about her."

"No, I'm not."

"You are."

"No, I'm not," I insisted. "Let's get back to work."

* * *

It took the court-appointed DNA analysts, Stefano Conti and Carla Vecchiotti, six months to reach any definitive conclusions, in part because they had to battle as hard as we did to see the raw data from Dr. Stefanoni's original tests. The court issued an order to produce the data, which Stefanoni contested, saying the extra information would add nothing of significance. Not until May 2011 did her office finally exhaust the legal process, raise a white flag, and hand everything over.

In the meantime, Conti and Vecchiotti had an opportunity to analyze my kitchen knife—something our experts had been denied. Not only did they confirm there was no blood on the blade, they also discovered traces of rye starch, presumably from bread Amanda or I had cut. Starch absorbs blood, so the discovery was a huge point in our favor: even if we'd scrubbed the knife clean with bleach, as the prosecution imagined, the residual starch would have given the game away. Instead, it demonstrated what we already knew: that the knife had nothing whatsoever to do with the murder.

We presented other exculpatory evidence, none more satisfying than the research Luca Maori's office had done to destroy Antonio Curatolo's credibility as a witness. Curatolo was the street bum in Piazza Grimana on whom the prosecution had relied to place Amanda and me outside in the late evening of November 1. He had remembered, though, that it was Halloween, with people in costumes and masks and students massing around buses laid on specially to take them to and from the city's discotheques. November 1 was not Halloween; it had been the night before. We called the owners of several bus companies and proved conclusively that they had provided no service on the night of the murder because it was a holiday and the discos were closed. If Curatolo had seen us on October 31, which we doubted, it proved nothing.

When Curatolo took the stand in late March, he more or less self-destructed. Many of his most damaging answers weren't in response to cross-examination by my lawyers; he did it all himself. Mignini asked when Halloween was, and he responded, "It must be the first or second of November, the day we celebrate the dead." If Mignini was embarrassed by that, he didn't show it.

Moments later, Judge Zanetti asked how Curatolo ended up on the streets, and he said it was by choice. He was an anarchist. "Then I read the Bible," he added, "and I became a Christian anarchist." The streets, he explained, were a way to follow the example of Jesus.

Was he still on the streets? No, he was living at "home." Giulia Bongiorno, chiming in between the other lawyers and judges, got him to admit that "home" was in fact a prison, and that he had a lengthy criminal record for drug-related offenses.

Zanetti asked if Curatolo had been using heroin at the time of Meredith's murder. He admitted he had, but added, "I'd like to point out that heroin is not a hallucinogen."

This was the prosecution's star witness? One of the things Maori's staff discovered was that Curatolo had testified in at least two other recent murder trials in Perugia. Clearly, the prosecutor's office found him useful, despite the obvious strikes against him. We had to wonder, was he some kind of informant? Had he been promised a deal on his sentence in exchange for his testimony? After this performance it didn't matter. Judge Hellmann was so flabbergasted by the hallucinogen answer he sent Curatolo packing, and he never troubled us again.

* * *

The next person to self-destruct, at least partially, was Mignini himself. In May he gave an interview to a British journalist named Bob Graham and appeared to be taken by surprise when Graham put him on the spot about how the crime took place.

Was it possible, Graham asked, that I was not involved at all? (The interview, conducted through an interpreter, was recorded and later transcribed.) Yes, Mignini responded after some hesitation, that was a theoretical possibility, except that Curatolo—Mignini was still relying on Curatolo—had placed Amanda and me together on the night of the murder. Amanda, for Mignini, was the principal instigator of the murder; either Amanda on her own, or Amanda and Guede together.

Why was the sperm on the pillowcase never tested for DNA? "We had to make a choice," Mignini answered lamely. "We couldn't analyze everything."

Then Graham moved in for the kill. He said he had spoken to numerous forensic experts, veterans of Scotland Yard and the FBI, and they agreed it was a physical impossibility that someone involved in the murder could have left no trace in Meredith's room.

"In that room, there isn't a single trace of Amanda," Graham noted. How come?

"But there is a trace," Mignini said. "There's the bra clasp with Sollecito's DNA."

But what about Amanda?

"The two of them say they were together—there's a witness who saw them together. So Sollecito was there. Therefore Amanda was there."

This was extraordinary, circular logic. It was a theoretical possibility, according to Mignini, that I wasn't involved, but the only proof that Amanda, the "main instigator," was at the scene was a controversial biological trace attributable to me!

Graham did not let up the pressure. "That's not good enough. Where's Amanda in all this?"

"Amanda is there because of the knife."

"But you didn't find the knife in the room."

"Listen, listen . . ." Mignini was clearly scrambling. "I think there probably were traces but the police couldn't see them. . . . The police didn't analyze all the traces they found. They made choices."

Graham went back to his experts. According to them, he said, standard procedure in such cases is to search exhaustively for traces of the most likely suspects. If at first those traces don't materialize, you go back in and keep looking. "So we're left with two possibilities," Graham said. "Either she wasn't there, or the analysis was not done properly. It has to be one or the other."

Mignini was once again flustered. He cast doubt on the reliability of Graham's experts. But he also raised a further, extraordinary possibility. "Theoretically, Amanda could have instigated the crime. . . . Someone could have instigated the crime standing in the next room." He then said my name several times as if to suggest—though he did not say so explicitly—that I was her robot and murdered Meredith on her instructions. Somehow, according to Mignini, this related to the version Amanda had been forced to give in the Questura when she said Patrick had murdered Meredith and she was in her bedroom blocking her ears.

My family and I read this with our jaws hanging open. Would Mignini dare raise this new theory of the crime in court? We were half hoping so because it was so inherently absurd. But Mignini did not dwell on it and changed the subject as soon as Graham allowed him to.

Mignini preferred to focus on what he said were indications of our presence *outside* Meredith's room: footprints, shoe prints, bloodstains. Our experts had countered a lot of these already; the shoe prints and all the footprints, except those made by Amanda after her shower, were Guede's. And we would soon learn that the footprints supposedly made in blood—something Mignini had argued for and Judge Massei had accepted—were no such thing. The most Patrizia Stefanoni had said on the stand was that she hadn't tested the prints for traces of blood. But even this was not true.

As her own documentation now showed, she *had* tested the prints for blood, and the tests came back negative.

* * *

Sometime that spring, I made friends with a Neapolitan named Corrado, a former policeman now in solitary confinement for raping a prostitute. He reached out to me, for some reason, and I saw him on the exercise yard for games of soccer during the few hours a day when he was not forced to be alone. In one game, Corrado got hurt; he argued furiously with some of the other players about who was to blame and filed a formal complaint.

The others found this unforgivable and beat the crap out of him the next time they saw him. The guards rushed over, and again Corrado's fellow soccer players were written up.

I wasn't involved, but I got an earful from both sides and found myself caught awkwardly in the middle. One day, out on the yard, the old Neapolitan gangster Vittorio Vespa approached me and explained that a group of Neapolitans and Tunisians were planning to stab Corrado as we climbed the steps back up to our cells after the game. "Whatever you see on the steps," Mosca advised, "keep walking. Don't look at what is happening."

I decided to tip off Corrado, which I did as discreetly as I could. As soon as the game was over, he ran up the stairs at full speed, as I had suggested, and escaped. The men who were supposed to stab him were confronted by some of their fellow prisoners and beaten up as punishment for failing to fulfill their mission.

Fortunately, nobody found out what I had done. And Corrado never showed his face on the exercise yard again.

* * *

At the end of June, the defense teams made an all-out effort to discredit one of the stranger witnesses who had produced testimony against us: Rudy Guede. I say "produced testimony" because he had not, to this point, actually testified in court. Rather, he had changed his version of the murder several times, making no mention at first of Amanda or me, and then belatedly "confirming," in a letter to Mignini, that we were the culprits.

My lawyers had never been given a chance to cross-examine him. So they could not demonstrate, for example, that when he chatted with his friend, Giacomo Benedetti, in the days before his arrest, he had said categorically that Amanda had nothing to do with Meredith's death. Nor had they had a chance to correct the public perception—as reported in the newspapers—that Guede had "identified" me as a culprit as early as April 2008, just before our hearing before the Corte di Cassazione. (The reports, as we learned once we were shown the official documentation, were flat-out wrong.) Now a number of Guede's cellmates had come forward in the wake of our lower-court conviction and said he had confessed parts of the murder to them. We had a handful on the witness stand ready to repeat their stories.

This was one of the tensest episodes in our whole legal saga. One of the witnesses Amanda's lawyers wanted to question was Luciano Aviello, the gangster who had befriended me in prison and later blamed the murder on his own brother. He had gone on to spend time with Guede in a prison in Viterbo. Giulia Bongiorno was vehemently opposed to calling him because she didn't believe the story about his brother and didn't expect the court to either; his testimony risked casting a shadow on the credibility of the other witnesses. She exchanged words with Amanda's lead counsel, Carlo Dalla Vedova, but to no avail. Dalla Vedova appeared to think that any testimony blaming someone other than his client was worth having in the trial record. And so Aviello appeared.

The prosecution went into overdrive to stop any of the witnesses talking. When the first one was called—his name was Mario Alessi—he began to describe how he had held lengthy discussions of the crime with Guede, only to be swiftly interrupted by the lead appeals prosecutor (not Mignini, who remained actively involved, but Giancarlo Costagliola). In a spectacular intervention, Costagliola informed Alessi that, based on just the start of his testimony, he was now under investigation for lying.

Alessi asked for a minute or two to consult with his lawyers, at which point he fell entirely silent. The next witness, Aviello, was similarly told he was under investigation, in his case for slandering his brother. Clearly the prosecution intended to cow each of the witnesses by any means at their disposal.

Then Judge Hellmann stepped in and issued an order not only insisting that the witnesses be brought back in, but also stipulating that they would not be granted the usual right to remain silent. They had come to testify, Hellmann insisted, and he wanted to hear what they had to say. As long as they were in his courtroom, they would enjoy a modicum of protection.

This was excellent news, not because these witnesses were necessarily all that reliable, but because they indicated that Guede was completely *un*reliable. They also added alternative explanations for parts of the case that had either gone unexamined or had simply been blamed on us. Most useful in this regard was Alessi, who said Guede had talked about masturbating over Meredith's body during the fatal attack. If anyone wanted an explanation of the semen stain on the pillowcase, this could be it.

A little over a week later, Guede himself took the stand. He was invited to offer specific rebuttals to the prison-house witnesses' testimony, but he refused. Mignini revealed the existence of a letter Guede had written in response to Alessi and the others, and invited Guede to read it to the court. He said he had trouble deciphering it. So, farcically, Mignini read it himself. The letter was full of rhetorical flourishes about "blasphemous insinuations" and "scurrilous gossip," as well as acrobatic uses of the subjunctive and other verbal sophistications that seemed entirely beyond a person like Rudy Guede. We could prove nothing, but our impression was that Guede had considerable qualms about saying, under oath and in his own voice, that the prison witnesses were lying.

We would have much preferred him to speak up. Amanda and I were particularly incensed that Guede refused to answer questions directly addressing his role in the murder. Somebody needed to rebut his most recent contention that we'd all plotted the murder together. So Amanda and I both rose and gave impromptu statements.

Amanda went first. "The only times that Rudy Guede, Raffaele, and I have been together in the same place," she said, "is in a courtroom." The prosecutors glowered; this was one of the few points that Judge Massei had conceded to us, and raising it again was clearly effective. I mentioned the fact—also incontrovertibly in our favor—that Guede had not originally incriminated either of us. "How am I supposed to defend myself [from Guede's accusations]," I added, "if he won't answer any questions?"

Honestly, I didn't even want to think about Guede. But I wasn't about to let him spread lies so he could pin his murder on Amanda and me. Our indignation did not go unnoticed.

* * *

Two days later, Conti and Vecchiotti issued their report. It was even better than we could have hoped. Not only was there no trace of blood on the kitchen knife, they wrote, but the way in which Stefanoni and her colleagues had examined the tip for traces of Meredith's DNA violated international protocols for "low copy number" DNA testing and could not be regarded as reliable. They were equally scathing about the bra clasp: they cited multiple reasons why the evidence might have been contaminated before it was analyzed and said there were at least three Y chromosomes on the clasp, not just the one we knew about, pointing to any number of possible male subjects besides me.

We had to wait almost a month before Conti and Vecchiotti could be brought into court to present their results in person, and when they did, it was devastating to the prosecution. They took turns reading out chunks of testimony from the transcripts of previous hearings and overlaid them with extracts of the police's own video footage, which they projected in the courtroom. The disconnect was so stark that at times it made people laugh out loud. While Stefanoni, Finzi, and others were quoted giving assurances that they used clean gloves at all times and observed all the appropriate protocols, the images gave a very different impression of police officials coming and going without gloves, without face masks, sometimes without protective clothing of any kind.

Members of the Polizia Scientifica were shown using the same swab to take samples of as many as three different bloodstains. We saw how they touched Meredith's body and even her fatal wounds with their bare hands. Sometimes they used tweezers to place samples in evidence bags, but sometimes they used a finger—gloved or ungloved—to shove them a little further.

Conti and Vecchiotti explained that the kitchen knife had been put in a plastic bag, even though the FBI and other agencies around the world advise in no uncertain terms not to use plastic bags for such evidence. The knife was then left sitting around the Polizia Scientifica's lab in Rome for six days before it was examined—another no-no because other items with Meredith's DNA were being analyzed close by, and the risk of cross-contamination was considerable.

The most incriminating visual evidence of all, and the thing that made all the headlines, was footage Conti and Vecchiotti showed of someone's dirty glove handling the bra clasp when it was finally recovered from Meredith's room on December 18, 2007. This, on its own, was prima facie evidence of contamination. But there was more: the video footage showed that no attempt had been made to seal off Meredith's room from the rest of the house. The contents of the room had been tossed in all directions before the clasp was recovered. The clasp itself had grown rusty over time and was now unusable as a forensic sample. Conti and Vecchiotti concluded that there was no way the clasp could be used as evidence against me, or anyone else.

* * *

The prosecutors were beside themselves, and they let it show. They talked among themselves during trial testimony, threw their judicial robes onto their table in apparent disgust, and spent extended periods out of the courtroom altogether. At least once, the bailiffs had to go looking for them so the trial could continue.

I think it's fair to say that Mignini, Comodi, and their colleagues were blindsided. They tried to poke holes in Conti and Vecchiotti's work, without great success. They even gave the court a letter in which the head of the Polizia Scientifica objected to the way his team had been "stigmatized." Judge Hellmann read it aloud and moved swiftly on. After the inevitable summer break—more agonizing waiting—the prosecutors recalled Dr. Stefanoni so she could defend herself, to no great effect, and they put in a formal request for yet another independent analysis of the DNA evidence because they weren't satisfied with Conti and Vecchiotti's work. Judge Hellmann not only turned them down; he declared the evidentiary phase of the trial over and ordered the lawyers to prepare closing statements.

I didn't want to hope too much, but even in my most fearful moments I could feel the tide turning decisively in our favor. As the appeals process neared its end, the number of friends and family members in attendance steadily grew. The anticipation was palpable. At one point, a group of my childhood friends asked Vanessa—the family Cassandra and uncompromising bearer of bad tidings—what she thought would happen. After all, she had been in law enforcement and had predicted the outcome all too accurately last time around.

"I don't know for sure," she told them cautiously, "but I think that this time we're going to win."

* * *

The single most atrocious moment of the appeal came when Francesco Maresca, the lawyer representing the Kercher family, flashed brutally graphic photographs of the crime scene in open court, including images of Meredith's near-naked body and the ghastly wounds to her neck. Amanda and I instinctively turned away, not because we had not seen such images before—we had—but because the moment seemed to be in such unforgivably bad taste. Maresca had spent years accusing us and our defense teams of exploiting Meredith's death and soiling her memory, but here he was doing the very thing he was so fond of condemning in others. "Meredith was butchered, like victims of Mafia killings are butchered, in revenge for some wrong," Maresca thundered as the gallery gasped and the press photographers snapped away. "I'm showing you these photos so you can see how she suffered as she died."

These images had been shown by the prosecution during the evidentiary phase of the first trial, but when they did it, they at least cleared the public gallery and gave due warning. This time, in the words of the former FBI agent Steve Moore, who was in court, it was "without warning, without dignity, without any apparent concern for Meredith or her grieving family, without decency."

Extraordinarily, a few days later, Mignini tried to assail Amanda and me for shying away from the photographs, as though we were somehow betraying our guilt. "Why did Amanda and Raffaele not have the strength to look at Meredith's martyred body?" he asked.

I can tell him why. Because the crime sickened us, as it sickened everyone. Because we had been victims of tabloid justice—lurid, headline-grabbing tactics uncorroborated by the facts—for four years now and were revolted by it. Meredith's suffering had occupied my dreams and filled my prayers; I was not a lawyer, and her death was not a career opportunity. I derived no benefit from it, only pain, and I had no desire to dwell on it even for an instant. I had, in effect, been forced to stare at that ghastly crime scene every day since my arrest and come to grips with the fundamental absurdity of being held responsible for it. Enough was enough.

I had also listened, for hour upon hour, as my family and the consultants hired for my defense reconstructed the circumstances of Meredith's death in all its minutiae. My father, being a doctor, had taken a particular interest in the grisly physical details, all the better to make sense of the crime scene and exclude even more emphatically that I could have played a part. He would give demonstrations to whoever asked, grabbing people from behind as he believed Guede had grabbed Meredith, and talking through the knife play, the attempted sexual assault, the hasty effort to stanch the blood, the decision to finish her off, and, finally, her agonizing last moments lying on the floor as she simultaneously bled and choked to death.

The crime, I could have told Maresca and Mignini, was brutal but not complicated. Guede broke in through Filomena's window, started looking for the rent money, then went to the kitchen to help himself from the refrigerator. (He left forensic traces of all this, and his history indicated that he liked to make himself at home in the places he broke into.) He detoured to the bathroom when he developed an urge to go and sat there while Meredith came in through the front door and slipped into her room. He appears to have been startled by her entry, and did not flush to avoid tipping her off to his presence. Meredith must have been attacked quickly, my father and my defense team believed, because she had time only to kick off her shoes and put them in the closet before being interrupted. (Her shoes were the only things she wore that night that remained unstained by blood.)

Guede crept into her room and grabbed her from behind under the chin and yanked his hand up over her mouth to prevent her from crying out. He held his knife to the right side of her neck as he issued his demands, presumably for sex. In the ensuing struggle, he jabbed her twice, causing blood to spurt out. Our best guess was that he didn't set out to kill her, but at some point decided he'd caused so much damage he had no option but to finish her off. He tried to plunge the knife in farther but could not find the right angle. So he switched sides and stuck the blade a full eight centimeters into the left side of her neck, hacking back and forth in an effort to sever her carotid artery, which he missed.

As Meredith struggled for her life, her lungs filling with blood through the perforation he had made in her throat, Guede lost his right shoe and his foot started slipping around in the growing pool of blood. He waited for her to die, but her agony, according to the medical experts, continued for more than ten minutes. If Mario Alessi was correct, Guede may have masturbated over her body. He picked up his right shoe and walked to the bathroom to wash off his foot and sock before putting the shoe back on. That would explain the bloodstains on the basin tap and the bidet, as well as the consistent pattern of left shoes and right feet. When he realized Meredith still was not dead, he threw a duvet over her body, stole her keys, phones, and money and locked her door to make sure she had absolutely no means of escape and no way of raising the alarm.

Guede was apparently afraid to return to his house by the most direct route, via Piazza Grimana, because of the risk of being seen covered in blood. So he took a much more circuitous route, walking down Via Bulagaio into open country and on to Via Sperandio, past Elisabetta Lana's property, where he disposed of the phones, and back toward Corso Garibaldi and his apartment a few steps away from mine. He changed his clothes, got rid of the shoes and knife, and went out dancing to make it look as if nothing were amiss.

This was the crime. This was the sequence of events I was haunted by. I needed no reminder, no visual aid, and certainly no lectures from lawyers pushing their own agenda. On the contrary; it was little short of incredible that the prosecution had not put this together for itself, because all the evidence pointed to this scenario. Now that Conti and Vecchiotti had exposed the DNA evidence for the sham that it was, literally nothing was left to tie us to the murder. No physical evidence, no eyewitness testimony, and no plausible motive.

Giulia Bongiorno, in her summation, put it admirably: "Nobody here is disputing that this was a savage crime; nobody is disputing it was an unforgivable act. But the gravity of the offense does not translate automatically into more evidence against the defendants. If you're wondering whether those photographs were shocking, I say, yes, they were. But they are also not the point."

Bongiorno, even more than she had in Massei's court, spent an extraordinary amount of her final presentation defending Amanda.

She said the prosecution wanted to present Amanda as a real-life incarnation of Venus in Furs, a coldhearted, diabolical woman who had used me, her weak-willed wingman, to commit unspeakable acts. But that, Bongiorno said, was not the real Amanda. Rather, she was like Jessica Rabbit, the cartoon character from the half-animated, half-live-action film *Who Framed Roger Rabbit,* which has always been popular in Italy. Why Jessica Rabbit? Because, Bongiorno said, she was a good-hearted, loving woman who was falsely accused of a crime and, because she was beautiful, was wrongly assumed to have loose morals and an evil heart.

My misfortune was simply to have been Amanda's boyfriend, her *fidanzato*—her betrothed, as we say in Italian. At the time I was arrested, the only evidence tying me to the crime was the Nike shoe print that was quickly shown not to be mine. Everything else, the bra clasp and the rest, had been pretexts to keep on accusing me once the initial evidence fell away. "There are those who by getting betrothed acquire a family," Bongiorno told the court acerbically. "He acquired a murder case."

I was so worked up I badly wanted to address the court myself. Bongiorno talked me out of saying anything that pertained directly to the evidence, but I still have the draft of my original remarks. I felt I had been excluded from the proceedings so thoroughly it was almost as if I did not exist. I was, as I wanted to say, "Mr. Nobody," of no apparent interest except as someone to condemn to years in prison as an accessory; an accessory to Amanda, that is, not to the crime.

"Mr. Nobody is a shadow flitting through the night, present all around the murder scene yet without leaving a trace," I wrote. "Does Mr. Nobody exist? No, he does not, and if he does, he's certainly not me."

When I addressed the court, I focused instead on the FREE AMANDA AND RAFFAELE WRISTBAND I'd been wearing since the start of the first trial. I talked about how much it meant and how I had kept it as a badge of resistance to my imprisonment. At the end of the speech, I removed it and offered it to the judges as a symbol of my faith in their decision making. "*È arrivato il momento,*" I said. The moment has arrived.

* * *

The lawyer's final rebuttals took place on Friday, September 30, and Judge Hellmann insisted on waiting out the weekend before announcing a verdict, apparently to avoid the risk of civil disorder on a Saturday night. This final round of waiting was the hardest of all. I was back at Capanne, back in solitary confinement, unable to concentrate on anything except the knots of anticipation twisting my stomach.

When Monday rolled around, we were called into court for a short hearing, then we had to wait again, for what turned into eleven excruciating hours. I spent some time talking to my lawyers, but otherwise I was a nervous jumble, not knowing what to do with myself. Reading the newspapers was of no interest; they just aggravated me. I thought of my chess games with Carlo in the library at Terni, but there was no chess set here. I worked my way mindlessly through a few sudoku puzzles, only to decide they were a waste of time.

I heard that Rocco Girlanda, the Italian parliamentarian who had befriended Amanda, wanted to see me, but he was not allowed in. Still, the courthouse authorities were relatively lenient, perhaps sensing I would not be a convicted murderer much longer. I was allowed to roam into the corridor outside my holding cell, and I remember watching the sun set as a hare played nonchalantly outside. I stared at that hare and thought of the freedom he enjoyed. I prayed that I would soon be out there with him.

Shortly after nine thirty, we were ordered back into the courtroom. It was so packed I couldn't see my father or my other family members or Amanda. Every square inch was jammed with police officers, lawyers, journalists, friends, and supporters. Bongiorno told me not to make eye contact with the police, so I kept my gaze in the other direction. I felt too sick to speak.

Then the judge entered. We all rose, and I grabbed the nearest hand. It belonged to one of my lawyers, but I couldn't even tell you which one.

Judge Hellmann began, *"In nome del popolo italiano . . ."* In the name of the Italian people, the old cliché. The next phrase I grabbed on to was *"parziale riforma della sentenza di primo grado"*—partial revision of the lower-court sentence. Which part was *not* being revised? I imagined having a few years knocked off my sentence, no more, and felt desperation rise through my body.

Amanda, Judge Hellmann announced, was still guilty of slandering Patrick Lumumba. My heart sank a little further.

But that was all the bad news he had. On the main charges, of murder and sexual assault, we were acquitted *"per non aver commesso il fatto,"* because we did not commit the deed. On the charge of simulating a break-in, we were acquitted even more comprehensively, *"perché il fatto non sussiste,"* because no such crime took place. And then came the most beautiful words of all, Hellmann ordering our immediate and unconditional release from detention.

The room erupted in cheers. I had closed my eyes from the tension and now I reopened them to a scene of indescribable joy. Bongiorno hugged me; she was beaming. My other lawyers hugged me too. I couldn't see my father, but I later learned that he punched the air as our release was announced. Moments later, he wiped away a tear—using a tie originally given to him by his mother. I asked my lawyers if I could go and find my family, but they said there would be time to celebrate with them shortly; we needed to leave.

On the way out, I glanced at the police, who were lined up in their uniforms against a side wall. I wanted to see the dejection and disgust I knew must be written all over their faces, but they would not indulge me and looked away. It didn't matter; the victory tasted just as sweet.

Finally, I saw Amanda, who was weeping her eyes out, her body racked by great waves of relief, anguish, and sheer incredulity. All I wanted, in that moment, was to be alone with her, to wish her well, to reflect on everything we had gone through, separately and together, over four long years. But we were at the eye of a tremendous storm, a crowd of screaming supporters and flashing cameras and a sea of blue official uniforms trying to keep some sort of order. Privacy was impossible.

We did, though, have a few moments together in the basement of the courthouse waiting for the cars that would take us back to our prisons one final time. The crowds were behind us now; it was just us and a couple of guards making sure everything ran smoothly.

Amanda took my hand and squeezed it ever so gently. She was still in shock, as I was, but no longer bawling. "What will you do now?" she asked.

"I'll go to Bisceglie to be with my family, and then I'll get organized and continue my studies. What about you?"

"I think my family's already booked a plane to take me straight back to Seattle. I can't wait to see my house and my friends."

"You know something? I would have loved to see a huge, white Viking lady singing an operatic aria when the judge finished talking."

Amanda looked at me quizzically.

"You know, 'it's not over until the fat lady sings' . . ."

I think I got a hint of a smile out of her. But we were out of time.

"*Ciao,* Raffaele," she said as she climbed into the back of a four-wheel drive.

"*Ciao,* Amanda."

Our Italian adventure, one part love affair to ninety-nine parts nightmare, was over at last.

* * *

My family followed me to Terni in a great, noisy convoy. My childhood friends Francesco, Saverio, and Corrado carried Vanessa out of the courthouse in celebration (they were the ones to whom she had earlier predicted our acquittal). Everyone squeezed into each other's cars and they honked and yelled behind me all the way.

At the prison, the director herself came out to shake my hand. Behind her I could hear a tremendous din—prisoners banging pots against the bars of their windows and shouting to celebrate my release, which was all over the television. I wanted to go back to my section and say good-bye to everyone, but the director said it was not a good idea. So I asked one of the senior guards to retrieve my things, everything that I had packed in anticipation of this outcome. I'd left a few things unpacked—a belt and a pair of shoes—with the intention of leaving them for my last cellmate, a friendly Dominican named Dan Toussaint. As soon as the guard returned,

I changed into a pair of sneakers I had been barred from wearing in prison because they had metal embedded in their soles. My first little taste of freedom.

Then I walked, alone, toward the gates and the free world.

Luca Maori and Donatella Donati were there to greet me, their faces awash in tears. "Finally!" Donatella shouted. "I'm so happy!" What about my family? Before I could even ask the question, I saw my father rushing toward me, arms outstretched with a huge smile on his face. He didn't need to say a word. To hug his son as a free man was all he had dreamed of for four years.

* * *

We drove through the night, a carnival parade snaking its way down the Italian boot toward home. When we stopped at a highway service station, I asked for a beer, a Corona. It had been so long since I'd tasted one. Just the lights and displays in the service station were a thing of wonder. I couldn't stop touching things—the toys, the maps, the wrapped candy bars.

I realized I wanted something else besides beer, something to remind me of my childhood, and that was a lollipop. I asked my friend Francesco to buy a Chupa Chups; we used to eat them together when we were little kids. It was like tasting one for the first time all over again.

I remained in a daze of wonder and disbelief all the way home. Even before I crossed the threshold of my father's house, I was touching the plants and smelling the grass. I could have breathed them in until morning.

After everyone had hugged me and headed to their beds, I sat in the kitchen, alone, and opened the refrigerator. I marveled at everything inside and just stared and stared. Then I moved on to the washing machine and stared at that too. So many things I'd taken for granted. So many bounties in life I couldn't properly appreciate until they were taken away. It was overwhelming.

At length, Vanessa came and found me and asked if I wanted anything.

"Yes," I said. "A glass of water."

"Water? Sure."

I sipped at it gratefully. Vanessa seemed perplexed.

"You don't understand," I explained. "To me, this is like champagne. This is the first water I can remember that doesn't smell like a toilet."

Vanessa looked at me, and at the water. She had tears in her eyes. And she understood that my ordeal was truly over, at last.

I had a lot to get used to, a lot of things to relearn. But my life had just been handed back to me, and for that I would never stop being grateful. Like that glass of water, I intended to savor it to the last drop.

EPILOGUE

---

*One might ask, even if the prosecutor and the lower court did not,
how two innocent young people could spend four years in prison,
with the prospect of staying another twenty, without going mad.*

—Judge Claudio Pratillo Hellmann

Five and a half months after my release, I flew to Seattle and saw Amanda again. We were no longer criminal defendants stealing glances from each other across a crowded courtroom, but free people fully able to reflect on our experiences and the peculiar way fate had thrown us together.

That may sound like a perfect ending to our story, but in truth I wasn't at all sure it was a good idea to see her and I wavered back and forth even after I had booked my ticket. We had been through so much; perhaps we owed it to each other to live our lives and leave each other in peace. I had come out of prison to a world that was at once familiar and irrevocably altered. After the celebrations, the reunions, the nights out on the town accepting offers of free food and drink from friends and perfect strangers, I had to pick up the pieces of my interrupted life and forge forward. I was no longer the sweet, innocent, ordinary boy from Giovinazzo, but a scarred, more reflective ex-prisoner who could go nowhere without triggering some sort of conversation or expression of opinion. I couldn't stop wondering: Was it realistic for me simply to resume my studies, as if nothing had happened? Could I go out, make new friends, fall in love, and plan for the future like any other man in his late twenties, or would my past always be a drag on me, like some great, unmovable weight around my neck?

For several months, I lived a life on hold, slowly recovering my familiarity with daily life, relishing my freedom and thinking, tentatively, about what might come next. This trip to the United States, my first outside Italy since my release, was an opportunity to explore the wider world without feeling that all eyes were on me. It was also a temporary respite from the concerns I had about my lingering legal liabilities and the bills my family had to pay. I spent an idyllic few days in Southern California strolling the Venice boardwalk, sipping wine in outdoor cafés and driving to Universal Studios in a brightly polished convertible. Nobody bothered me; nobody recognized me. Meeting up with Amanda, by contrast, felt like a step back into the lion's den.

I wasn't just nervous about setting eyes on her again. I felt I was suffering from some sort of associative disorder, in which it became difficult for me to focus on my genuine and continuing fondness for Amanda without being overwhelmed by an instinctive, involuntary revulsion at everything the courts and the media had thrown at us. Two different Amandas—the real one, and the distorted, she-devil version I had read about and seen on television nonstop for four years—seemed somehow blurred in my unconscious mind. I couldn't think of the brief romance we had enjoyed, or the tenderness with which we had written and supported each other in prison, without also feeling deluged by the suffering and vulgar tabloid trash we had endured at the same time.

My apprehensiveness reminded me of the climactic scene in *A Clockwork Orange* when Alex, the young delinquent played by Malcolm McDowell, has his eyes forcibly held open and he is saturated with images of sex and violence until the very idea of touching a woman, once his greatest pleasure, induces immediate nausea. I wasn't a delinquent, but the artificially induced feelings of aversion were much the same. I felt brainwashed, and I imagined that everyone who followed the media coverage of Meredith's murder and our trials—especially those who obsessed over it and argued about our guilt or innocence based only on the media reports—must have been brainwashed to some degree too. Amanda and I had been ripped away from our real selves and forced to play the part of killers so vicious they would strike for no reason except their own amusement. It was these alternate selves who had been imprisoned, tried, and sentenced in Judge Massei's court. But of course it was the two of us, our flesh and blood, who had to bear the consequences. Did I want to relive all that just to be able to give her a hug and wish her well?

Fortunately, I had other reasons to go to Seattle, which were a welcome distraction from my anxiety. I had many supporters of my own there, and I wanted to meet them and thank them in person. I was also interested in Seattle the digital mecca and had a meeting lined up with a video-game manufacturer I'd been corresponding with. But I could separate myself from Amanda only so far; these were connections I had made largely thanks to her family. Much as I dreaded it, it seemed crazy to think I would travel all the way to America's Emerald City and not get together with Amanda, even briefly.

Paradoxically, the news media forced the issue. Word got out a few days before my visit that I was coming. My designated host for the weekend grew nervous about having paparazzi parked outside her front door, and I ended up staying instead with Edda and Chris Mellas, Amanda's mother and stepfather. They were experts at dodging the press and weren't afraid of them. I was given a special police escort out of the Seattle-Tacoma Airport, so nobody saw me arriving, and I was left in peace for the rest of the weekend.

Amanda was not at the Mellases' house when I arrived, but I was told she would be coming around shortly. My stomach hurt at the thought of it, but I kept my misgivings to myself. And then there she was, the old, familiar smile, those familiar blue eyes and shoulder-length brown hair. Her boyfriend, James, brought her around, but he was gracious enough to withdraw after saying his hellos and left us alone for a while. She seemed genuinely pleased to see me, and at last I was able to relax.

We talked about our continuing studies—she was back at the University of Washington, and I was about to reenroll at the University of Verona—and about our new relationships. She showed me pictures of herself with James, and I showed her pictures of the girl I'd been dating for a few months.

I could tell Amanda had changed. She was no longer the carefree, playful twenty-year-old I had met at that classical concert, but a more considered, mature, cautious, serious twenty-four-year-old.

"What's James like?" I asked her. "Are you happy with him?"

She answered, *"È bravo come te."* He's a good man, just like you.

* * *

Our legal troubles were largely behind us, but they were not over. Our acquittal would not become definitive until it had been endorsed by the Corte di Cassazione, so we had one more layer of justice to work through. Amanda faced not only the outstanding charge of *calunnia*—criminal slander—against Patrick, which the appeals court had upheld, but also a new trial for slandering the Perugia police while on the witness stand.

My family was still working through some minor lawsuits of

its own. I was sick of the whole judicial circus and couldn't wait to put it definitively behind me. But the nature of the Italian system meant that it would probably be years before my family or I could stop thinking about the ghastly mess or talking to lawyers on a regular basis.

Judge Hellmann's sentencing report was magnificent: 143 pages of close argument that knocked down every piece of evidence against us and sided with our experts on just about every technical issue. It lambasted both the prosecution and the lower court for relying on conjecture and subjective notions of probability instead of solid evidence. And it launched a particularly harsh attack on Mignini for casting aspersions on the very concept of proof beyond a reasonable doubt. Mignini had dismissed it in one of his court presentations as a self-defining piece of linguistic trickery. Hellmann pointed out that reasonable doubt was now—belatedly—part of the Italian criminal code. A case built on probability alone, he said, was not sufficient and must necessarily lead to the acquittal of the defendant or defendants.

The prosecution's rebuttal of the sentencing report, filed a couple of months later, was little short of astonishing. It accused Hellmann of indulging in circular arguments, the old rhetorical fallacy known to the ancients as *petitio principii*—essentially, starting with the desired conclusion and working backward. The criticism applied much more accurately to what the prosecution and Judge Massei had done themselves; everything, even the *absence* of evidence, had been a pretext for them to argue for our guilt. But the author of the prosecution document, Giovanni Galati, chose not to dwell on such ironies. Instead, he attacked Hellmann—I wish I were joking about this—for resorting to deductive reasoning. Making yet more allusions to grand rhetorical principles, Galati said he had a problem with the appeals court taking the available evidence and seeking to make each piece follow on logically from the last. I take it he is not a fan of Sherlock Holmes.

Galati seemed incensed that Hellmann had found the "super-witnesses" unreliable. He argued that Hellmann's problem with Antonio Curatolo, the heroin addict in Piazza Grimana, was not his failure to be consistent about the details of when and where he had supposedly seen us but rather Hellmann's own "unwarranted prejudice against the witness's lifestyle." Galati even dared to embrace Curatolo's argument that heroin is not a hallucinogen to insist he must have been telling the truth.

These arguments, to me, made a mockery of civilized discourse. I don't honestly know how else to characterize them. From my experience, I also know they are the bread and butter of the Italian legal system, the peculiar language in which arguments and counterarguments are formed every day. Not only do innocents go to prison with shocking regularity, while guilty people, equally often, win reprieve or acquittal; magistrates and judges who make the most howling errors rarely pay for their mistakes.

Paolo Micheli, the pretrial judge who didn't let his obvious intelligence and sharp questioning of Patrizia Stefanoni get in the way of keeping us locked up until the end of the trials, now sits in the civil section of the Corte di Cassazione. Giancarlo Massei, our lower-court judge, has been promoted to the Court of Appeals.

Giuliano Mignini, meanwhile, managed to have his conviction on abuse-of-office charges vacated on a technicality. He argued on appeal that Florence was not the appropriate trial venue because the judges there were too close to the Monster of Florence prosecutors. In theory, his case has now moved to La Spezia, the naval port halfway between Florence and Genoa, to be reheard from scratch. But in all likelihood Mignini will wait out the five-year statute of limitations and have the entire case thrown out by default.

We may have beaten him, but in an important and deeply depressing sense he has emerged a winner too. At least so far.

* * *

Amanda and I steered clear of any legal discussion; we'd avoided talking about the case in prison, and we weren't about to depress ourselves by starting now. Instead, we shared many of the normal, joyful things that had instinctively brought us together in the first place: our noisy, rambunctious, warmhearted families, and our love of friends, good food, and large gatherings. On my last night in Seattle, Chris and Edda threw a big party to celebrate our freedom and our reunion. We ate king crab and other delicious seafood, and I was presented with an all-American cheesecake to celebrate my twenty-eighth birthday.

Amanda's younger sisters and cousins were there, and so was her best friend, Madison Paxton, whom I'd seen many times in court. We took a lot of photos; unlike so many of the shots of the two of us taken at trial, we were smiling in every one.

I did manage to have snippets of serious conversation with Amanda amid the celebration. She told me she now relied on a small handful of close friends but otherwise did not go out much. It made her too nervous. She was recognized almost everywhere she went, and while most people were supportive, she dreaded the times when she would hear someone shout out hateful, negative things. She had even received anonymous threats.

I told her I sympathized. I'd gone through much the same thing. I, too, had days or weeks when I didn't feel like seeing old friends. I was dismayed, if not surprised, to realize that my family was as volatile as ever. Vanessa was still boundlessly opinionated, only more depressed now that she was living back home, her career in tatters, and tending horses to make ends meet. My father would alternate between infinite patience and understanding, and explosions of indignation at the choices I was making and the company I kept. Both Amanda and I were contending with contradictory experiences. We had to get reacquainted with normal life, with its frustrations and banalities as well as its pleasures and prospects for future happiness; but at the same time we had to acknowledge we were ourselves still far from normal.

I told her that when I was confronted with people haranguing me about the case, either to attack me or to presume more knowledge than they had, I ignored them. As a general rule, I tried to give as little weight as possible to the opinions of others. We had to focus on living our lives, I said, because nobody could live them for us. "If I had had that attitude," I said, "if I'd allowed other people to dictate what I should do and think and feel, I wouldn't be eating seafood here with you. I'd still be in prison."

She agreed, and as our conversation continued, she looked visibly moved. "I want only good things for you, Raffaele. I'm very glad you came." She gave me a monster hug, the sort that only close friends or siblings give each other, people who share a special, unbreakable bond.

Amanda and I will forever be associated, for better and for worse, because of what we went through. I'll never be entirely comfortable with that, because of the memories it inevitably dredges up. But Amanda herself will always be a treasure. She was good to me from the beginning, and she stood by me when I needed her most, just as I stood by her. We are free today because of the support we were able to offer each other in our darkest moments. The romance that made headlines around the world was a fleeting thing, but that deeper trust, the inherent faith we had in each other even as others dragged us endlessly through the mud, defines us as human beings.

It's what kept us sane for four long years in prison. And, I am quite certain, it will endure.

Acknowledgments

I would like to thank everyone who stood by me during my long and difficult journey. Many people's lives were changed by the horrific miscarriage of justice that Amanda and I went through, and while we and our loved ones went through hell, the experience also led to many friendships and associations between people who might never have met otherwise. All of them helped me keep my desire for truth and justice alive. The list is long, so I apologize in advance to anyone I may inadvertently have left out.

I want to offer my deepest thanks to my family, who always stayed close to me in mind and heart and spirit, who fought for me and encouraged me never to give up hope. Foremost among them is my father, Francesco Sollecito, who always listened to me and fought from the beginning to stand by what I was saying, which was the truth. Even in my darkest moments I could always count on the moral support of my aunts, Magda and Dora Sollecito, my stepmother Marisa Papagni, my uncles Alfonso Colamaria and Enrico Errico, and my cousins Stefania, Giuseppe, and Carmela. Then there are those who, beyond that support, worked tirelessly on the case: my father, my sister Vanessa, my uncle Giuseppe Sollecito, my aunt Sara Achille, my cousin Annamaria, and my cousin Raffaele Sollecito. I also want to thank you, Mamma, for watching over me and protecting me always. I love you.

ACKNOWLEDGMENTS

I've been blessed with many dear old friends who also stood by me, corresponded with me and shared my emotional ups and downs: Corrado Tridente and his family, Paolo Genovese and his family, Milko Desantis, Mariano Demartino and his family, the Marrano family, Marika Galizia, the Mastroviti family, Damiano Stefano, Rita Bonserio, Andrea Gennaro Palmieri, Angelo Cirillo, Teresa D'Angelico, Francesca Amatulli, Gabriele and Francesca Traverso and their family, Mario Mastropasqua, Valeria Degennaro, Francesca Murolo, Gianfranco Chetta, Claudia Quercia, Fabrizio Siffredi, Ana Gomèz Cortèz, Maite Olmos Ureta, Silvia Parenti, the staff of the newspaper *La Piazza di Giovinazzo,* Paolo Coppa and his family, Francesco and Roberto De Robertis, Enrico Tedeschi, Lillino and Mariateresa D'Erasmo, and Don Michele Fiore.

Some friends not only corresponded with me but found ways to come and visit me in prison. They include Saverio Binetti, Corrado Decandia, Francesco Marrano, Antonella Petruzzella, Giovanni Stufano, Erica Milillo, Miriam Massari, Marta Marianna Modugno, Raffaele Mastroviti, Silvia Musarò, Bishop Luigi Martella, Don Raffaele Gramegna, Sergio Pisani, and Gabriella Marcandrea.

Along the way I acquired many supporters who, over time and many exchanges of letters, have become true friends themselves. Among them: Gilbert Baumgartner, Michael Krom, Maria Luigia Alessandrini, Joe Santore, Jessica Nichols, Chris and Edda Mellas, Madison Paxton, Cassandra Knox, Deanna Knox, Elisabeth Huff, Shirley Anne Mather, J. Tappan Menard, Martin Speer, Jason Leznek, Eric Volz, Steve and Michelle Moore, Leslie Calixto, Laura Buchanan Kane, Larry Kells, Jerry and Sue Alexander, Steven David Bloomberg, Eve Applebaum-Dominick, Francisco di Gennaro and Anna Rella, and Nigel Scott. Other supporters I'd like to acknowledge include Angela Benn, Karen Pruett, Judge Michael Heavey,

ACKNOWLEDGMENTS

Sunshine Tsalagi, Janet Burgess, Alexander Jackson, Maria Alamillo, Candace Dempsey, Paul Smyth, Patrick King, Joe Starr, Mario Spezi, Douglas Preston, Mark Waterbury, Bruce Fisher, David D. Kamanski, Jerry Morgan, Bruce Locke, Jodie Leah, Michael Scadron, Pawel Bukowski, Michael Smith, Jake Holmes, Michael Rabold, Bern Vogt, Joe Bishop, Kate Lee and Willie Grey, Diana Navaro Botero, June Easterly O'Brien, Margaret Ralf, Werner Gompertz, Anthony Giorgianni, Terrie Connell, Colin Connaughton, Dave Tupper, Dale Gridalt, Hayes Whitt, Hilde Conradi, Charlotte Olson, Rebecca Springer-Seeman, Raymond and Betty, L. Schwab, Jim and James Rocca, and Colleen Conroy.

I was lucky to have a crack legal team who showed their devotion to the truth and, in some cases, did not even request payment. The team of lawyers and consultants included Adriano Tagliabracci, Francesco Vinci, Bruno Pellero, Francesco Introna, Giulia Bongiorno, Maurizio Parisi, Daniela Rocchi, Luca Maori, Donatella Donati, Marco Brusco, Aldo Poggioni, Delfo Berretti, Tiziano Tedeschi, and Antonio D'Ambrosio.

A special thank-you goes to Professor Alfredo Milani, who is not only a wonderful person but also a great friend and was a key part of the defense on computer-related issues.

Heartfelt thanks, finally, to my literary manager, Sharlene Martin of Martin Literary Management and everyone at Simon & Schuster—in particular, Louise Burke, Jennifer Bergstrom, Tricia Boczkowski, and Alexandra Lewis—who made this book possible and gave me the vehicle to tell the world what really happened.

* * *

Andrew Gumbel would like to thank Dana Newman, who made a crucial introduction at the start of this project, the indefatigable

Sharlene Martin, the ever gracious Gail Ross, the boundlessly generous Steve and Michelle Moore, my favorite *pugliese* Anna D'Elia, Peter Popham, Robert Adams, and of course the rocking, supertalented team at Simon & Schuster/Gallery who were never less than a pleasure and kept me sane against a tight deadline. Thank you, Jen Bergstrom, for believing in this book from the get-go, thank you Lisa Rivlin and Alex Lewis, and thank you, Trish Boczkowski, for your brilliant editing and infectiously good company. That's amore!

This was a group effort all around. The Sollecito family, not just Raffaele, opened up their lives and their souls with remarkable candor. Thank you, in particular, to Francesco and Vanessa for days of fascinating conversation, for your dedication to getting every detail just right, for compiling exhaustive time lines, and making sure that material reached me promptly. Donatella Donati in Luca Maori's office gave up many hours to make the official documentation available and to present it all in a cogent order. She's a largely unsung hero in this story and deserves recognition for her extraordinary efforts on Raffaele's behalf. Giulia Bongiorno, Luca Maori, and Tiziano Tedeschi answered questions and made comments on parts of the manuscript.

Heartfelt thanks, also, to my family, who not only put up with my long hours at the computer but cheered me on. My older children, Max and Rara, made me laugh and followed every step of the story. Sammy took me on fabulous walks every evening, nodded sagely even at ungodly hours of the night, and positively drooled with enthusiasm. And Naomi was spectacular, as always—every writer (and husband) should be so lucky.

Photo Credits

pg. 1:
top: GianCarlo Belfiore
middle: MediaTake
bottom: MediaTake

pg. 2:
top: MediaTake
bottom: Dott. Francesco Vinci

pg. 3:
all: GianCarlo Belfiore

pg. 4:
top: MediaTake
bottom: GianCarlo Belfiore

pg. 5:
top: GianCarlo Belfiore
bottom: Steve Moore

pg. 6:
all: GianCarlo Belfiore

PHOTO CREDITS

pg. 7:
all: GianCarlo Belfiore

pg. 8:
all: The Sollecito Family